# THE
# CAPTAIN

# THE
# CAPTAIN

## - A MEMOIR -

# DAVID WRIGHT

## and Anthony DiComo

**DUTTON**

Dutton
An imprint of Penguin Random House LLC
penguinrandomhouse.com

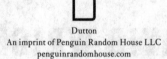

Previously published as a Dutton hardcover in October 2020

First Dutton trade paperback printing: June 2021

LIBRARY OF CONGRESS CATALOGING-IN-PUBLICATION DATA
has been applied for.

Dutton trade paperback ISBN: 9781524746308

Printed in the United States of America
1st Printing

BOOK DESIGN BY KRISTIN DEL ROSARIO

This book is dedicated to all the Mets fans
who welcomed a twenty-one-year-old kid from Virginia
into their lives and, through their love and support,
made him a New Yorker.

# CONTENTS

||||||||||

# THE
# CAPTAIN

# INTRODUCTION

||||||||||

I thought I was going to throw up.

By age thirty-five, I figured I had experienced most everything one could on a baseball diamond. I was a first-round draft pick who had been to a World Series and seven All-Star Games. I had twice represented my country at the World Baseball Classic, wearing the letters "USA" across my chest. I'd swung my bat thousands of times for the team I'd grown up loving. I'd stared down the greatest closer who ever lived on one of the game's most pressure-packed stages. But until this day, I had never felt the emotion of standing in uniform, knowing I was wearing it for the final time.

Seven years earlier, I'd fractured my back on a hustle play at third base, beginning a health spiral that would ultimately end my career. In 2015, doctors diagnosed me with stenosis, a degenerative narrowing of the spinal canal. Twice a day that summer, I ground through the monotony of physical therapy, trying to will my body to cooperate. It worked, at least temporarily; I made it to the World Series for the first time that autumn, even hitting a go-ahead home run early in Game 3. But the injuries never ceased. The next year, my neck required surgery. Then my shoulder. Then my back. Late in 2018, I finally admitted to myself that I would never truly return to the field on my terms. So the Mets and I hatched a plan: I would suit up for two final games before calling it a career.

That is how I found myself in the on-deck circle at Citi Field in New York City, bent in a crouch, trying to prepare for my first at-bat in twenty-eight months. I remembered being nervous for my big league debut and the World Series, and for dozens of moments in between. But I had never felt like this, physically sick, unsure if I could stand up and make the short walk to home plate. My legs wobbled as a sold-out crowd chanted my name. I took a couple of practice cuts and then the inning ended with me stranded on deck. Back to the dugout I retreated, hoping to regain my composure.

From the time I was young, baseball meant everything to me. My father helped introduce me to the game in our backyard, installing a homemade tee made out of concrete, a PVC pipe, and a little bit of rubber, and hanging a fishnet between two trees so I could hit balls into it. Growing up, I attended minor league games in my coastal Virginia hometown, then watched on television as those players broke into the majors. I wanted badly to become one of them, and eventually I succeeded, playing for the only team I'd ever rooted for as a kid.

Maybe from the outside, it seems like things came easy to me. They didn't. As much as I tried to do everything the right way, my career wasn't about skating by without adversity. It was about refusing to let pain define me. It was about the value of hard work, of perseverance, of living life in a manner that leaves no room for regrets.

As the years passed, my body failed me, making it impossible to go out on my terms. But at least I could dictate a small part of my ending. After another half inning passed that night at Citi, I grabbed a bat and walked back onto the field, steeled a bit better this time to keep the crowd from frazzling my nerves. I made my way back into the on-deck circle, looped my bat in an arc around each shoulder, then dropped into a squat to survey the field—the site of some of my greatest triumphs as a baseball player, and also some of my most jarring failures.

Then I stood back up and strode to the plate.

# ONE

# THE PUDGY KID AT SHORTSTOP

To this day, my father isn't sure quite what possessed him. Shortly after I was born, once the initial bursts of elation and exhaustion and emotion had faded, my dad, Rhon, had a chance to steal away from the hospital for a few hours. Intending to drive straight home for a bit of rest, he instead found himself pulling into the parking lot of a local department store. This was a few days before Christmas, and as he puts it, the shelves were mostly bare— but there was my dad, rummaging around them long enough to find a plastic glove, a kid-sized Louisville Slugger, and a cheap baseball.

Rhon Wright was never much of an athlete, too short for basketball and too small for football, but he did play baseball and enjoyed the game. He wanted to instill that same love in me.

In the weeks that followed, my grandmother constructed a

wooden plaque with prongs sticking out of it to hold the bat, as well as spots to store the glove and ball. That contraption hung on my bedroom wall from the first days of my life until I was old enough to go play outside with them. They were perfect. At first, I could barely lift the bat, but I never got tired of trying alongside my father and grandfather in the backyard. When I got older, my dad told me to swing it underwater, because he had read that that was how Gregg Jefferies trained. I was probably better equipped to handle a Wiffle-ball bat, which I often did, standing with my back to my grandfather's pool and trying to hit his looping pitches for hours.

To say I was predisposed to a love of baseball would probably be an understatement. From the time that I could walk, everything on both sides of my family revolved around a ball and a bat.

So enthused was I about the game that, one afternoon, when my mother, Elisa, spied a Little League team playing, she stopped the car, got out, and asked someone at the field how old I had to be to register. Turned out I was a year too young, but the next spring, I was out there in uniform, ready to make my Green Run Little League debut. I showed up with the same wooden bat my dad had bought on his way home from the hospital, which embarrassed him only a little when he realized all the other kids were swinging aluminum.

We learned that sort of stuff on the fly. Quickly, Saturday turned into the best day of the week. I would wake up and spend all day at the field. I would eat breakfast, lunch, and dinner at the concession stand, watch the other games, and play in mine, loving every second of it. Three younger brothers—Stephen, Matthew, and

Daniel—eventually came along, one every three years. We all played baseball. None of us could get enough.

What's amazing to me now, looking back, is how much my parents sacrificed to help make that possible.

|||||||||||||

My dad was raised in the Hampton Roads region of Virginia, which in those days was generally just referred to as Tidewater. It encompasses Norfolk, the biggest city in the area; Virginia Beach, where I grew up; Chesapeake, where we moved when I was a teenager; and several other communities. Dad met Mom at a local roller-skating rink, convinced her to go on a double date with two other friends, and managed to turn that one date into many more. Rhon and Elisa became high school sweethearts. In 1978, when she was nineteen and he was only eighteen, they got married.

At the time, my mom was working at the local Navy Exchange store, while my dad was earning some cash at an auto dealership with his uncle, selling muscle cars, which were all the rage. Within a couple of years, they switched: She started working at the dealership, doing bookkeeping and other tasks, while he worked security at the Navy Exchange, rooting out shoplifters. That sparked Rhon's interest in law enforcement, and once he was eligible at age twenty-one, he applied to the police academies in Norfolk and Virginia Beach. Norfolk, a much more urban area with some relatively high crime rates, called him back first. A career was born.

Until I grew older, I wasn't really aware of the dangerous nature of my father's work. Flipping through channels as a kid, I watched *Cops* and saw the officers busting down doors and catching bad guys, but my brothers and I always thought there was no way my dad did that sort of stuff. When we all sat together for family dinners, my father never talked about his work. My parents completely shielded us from it, even if that wasn't totally on purpose. To Rhon, the work didn't always seem all that dangerous. To me and my brothers, it was just what he did. Our biggest thrill was having him flip on the siren for us as we drove around town in an unmarked police car. Sometimes, we'd get to wear screen-printed T-shirts that the officers made to celebrate successful missions, even though we didn't really know everything that went into them.

It wasn't until I was an adult that I learned the truth from a couple of his partners at a local gym.

"Your dad was a bad dude," one of them told me.

"*Him?*" I replied, incredulous.

Him. I had always pictured Rhon with his feet up at the local precinct, donut in hand, pushing paper from behind his desk. But when his friends started opening my eyes with stories of his time on the beat, I learned that he actually *was* that guy in *Cops,* breaking down doors and catching bad guys. Rhon started out on precinct patrol, wearing a uniform, driving his cop car around town. Eventually, he worked his way into the K-9 unit, which doubled as the Norfolk Police Department's SWAT team. If the situation required advanced weaponry or tactical expertise, my dad would get the call.

Promotions throughout the 1980s took him out of uniform but not out of danger. Going undercover for the department's vice and narcotics division, Rhon eventually took charge of that entire unit, leading armed missions involving informants and search warrants and criminals hawking drugs. On one such mission, a fleeing perp shot at him from a distance in a city park. Another time, my dad and a partner wrestled a man brandishing a knife to the ground. There were plenty of other scrapes along the way. Rhon didn't reach the paper-pushing, donut-eating phase of his career until much later, when he topped out as Norfolk's assistant chief of police. At that point, I was really only just beginning to understand the nature of his previous work.

My dad took his job seriously and was very, very good at it. That translated to life at home, where he created the type of culture you might expect from a cop. My brothers like to joke that we lived in the strictest home in Virginia, and as the oldest of four boys, I had it worst. We were taught to say, "Yes, sir," and "No, sir," to the adults we encountered. We were taught to shake hands and look people in the eyes. Curfews were strict. Punishments were no joke, often involving my parents' threatening to take baseball away from me and my brothers. At that age, I'm not sure I could have imagined a more terrifying fate.

My mom, Elisa, eventually moved from her work at the car dealership to jobs as a teacher's assistant and a school security officer, where she spent all day dealing with kids. She was definitely the more lenient of our parents, so we often went to her to try to plead down punishments. We simply couldn't get anything past Dad, who could sense the smallest fib. He was strict and punctual. If he told me to be home by ten o'clock and I snuck upstairs at 10:04, he wouldn't say anything that night. Instead, he'd wait until the next morning to ask what time I got home.

"Ten o'clock," I'd tell him.

"Did you?" Dad would reply.

"Yeah," I'd say.

"Did you?" he'd ask again.

A pause. "No," I'd admit under the pressure of his questioning. "It was ten oh four."

And 10:04 wasn't okay. That was his nature. He'd ask simple questions about things like schoolwork, allowing us to bury ourselves with our answers. If I made a B in one of my classes, I always knew the question would come: "Could you have done better?" I couldn't say no, because there was always something more I could have done. That lesson was always there, always lurking in the back of my mind. He wanted us to fulfill our potential. He wanted to make sure that we didn't have regrets. He wanted to make sure that we maximized our abilities, and without that sort of upbringing, I'm not sure we would have.

As one of our Little League coaches, my dad was also tougher on me than on anyone else on the team. I thought I deserved to play shortstop, where all the best athletes played. Instead, Dad put me in the outfield, saying I needed to earn my way onto the dirt. I was upset, but that's just the way he was. He made me earn everything, which I eventually did—my claim to fame as a youth baseball player occurred when I hit two home runs in a Little League All-Star Game. Doing that, while getting to wear the cool jerseys, made for one of the best days of my young life.

Looking back now, the sort of discipline my dad instilled in me was pretty critical to my development. Even once Rhon let me play the infield, I was no natural-born athlete. I was actually a little round as a child, which made for some early life lessons when I started playing football in addition to baseball. Teams were decided by weight, not age, and if I wanted to play within my normal age group, I had to tip the scales at a certain amount.

When that became an issue one autumn, I found myself at risk of having to move up a level. My dad used it as motivation, teaching me about my body and the things I would need to do to become an elite athlete. That summer, he was working on the SWAT team at the police department, so it was paramount that he keep in shape. Rhon went jogging daily, usually for up to five miles at a clip, in addition to all the running he did at work. While he never made me go with him, let's just say he lovingly recommended it. Inevitably, on those runs, I'd fall behind and my dad would snap his fingers loudly, encouraging me to catch up. It worked, helping me cut weight and learn about my body. But it wasn't all that fun. I remember some days I'd come home from school and shower by five P.M., thinking if I had already showered, I wouldn't have to go jogging.

On weekends, we'd run charity 5Ks and 10Ks. Again, this wasn't my favorite way to spend a Saturday, but I could see the transformation in my body. I made weight at football, building the foundation I would need to stay in shape throughout my big league career. During the off-season, I became a runner myself, sometimes dragging my brothers with me to an old landfill in Virginia Beach called Mount Trashmore. We would sprint up, jog across the top, do sets of push-ups, and run down. Football might not have worked out as a career, but it wasn't because of my weight or my effort. It was because I hated getting tackled. What can I say? I was soft.

I was also fast and athletic, despite my weight. In one youth game, an opposing coach came up to my coach at the time, Allan Erbe, and said, "I wish my team would hit more balls to your pudgy shortstop."

"I wish they would, too," Erbe shot back.

It's easy to look back on those years and see how lucky I was, but at the time, I don't think I appreciated the discipline and structure my parents instilled in me and my brothers. I might not have fully realized how important it was until I wound up having kids myself. Back in those days, it could be infuriating when my dad was tough on me. I probably slammed a lot of doors around the house. I probably cursed under my breath quite a bit. I can't even count the number of times I was fuming mad because I felt like the punishment for some transgression didn't fit the crime. But when I look back now, I understand the discipline helped me make choices that I might not have made had my parents raised me differently. I doubt I would have accomplished what I did without that grounding in my youth.

That doesn't mean I always avoided trouble. When I was in middle school, as my paternal grandparents' health was starting to fail, we decided that we would sell our house, they would sell theirs, and we would all move together to a new home in Chesapeake. While my grandparents were in the process of selling their home, we went over there and played some basketball in their driveway. My brother Matt lofted up a shot that I knew I could block. Despite the fact that he was six years younger than me, those old competitive juices started flowing, and I crushed the ball directly into one of the garage windows, smashing it to pieces. Neither of my parents was too happy with that one.

I did survive that punishment and made it to high school, where

I ran into one other little bit of trouble. One day during freshman year, a couple of my friends were goofing off in the cafeteria, flicking scraps of food at me. I was tired. I was in one of those moods. I just wanted to eat, but they wouldn't stop getting on my nerves.

Two important points to remember here. One, I had a bit of a short fuse. Two, I was a baseball player, so I had a pretty good arm. I stood up, balled a sandwich in my hand, and just let it rip at one of my friends.

Bad idea. I got slapped with an in-school suspension—me, son of a cop, who had never been disciplined at school in my life. I was petrified. Going home to tell my dad was probably one of the scariest things I had ever done. In situations like that, I knew it was bad when Rhon stayed quiet. When my dad was screaming and yelling, I could typically handle the punishments. When he was calm and measured, that's when I knew I was really in trouble. That's when he was livid. Needless to say, the food fight punishment was harsh and I deserved it. Messing up in school, which was so much higher on his list than anything else, was a surefire way to earn the wrath of Rhon Wright.

||||||||||||||

Of course, my dad's status as a Norfolk police officer resulted in more than a strict upbringing. It came with perks, too—and not just the thrill of having him click on his siren every once in a while. I mean the type we really cared about—baseball perks. To this day, in my parents' home, there's a picture of him as a plainclothes police officer, posing with some of his coworkers during an undercover mission. In the middle of the photo is my dad, wearing a Mets jacket.

That was no coincidence. Lots of locals were Mets fans due to the presence of the Norfolk Tides (originally called the Tidewater Tides), the local Triple-A team affiliated with the Mets from 1969 to 2006—a period that just so happened to include the entirety of my childhood. To handle security at the stadium, the Tides used to hire off-duty Norfolk police officers looking for some extra cash. Invariably, my dad would run into one of his police officer buddies there, and they would either sneak me a foul ball or bring us down to the field and introduce us to a player. Anytime the Tides participated in community events, my dad would badge his way in with the Wright boys in tow. At the stadium, he would send us down to lean over a railing, trying to get the attention of players.

I'm not sure I ever convinced anyone more famous than the mascot, Rip Tide, to sign a ball. It didn't matter. At that age, there was no greater thrill than taking a picture of someone, turning on the TV a couple weeks later, and seeing that same player up with the Mets at Shea Stadium. It was surreal. As a kid, those guys were our heroes.

Think about the impression that made on me, watching some of the best players of that era stop through Norfolk on their way to the majors—guys like shortstop Rey Ordóñez, a hot prospect who played my childhood position; outfielders Alex Ochoa and Jay Payton, the latter a star at Georgia Tech, where I would commit to play college ball; big-time power hitters like Todd Hundley, Butch Huskey, and Jeromy Burnitz; the Mets' "Generation K" trio of pitchers, Jason Isringhausen, Bill Pulsipher, and Paul Wilson; and more.

Even Dwight Gooden made a cameo there one year on a rehab assignment. Sometimes, at the end of spring training, the entire big league team would stop in Norfolk on the way back up to New York, and we'd get to see Gary Carter, Darryl Strawberry, and other superstars. My heroes, right there in my hometown.

The thought of one day playing for the Tides myself seemed like a dream. It took years before I realized I would have a chance at that homecoming—years of Little League, years of camps at Virginia Wesleyan and Old Dominion University, years of travel games in Virginia and beyond. Each summer, baseball was like day care for us. In the morning, my mom would load us all into a three-row Ford Expedition—she racked up more than three hundred thousand miles on that thing over the years—and drop us off at one camp or another. In the afternoon, she'd pick us up. As the oldest, I'd ride shotgun. Then the Wright brothers would head home for another round of basketball, Ping-Pong, Nintendo 64, whatever. It didn't matter as long as we were with one another, competing.

|||||||||||||||

One of the first baseball camps I attended was at the nearby Greenbrier Christian Academy, which at that time was run by a local baseball legend named Marvin "Towny" Townsend. A Philadelphia native, Townsend played parts of two seasons as an infielder in the Red Sox organization from 1974 to '75, topping out at Winston-Salem of the Class A Carolina League. He took his first coaching job two years later at Virginia Wesleyan University, a Division III program that has produced six major league draft picks. In three seasons there, Towny won his conference's Coach of the Year award twice. About a decade after leaving that job to pursue a master's degree and a career in private business, Townsend resumed coaching at his Norfolk alma mater, Lake Taylor High, turning a historically losing program—the school had won three games in three years before Townsend came along—into a perennial winner. He moved from there to Greenbrier Christian Academy, where he coached future big leaguer B. J. Upton, went 112-19 in four seasons, and won a state private school championship.

Townsend also played men's league baseball on a team called the Blasters, which became the inspiration for an Amateur Athletic Union (AAU) program that he eventually established. A true athlete, he could light up the radar gun with high-eighties fastballs even as he approached his fortieth birthday. Townsend was the only person we knew who had played in the minor leagues, which was about the coolest thing on earth. To us, Towny had street cred.

By the time I was old enough to start playing baseball, Townsend was omnipresent in the Tidewater baseball community, running summer camps with his friend, former big league pitcher Gary Lavelle, and teaching at a local batting cage called Grand Slam. Townsend kept a video of my first lesson there, of a pudgy six- or seven-year-old hacking off a tee. The film depicts my taking a series of huge cuts, knocking the tee down each time, maybe hitting the ball squarely one out of every ten tries. It didn't matter. After every swing, I waddled over, picked the ball up, and swung again. The tee usually went farther than the ball.

As a coach, Townsend was a fierce competitor with a loud,

outgoing personality—a true type A—and a baseball mind that was ahead of its time. The drills Townsend used were similar to what my coaches had me do when I made it to the minor leagues myself. He used to fill up giant plastic bouncy balls with water and have us haul them around as if they were medicine balls. He also used baseball as a vehicle to teach us life lessons, which was right up my dad's alley. Towny was intelligent and articulate and a little bit crazy, in a good way. One week, he made us memorize the famous Ernest Thayer poem "Casey at the Bat." Every day, Townsend brought something new like that to the table, sitting us down at the field and teaching us trivia, poems, other oddball things. He had a strange way of coaching the game, but I liked it. I liked it a lot.

More than anything, Townsend had an uncanny ability to make players believe in themselves. He took care of us, especially those who came from rougher upbringings, often hosting meals and other events at his home. Most of Townsend's players would have gone straight through a wall for him, and he returned the favor with time and love. His wife used to joke that when she wanted him to spend more time at home, she used glove oil as perfume.

Townsend made things fun, constructing a makeshift Slip 'N Slide out of a polypropylene plastic sheet and a garden hose, which we used to practice slides. We threw water balloons to each other to keep our hands soft. But he was known best for his other must-have training tool—something available in any grocery store.

Growing up, Townsend trained by using a broomstick to hit bottle caps that his father flicked toward him. When he became a coach himself, Townsend went bigger, peeling the tops off coffee cans and Cool Whip tubs and flipping them to us as if he were soft-tossing baseballs. It became a game to see how many in a row we could hit, and he always had little prizes for the winners, like pieces of gum. The first five or six lids, Townsend tended to toss right down the middle; then he'd start putting all sorts of crazy spin on them. For those of us who attended his camps, our parents received a discount if they sent us to the field with a certain number of lids from our kitchen cupboards. Those lids were so valuable because we could hit them anywhere—on the field, in the batting cage, even in our own homes. During one rainy tournament weekend, we hit them in an empty hotel conference room to stay sharp. If you could hit a lid fluttering in all sorts of crazy directions, you could hit anything.

Later in life, Townsend worked with a local plastics company to develop his own lid—flexible enough to stand up to getting smashed with a baseball bat, strong enough that it wouldn't flutter in the wind, weak enough that it wouldn't go flying back at the pitcher's head. I was in the big leagues at that time and made a video for Townsend to help market the lids, catching one of them and saying, "I would not endorse something that I don't believe in one hundred percent." That's how much I loved hitting those lids and how big an impact I felt Townsend had on my development. The lid drill was very competitive, sticking with me throughout amateur baseball. But no one could throw the lids like Townsend, who was masterful at making them spin, dip, and dive to simulate curveballs and changeups.

For a while, I just assumed all young hitters learned by whacking Cool Whip lids. It wasn't until I turned professional that I realized that's not the case. When I brought a bunch of them with me to my first stop in the minors, nobody knew what they were or why I had them.

It was around that time that I fully began to realize how lucky I was to have a baseball mind like Townsend in my home region. In addition to his coaching skill, Towny had ambition and long-term vision. One day after camp, I was about to head home with my grandfather when Townsend stopped us, asking for a minute of our time as we walked to our car.

Then Towny Townsend changed my nine-year-old life forever.

He said he was gathering as many of the best Little Leaguers in the area as possible to form a pair of All-Star teams, Tidewater Red and Tidewater White, to compete in a tournament two hours up the road in Varina, Virginia, just outside Richmond. Even though I was younger than most of the other kids, Townsend wanted me on one of the teams, and my parents obliged. I hit a home run that first tournament, and although we lost, we were all hooked.

Those teams would form an Amateur Athletic Union team called the Virginia Blasters, which became home to a talent mine unlike anything the region had previously seen. Between the Blasters and the Drillers, another Townsend brainchild that still exists today, the fledgling Tidewater AAU circuit produced five first-round draft picks and six starting major league position players over an eight-year span. From 2007 to 2015, all six of us played in the big leagues at the same time.

In addition to me, there was B. J. Upton, a middle infielder who went on to become the second overall pick in 2002—ahead of guys like Zack Greinke, Prince Fielder, Joey Votto, and Curtis Granderson. While he never made an All-Star team, B. J. played twelve years in the big leagues, hitting over twenty home runs on four different occasions. When we played together on the Blasters, B. J. was so young that he mostly came off the bench as a pinch runner. His brother, Justin, was a bat boy who enjoyed even more success in the big leagues, going first overall in the 2005 draft and making four All-Star Games.

There was also Ryan Zimmerman, the fourth overall pick in 2005, who spent more than a decade and a half in the big leagues with the Nationals. Like me, Zimmerman played for only one team throughout his entire major league career. He started out with the Drillers, and although we didn't know each other well back then, our common background and time in the NL East turned us into lifelong rivals and friends.

A year younger than me was Mark Reynolds, a sixteenth-rounder in 2004 who hit nearly three hundred home runs in the big leagues. Reynolds played for both the Blasters and the Drillers.

The one we all looked up to was Michael Cuddyer. Even though Cuddyer was too old to play for either AAU team, he was one of the first big leaguers of our generation to learn from Townsend at his camps and various other tournaments.

Once the Blasters were fully formed, I continued to play an age level up for a time, holding my own but never really excelling. It wasn't a perfect situation, so less than a year later Townsend and my dad talked it over and said they thought it might help my development to play with kids my own age. When my dad broke the news to me, it didn't really bother me. The reasoning made sense. If it meant improving my chances of becoming the next Cuddyer, I was all for it.

Still, moving down a level meant meeting an unknown coach and a new set of teammates. On that front, I wasn't sure what to expect.

# TWO

# TIDEWATER BOYS

Allan Erbe gave us a Harvard education in baseball when we were eleven years old.

The best way I can describe Coach Erbe is as a baseball genius for kids. At that age, the last thing any of us wanted to do was practice defense and fundamentals, which were the first things on Erbe's mind. Those initial years with the Blasters, we practiced on a sandlot field with rocks dotting the infield and grass up to our shins. For hours, Erbe smacked ground balls at us, giving us wooden blocks instead of gloves to teach us how to keep our hands soft. You can't catch a ball with a wooden block unless you're delicate with it, snapping your cover hand over the top. So we snapped and we snapped until we all perfected the art.

Like Townsend, Erbe had been a decorated amateur player in Virginia. He then became a mainstay on the local semipro circuit before touring South Africa and Rhodesia with the American Eagles USA team in 1976. He never stopped playing; in the 1990s, Erbe became the starting first baseman for a local men's league team that Towny Townsend established—the original Blasters. By that point, Erbe had a son of his own, who was my age. Townsend, who had already created his first AAU team, asked Erbe if he would be interested in coaching a younger version featuring his son Elliott. He was. So when Townsend and my dad decided it was time for me to drop down and play with kids my own age, I joined that team and met Erbe.

Erbe taught us bunt plays, pickoff plays, first-to-third plays—all sorts of things most kids don't learn until high school at the earliest. Years later, when I turned pro, some of my new teammates didn't know what a bunt defense was. With the Blasters, we ran seven or eight of them. Our sign system for calling plays had to be the most complex in the state, involving careful attention and arithmetic. We practiced so much that missing a sign just didn't happen. Erbe never dug too deep on hitting or pitching mechanics, the things that are so important on the travel circuit these days. For us, it was all about defensive fundamentals and mental training.

After practices, we crowded around Coach Erbe in the summer heat as he showed us photographs of baseball cards, Xeroxed nine to a sheet. In the margins were Erbe's handwritten notes, offering comments and criticisms. If one of our outfielders was getting lazy, catching fly balls with one hand, Erbe would find a card with an outfielder using both. If one of our hitters had a problem keeping his batting mechanics clean, Erbe would photocopy an image featuring the proper form—a picture of Jay Buhner with the words "HEAD

DOWN/EYES ON BALL" scribbled in all caps, or a photo of Robin Yount with the inscription "STIFF FRONT LEG, 3,000 HITS." He was crazy like that—the type of guy who could have total recall of a baseball tournament that happened decades ago but not remember where he put his car keys. On more than one occasion, he and his son had to search baseball fields by flashlight to find them.

After practice, there were written quizzes with all sorts of questions. Erbe tested our knowledge of things like the proper base to throw to in certain situations or all the ways to score with a runner on third and less than two outs. He taught me how to catch a lead base runner napping by faking a throw to first to bait him into venturing too far off second or third. Erbe often scheduled two-a-day practices; in the time in between, we sat with our eyes closed, visualizing situations and learning about the mental side of the game. Erbe's background was in psychology, with a master's degree in rehabilitation counseling from Virginia Commonwealth University. When I look back now, I realize Erbe probably could have been coaching more advanced levels of baseball with the knowledge that he had. But he was happy instructing us kids, and we were happy to have him.

About the only thing Erbe outlawed was batting practice, figuring we would all just do that on our own. He was right, of course. We hit plenty in our free time.

Like my dad, Erbe helped instill discipline in me. We signed contracts to play for the Blasters, promising to follow certain rules and maintain at least a 2.5 GPA in school. After each season, Erbe shared performance reviews with our parents, grading us for everything we did both on and off the field—things like power hitting, defense, coachability, and more. It was pro-style stuff from Erbe, who worked on the side as a bird-dog scout for the Cubs. (Essentially, that meant putting the first set of eyes on players that Chicago's area scout might consider pursuing.) Everything we did was professional.

Erbe was strict about equipment, going as far as to ask us to polish our shoes before each game. (That one didn't last long, considering the parents wound up doing most of the polishing.) I spent some time as a catcher for the Blasters, and there was a rule in the league that catchers, who had to strap on their equipment between innings, could always receive a pinch runner without penalty—something I had little interest in. I may have still been a little chubby at that time, but I was fast. So when I reached base one day and Erbe signaled for a pinch runner, I was livid. I spiked my helmet to the ground, understanding immediately that my reaction was the wrong one.

"Are you going to tell your dad," Erbe asked me, "or am I?"

I was petrified, knowing this was a lesson both Rhon and Erbe had taught me many times. If I went 0-for-20 with twenty strikeouts, that wouldn't matter. If I went 19-for-20 but pouted after the out, I would get a talking-to. How I carried myself made a difference, and that's a lesson I always tried to take with me throughout my career and life.

|||||||||||||

The Blasters changed the equation for me at a time when the youth baseball season, even for the most talented All-Stars, typically ended in June and didn't start again until the following spring. This was before travel leagues and tournaments like Perfect Game became big business, driving the country's amateur baseball agenda. Back in those days, fall ball didn't exist. Until high school, Little League was all we had. The Blasters and the AAU circuit sparked the beginning of a new wave, giving us an opportunity to play nearly all year round. It was amazing to travel across the state and the country playing games under the instruction of Erbe and his assistant coaches, Ron Smith and Rob DeMara. The kids who were on that team remain some of my closest, lifelong friends.

The Blasters also gave me perspective on how I stacked up compared with other kids. As we began traveling to tournaments in Virginia and the Midwest, competing against some of the best teenagers in the country, I realized I was usually one of the top players on the field. While I was never totally sure and often harbored doubts about my ability, I began to understand how I compared to the kids in Florida or Texas or California—a lot of them players who would go on to become high draft picks. With each tournament I attended, my confidence increased. I grew stronger and leaner, getting rid of some of that childhood chubbiness. I started to figure out my place in the baseball world.

One advantage of being a bigger kid was that I was able to use heavier bats, sometimes even trying out wood bats even though I had no business using them in games. (My coaches thought the wood bats would refine my swing, and they very well might have, helping me grow proficient at driving balls to the opposite field.) No bat was too big for me. When we were about twelve, one of my best friends, Matt Smith, received a new metal bat for his birthday: thirty-one inches and twenty-two ounces, a pretty typical size for someone that age. So imagine his reaction when that Christmas, Santa brought me an Easton C-Core: thirty-three inches and twenty-eight ounces. I showed it off to everyone. I felt like I was really going to do big things with this bat, like this was the secret weapon I had been missing.

"Dude," Smith told me when I showed him. "There is no way you can swing that bat."

"Yes I can," I replied.

And I could. I swung it well enough to create controversy when we attended an AAU tournament in Rocky Mountain, North Carolina. Our opponents were accustomed to using skinny-barrel bats because of their local Little League regulations. When I walked up to home plate lugging my C-Core, their coach complained so vociferously that the umpires made me use a thinner model. The next pitch, I drilled a skinny-bat home run. I didn't even know what pimping a homer was back then, but I definitely pimped that one. That home run felt good.

Smith joined the Blasters the same day I did, mostly manning second base because B. J. Upton was still too young to play there full-time. (Like me, he would eventually drop down to his own age group.) Quickly, Smith and I became inseparable. Another Christmas, I received a soft-toss setup for my garage, with a sock net to hit baseballs into. Smith and I hit until one A.M. that night, and it wasn't long before he had the same setup at his house. Coach Erbe was right about our not needing to take swings during Blasters practices. In our free time, we hit plenty.

We also won plenty. The Blasters took five trips to the national AAU tournament, at a time when teams couldn't buy their way into those events. The only way there was to win a state tournament, earning the chance to go up against the best teams from around the country. In one national tournament in Minnesota, we played a team called the California Bums, featuring a couple of future big leaguers. Andy Sisco, who went on to play parts of three seasons for the Royals and White Sox, started that game and was throwing hard. But we rallied in the ninth inning, and I came through with the game-winning hit.

Back then, just getting my name in the local newspaper was a big deal, but as my skill level grew, so did my goals. Thanks to Townsend, Erbe, and other coaches, the level of youth baseball in the area was so high that we all couldn't help but improve on a regular basis. In the grand scheme of things, the Tidewater area is tiny compared to baseball hotbeds in California, Florida, and Texas—and that's not even mentioning Japan, Puerto Rico, the Dominican Republic, you name it. To have one little slice of Virginia so saturated with talent might have been lucky to a certain extent, but the perfect coaches were in place to nurture it.

By the end of my Blasters tenure, scouts were starting to hang around—at least partially on the recommendation of Erbe, whose bird-dog job gave him connections to the higher levels of baseball. The first game I ever played in front of a scout was at a Moose Lodge in Manassas, Virginia.

Featuring a strangely configured outfield, the Moose Lodge had a huge, deep center field and lots of room in right-center. I took advantage of that gap to hit six triples that day. Six! Late in the game, I hit what seemed like a surefire double. Even though the game was a blowout, Erbe, totally out of character, waved me around second base in an attempt to get me that elusive seventh triple. By the time I rounded second, the cutoff man had the ball in his glove, allowing him to throw me out by a good thirty feet. If it had been a big league game, the other team probably would have drilled me for attempting a stunt like that. Instead, we all got a good laugh out of it—especially Erbe, whose scout friend filled out a report on me that day.

I was playing baseball constantly and loving it, though things became a little turbulent as I tried to balance my AAU commitments with high school baseball, travel showcases, and the influx of scouts and college coaches who started to come calling. One weekend when I was a sophomore in high school, the Blasters were set to play in the AAU Junior Olympics in Ohio. Scheduled that same weekend in Wilmington, North Carolina, was the East Coast Professional Showcase, which is a big deal for players hoping to get drafted. For me, the decision seemed like a no-brainer. The way I looked at it, Coach Erbe and his staff had succeeded in getting me invited to those types of showcases—now it was my responsibility to play in them. But when I let them know I was going to miss the Junior Olympics to attend this one, they told me they didn't agree and tried to dissuade me from going. That caught me off guard. So I compromised, heading out to Ohio for half the weekend before driving back to attend the showcase.

That AAU tournament wound up playing host to one of my most memorable amateur moments. I hit a home run to right-center, a line drive that just kept going and going until it struck a tree branch. As I rounded the bases, the branch fell to the ground in what my teammates compared to the light-tower moment from *The Natural.* The moment was just really cool, even if it wasn't *quite* as dramatic as the movie.

I also performed well in the second half of the weekend at the North Carolina showcase, which included an amazing collection of talent. Playing for Billy Swoope, a local Cubs scout who had assembled the event, I was on the same team as future big leaguers Rocco Baldelli and Brandon Guyer. My performance made a big impression on all the scouts in attendance, and suddenly, I found myself on the draft radars of multiple teams. Looking back, I realize how much my parents and grandparents sacrificed, both financially and otherwise, for me to appear in those showcases across the country. And guys like Townsend and Erbe gave up countless hours of their lives to coach us. I'm forever grateful for all of that.

The following autumn, I played on a travel team with Ryan Zimmerman, Mark Reynolds, and B. J. Upton (B.J.'s younger brother, Justin, also hung around and practiced with us), driving to different colleges in the area, sometimes even staying on campus and getting a taste of university life. Those experiences spotlighted the goal for all of us. Turning pro was a dream; going to college was realistic. I thought much more about using baseball as a vehicle to land a college scholarship than I did about getting drafted.

Because I grew up near Upton, Zimmerman, and Reynolds, people assume we were teammates during our entire climb up the youth baseball ladder. In reality, that fall was the first and only time we all played together. Since we were all shortstops, we rotated game to game. Sometimes, I manned third base, B. J. Upton played short, and Zimmerman was at second. Other times, I took shortstop with Zimmerman or Reynolds at third.

Regardless of where this baseball path would take me, I was on my way, with more and more showcases to attend. The tournament that really helped cement my status was the Area Code games, which brought together the best of the best amateur players in the country. In my junior year of high school, my parents bought me a plane ticket to Los Angeles to fly out there by myself. Traveling alone for the first time in my life, I was scared to death. The logistics were hairy; I had a connection, and upon arriving, I was supposed to catch a shuttle at LAX to take me to the tournament in Long Beach.

I couldn't find the shuttle. I didn't have a cell phone. So there I was, standing with my baseball bag and personal luggage, calling my dad on a pay phone, close to hysterical because I had no idea how I was going to get to the La Quinta Inn an hour away. Finally, I saw another kid with his family carrying a baseball bag, so I gathered enough courage to go up and ask them, "Do you know where you're going?"

His parents gave me a ride straight to the field, where I received my tournament gear right before game time. Because I was the last kid to arrive, I had last pick of uniform, forcing me to play in pants that were way too small for me. Still, I hit a home run and a double my first two at-bats, well aware of all the scouts there to see it.

# THREE

‖‖‖‖‖‖‖

## "ADULT STUFF"

Hickory High School was not established until 1996, which probably diminishes this achievement a bit, but I'm proud of it nonetheless: The following year, I became the first freshman in school history to make the varsity baseball team.

Having established a relationship with coach Steve Gedro after playing for him at a local basketball camp, I actually played on the varsity team in eighth grade as well, splitting time with a sophomore shortstop—an experience that taught me how to be even more competitive and take nothing for granted. Then, when I made honorable mention for the all-district team my freshman year, I established a goal of making the first team the following season. I was obsessed with working longer and harder than everyone else, especially as I began understanding that baseball could be a way to attend a college of my choosing on scholarship. With that opportunity hanging right there in front of me, I needed to do everything possible not to blow the chance.

It helped that I had a firsthand look at the potential spoils of my hard work. That year, when I was in in eighth grade, Hickory High didn't have its own field yet, so we split a practice venue with our rival, Great Bridge High School. The star of that team was Michael Cuddyer, a senior well on his way to becoming a first-round draft pick. Cuddyer's team always had the early practice slot, which led to this comical scene: As we stretched to prepare for our own work, we routinely had to duck away from balls screaming toward us during batting practice. I had always heard about Cuddyer growing up, even meeting him a few times due to his association with Towny Townsend. Still, seeing him hit in person was eye-opening for an eighth grader like me. This guy was the real deal, and we all knew he was going places.

That same year, I moved from Virginia Beach to Chesapeake. Because the school system syllabi weren't quite identical, my middle school ran a program where they put me on a bus to Great Bridge High for math and Spanish classes, so I wouldn't have to repeat the lessons I had already learned in Virginia Beach. That was how I found myself in the building the day the Twins drafted Cuddyer ninth overall in 1997. As someone made the announcement over a loudspeaker, the entire school ground to a halt. Everyone started cheering and yelling in one of the coolest scenes of my young life.

If any doubt remained, I knew right then and there that I wanted to be the next Michael Cuddyer. He was a perfect role model for me to say to myself, *Okay, this guy from Chesapeake just did it. Why can't I do it, too?* I understood the path forward would involve hard work, and I wasn't going to shy away from that.

So I worked and I worked and I worked. When I was in high school, my friends and I began spending our free time at a batting cage in Virginia Beach called Grand Slam (the site of my first lesson as a kid with Towny Townsend), which eventually opened a second location right by my house in Chesapeake. I struck a deal with them. Each day, I spent a couple hours selling tokens to customers and cleaning up balls from the cages. In exchange, they let me hit for free.

Eventually, the owners of Grand Slam gave me a key to the place. My friends and I would wake up around five A.M., let ourselves into the cage, put on some music, and hit before school. No number of swings was ever enough. My parents had raised me on the foundation that good things happen to people who work hard. I wasn't sure at that time if I was going to make the big leagues, but if I failed, it wasn't going to be for lack of effort. When that effort paid dividends, I doubled down on it. I tripled down on it. I set the Hickory High School record with a .471 batting average as a sophomore. As a junior, I put together a twenty-one-game hitting streak to break my own record with a .474 average, then I broke it again by batting .544 as a senior.

By the time I'd become an upperclassman, scouts and college coaches were regularly coming out to watch me play. Every Hickory High game became like my personal World Series. I wanted to stretch and get loose at six A.M. for a five P.M. game, which made perfect sense in my mind. I became obsessed with the idea of playing at the next level. One of the greatest adrenaline rushes of my life was walking behind school to the baseball field and seeing college coaches and scouts lined up for the first time.

Preparing for those visits became a second job. Dozens of colleges sent me questionnaires. No matter if it was Georgia Tech, North Carolina, or some random Division III school I had no intention of attending, my parents made me fill out each questionnaire as if it were my top choice. Those forms typically included a spot for height and weight. Before completing them, my dad brought out the tape measure and scale to make sure we were noting the most accurate information possible, even if I had just recently measured myself earlier in the week. To prepare for the first day that collegiate coaches were legally able to talk to me, we set up a second answering machine in our house. As both tapes filled up, my parents made certain that I responded to every message.

I don't think my parents ever let me believe I was going to get drafted; the idea of receiving a college education was paramount both for me and for them. Largely, I enjoyed the process of sifting through schools. Outside of playing in my Hickory High games, the highlight of those days was running out to the mailbox and seeing which colleges had sent me letters. I'd examine them to see which ones were personalized and which were just form letters with my name inserted in the proper spot. I received multiple pieces of mail per day from schools all over the country, and as those flowed in, my dad and I cross-referenced their academic and baseball rankings with a college-prep book he had bought.

We made a spreadsheet ranking my top twenty schools, complete with notes on who the starting shortstop and third baseman were at each college, how old they were, how good they were. Make no mistake: I wanted to play. I'd rather have gone to a lesser baseball school where I could start, as opposed to sitting on the bench at my top choice. So every week, as more letters came in, Dad and I added to the spreadsheet and reranked everything. Sometimes, I'd complain that nothing had really changed. My dad would have none of it. We spent time on that spreadsheet every single week.

High school players back then were allowed only five official visits to college campuses, so I scheduled mine for Florida State, Duke, North Carolina, Auburn, and Georgia Tech. I liked Florida State because that was where Cuddyer had committed before turning pro, but I fell so head-over-heels in love with Georgia Tech that I canceled all the other trips after visiting Atlanta. Not only did I know it was the school for me, I was pretty certain I was going to go there instead of the professional ranks. My parents went as far as to buy me a set of Yellow Jacket bedsheets and a Georgia Tech shower caddy.

The day I signed my national letter of intent was something I'll never forget. Hickory High threw a signing party for me, with cake and pizza, sort of like the reception Cuddyer received when he got drafted. I was allowed to miss my last class and invite friends and family to come to the school, where I put on a Georgia Tech hat and the one suit I owned, posing for pictures with a pen in my hand as I signed the letter. My parents bought black-and-yellow balloons and a huge banner. I felt like I was a really big deal.

Still, the idea of turning pro lingered in the back of my mind. My dad bought a book, the *Baseball America* almanac, which we used to put faces to the names of scouts who came to watch my senior season at Hickory High. There were Gary LaRocque, scouting director for the Mets; Jim Hendry, general manager of the Cubs; and plenty of others. When those guys showed up, I wanted to be able to look them in the eyes and call them "Mr. LaRocque" and "Mr. Hendry" and show them I was the type of person they could rely on. When guys like LaRocque came out to watch me play, it was a big deal—scouting directors and other high-ranking executives tended to watch in person only if their area scouts and cross-checkers had signed off on a prospect. In other words, his presence alone meant I was a legitimate draft target for the Mets.

The first time LaRocque came to Hickory High, he was waiting in the bleachers when I walked out of school around one P.M. to take early batting practice with one of my teammates. Each of us carried a bag of balls, taking turns pitching to each other and going through our usual batting practice routine—hitting first to the opposite field, then up the middle, then finally trying to pull for power. When we were done, we walked over to the other side of the fence to collect all the balls we had hit. Before heading back inside, I made sure to thank LaRocque for coming.

I didn't realize it then, but those simple acts of politeness impressed LaRocque as much as any of my results in the game that day. At the time, I didn't know all that much about my draft status. This was 2001, back in the days of dial-up Internet, long before *Baseball America* and MLB.com were publishing regular online mock drafts leading up to the event. The publications that did exist, such as *Baseball America*'s print magazine, had me ranked anywhere from the first round through the fifth. At one point, a scout from the Expos called to ask if I would accept tenth-round money.

*Oh wow,* I thought. *I'm not going to be a major league player. The money's not going to be there so I'm going to go to college instead.*

Other experiences made me think differently. I received one of my biggest thrills when Randy Milligan, one of the players I had grown up rooting for with the Tides, came to my house as an area scout representing the Mets. His nickname was Moose, and every time we watched him play as kids, we would all yell, "MOOOOSE!" So imagine my excitement when the guy I screamed for as a kid—"MOOOOSE! MOOOOSE!"—came to my house with a pre-draft questionnaire to see if I had the right type of talent and makeup for the Mets.

As the draft grew closer, I huddled with my parents and my advisors and decided to set a walkaway point around the third round. If a team drafted me by that point, I would turn pro. If a team selected me later, I would go to Georgia Tech.

I at least had an idea of which teams might be interested—led by the Mets and Cubs—even if I didn't really know the extent of that interest. As it turned out, the Cubs wanted me badly, but they spent the number 2 overall selection on future All-Star pitcher Mark Prior and didn't have another pick until the second round. The Mets took Notre Dame right-hander Aaron Heilman at number 18 overall but had a compensatory pick later in the first round for losing Mike Hampton to the Rockies on a then-record eight-year, $161 million free-agent contract.

That afternoon, I had an anatomy and physiology exam, so I missed the first couple dozen picks of the draft. Once I finished the test, I rushed home to listen to the draft feed on our dial-up Internet

connection. There was no video or analysis, just a scratchy recording of each selection as it was announced. Because no one in my
family rushed over to congratulate me when I came through the
door, I knew right away that I hadn't yet been picked.

The supplemental round began soon after I arrived. Because
the Mets had the eighth pick in that round, thirty-eighth overall, I
knew there was at least a chance I could go off the board at that
point. I listened as Jeff Mathis, a premium catching prospect who
wound up spending close to two decades in the majors, went to the
Angels. I heard the Mariners take Michael Garciaparra, Nomar's
brother. The draft feed kept cutting in and out, but we got the gist
of it. Finally, it was the Mets' turn at number 38. I heard someone
on the feed say my draft ID number, identifying me as "Wright,
David Allen, Hickory High School, Virginia." And then my mom
broke down crying, jumping up and down in our kitchen. I started
jumping beside her. My dad came over for a hug as the entire family
went nuts. It was just a magical, magical moment.

|||||||||||||

From that point forward, I knew I was going to sign a contract and
begin my professional career. The Mets drafted me well before the
third-round cutoff that I had set for myself to sign; as much as I had
been looking forward to going to Georgia Tech, I simply wasn't going to turn down first-round money. Shortly after the draft,
LaRocque invited me to a Tides game to show me what minor
league life could be like. John Gibbons, the Norfolk manager at the

time, joked that he had an extra uniform available if I wanted to sign right then and there. Believe me, I was tempted.

My patience for the negotiations was nonexistent. I hired an agency, ACES, to do that work for me, choosing them in part because they represented one of my idols, Scott Rolen. I started growing close with one of my new agents, Keith Miller, who was a friend of Moose Milligan's. He kept telling me to hold tight, but weeks felt like months. I set a deadline for the agency to negotiate the best possible deal, telling Miller I'd sign whatever he had for me at that point. He was convinced that dragging out the negotiations could have netted me more money, but I was plenty happy with the result: $960,000, plus a guarantee that the Mets would pay for my college education if I decided to matriculate within two years of retiring— regardless of whether that happened at age nineteen or thirty-nine. That part was of utmost importance to my dad.

From my perspective, I was never going to turn down that sort of money. We were a squarely middle-class family. When somebody offers you close to a million dollars to play baseball, you go play baseball.

My dad, who had helped guide so many decisions in my life, left it all up to me. He instructed Miller to talk to me, not him, calling it "adult stuff."

"You're a kid right now," Rhon said, "but once you get drafted, you're going to see how quickly you become an adult."

# FOUR

# THE GRIND

When the Commonwealth of Virginia issued my first temporary license after I turned sixteen, I used it to drive a 1985
S10 Chevy pickup truck—a big, hulking stick shift. Sadly, that beast
had lived out its best days by the time I was a senior in high school.
After I committed to Georgia Tech, on my mom's birthday, we went
to a local Ford dealership that offered great prices for police officers
and their families. I drove a brand-new blue 2000 Ford F-150 off the
lot. Not long after, I pointed it west across the whole of Virginia.

I was bound for Kingsport, Tennessee, and a professional baseball career.

This was before the days of Waze or Google Maps, or even
those GPS units people used to stick on their windshields. Before
my trip, my dad and I went to AAA to create a TripTik, which was
basically a bunch of road maps all mashed into one. I drove until I

reached the end of the first map, then flipped it over to the next portion, and so on and so forth all the way from Chesapeake to Kingsport. Throughout the entire ride, I kept thinking about how my responsibilities were about to transform. No more Mom to do my laundry. No more Hot Pockets in the freezer. Everything on my own. It all just hit me as I was driving away in that blue Ford pickup: Welcome to adulthood. Here goes nothing.

There were indeed no Hot Pockets, but at least there was cereal in the pantry and milk in the fridge. The Mets assigned me and one of my teammates to live with a host family, an elderly couple named Peggy and Jim, who took a small cut of my paycheck in exchange for room and board. That was certainly a bit of culture shock for me, at a time when all my friends were going to college, moving into their freshman dorms with beer and parties and soon-to-be lifelong buddies as roommates. This decidedly wasn't that. Peggy and Jim were big, big smokers. The house was always filled with cigarette smoke, which took some getting used to. So did being on my own for the first time. Here I was starting a professional baseball career that I hoped would be illustrious, living in a small town with a group of total strangers. But they were great people who welcomed me with open arms and kept in touch with me throughout the minor leagues.

Kingsport was the longtime landing spot for Mets high school draft picks, and I was no exception. When I arrived, the team kept me inactive for a couple days, budgeting some time for me to take batting practice and ground balls and get the lay of the land. Goodness knows I needed the adjustment period. My first day at the ballpark, team stretch was scheduled for 4:00 P.M. I showed up at 3:50, thinking that was totally fine, and got chewed out by the veterans on the team. I had no idea I was supposed to report to work way sooner. At just eighteen years old, I had a lot to learn in this strange world of adulthood. I had a lot more to learn about professional baseball culture and clubhouse etiquette.

I learned rapidly, though, as the Kingsport Mets quickly became my entire life. Returning home from each game, I was on such an incredible high, beyond excited to be playing in the minor leagues. I often fired up my email late at night to see a message from one of my old AAU coaches, Allan Erbe or Ron Smith, or from one of my buddies saying congratulations or asking me about life in the minors. I always responded that everything was great. For the most part, it was. Especially if I had gotten a couple of hits that night—forget it. My adrenaline would be through the roof. I wouldn't fall asleep until one or two A.M. I'd stay in bed until eleven A.M. or noon, get up, grab some cereal, and go straight to the ballpark. It was 24/7, constant baseball, which was exactly what I wanted.

It wasn't for everyone, sweating out those humid, oftentimes rainy summer days in the Appalachian League. There were times after games in those old stadiums when hot water was hard to come by. There were times when our bus broke down, times when we drove for hours across Tennessee or Virginia without any air-conditioning. It wasn't glamorous. It was so far from life in the big leagues. In those early minor league levels, I think a lot of coaches and organizations tried to weed out the guys who didn't really want to be there. For some, cold showers and hour-long bus rides did the trick. If you don't love playing and you don't have that passion for the game, day-to-day life in the lower minors can be miserable.

Financially, it can be tough as well, which often made me feel guilty as a first-round pick with a $960,000 signing bonus. My solution was to send the entire bonus to a financial planner, who squirreled it away for safekeeping. To this day, I've never touched a cent of that money. Instead, I lived on a combination of my minor league salary—around $800 a month—and some savings bonds that my grandparents gave me when I was born. Occasionally, I signed autographs for Topps to earn a few extra bucks, but mostly I lived the same way my minor league teammates did. Granted, I had this nearly million-dollar nest egg to give me uncommon peace of mind, so I tried to help out by buying dinners and things every now and then. One of my teammates the following year, Matt Galante Jr., jokingly established a rule that the highest draft pick always had to pay for dinner. I probably overextended myself a little bit, but I always felt for those guys who were grinding away without any financial guarantees.

In a lot of ways, I felt awkward as a first-round pick. Coming into Kingsport, it seemed like all eyes were on me, like I had to be this super-player because the Mets drafted me thirty-eighth overall. I felt like I needed to hit a home run every at-bat, make every play on defense. Quickly, I learned that sort of thing just wasn't possible in the professional ranks, where I was no longer facing the types of pitchers I'd hit .600 against in high school. I was used to being a big fish in a small pond; suddenly, I was surrounded by nothing but big fish. Learning to deal with failure was important. Learning to be responsible was critical. I wasn't going to get better if I treated this like a hobby, because baseball had become my job. My livelihood.

Living on my own for the first time that summer, I certainly could have found trouble if I wanted to. I never wanted to. I could have drunk away the nights, partied away the mornings. I never wanted to. Going back to the fact that my dad was a police officer and my mom worked at a school, that strict upbringing had a major effect on me. I feared telling Rhon about getting in trouble more than I feared the trouble itself. That, combined with the fact that I was hyper-driven to make it to the majors, kept me from pursuing anything harmful to my career.

Over the years, I saw guys with more talent than me, or equal talent to me, party themselves out of the game. It can be a temptation for some people. For me, that sort of idea was so far from my worldview. My life in Kingsport and up the minor league ladder was boring. I woke up. I went to the park early. I came home late. I went to sleep. I did it again.

I loved it.

Even that first season, I never felt like the routine, the grind, of professional baseball was too much to handle. I never felt like I couldn't succeed. I never felt overwhelmed. That summer at Kingsport, I hit .300 with four home runs, nine stolen bases, and an .850 OPS as one of the youngest players in the Appalachian League. It was a start; while I still had doubts about my ability to reach the top, I knew I was on my way.

IIIIIIIIIIIIII

It took me three seasons to advance beyond A ball, which is about the minimum for a high school player beginning his professional career at age eighteen. My second summer, I played on a full-season

affiliate with the Capital City Bombers in Columbia, South Carolina, which I loved because of our manager. Tony Tijerina was a
former Mets farmhand who had played at Capital City himself just
nine years earlier. Although he was young for a coach, just thirty-
two years old when I reached Columbia, Tijerina was old-school to
the bone. He looked out for us. In a game that spring, I hit a home
run, and the next at-bat, the pitcher hit me in the head. None of our
own pitchers retaliated, so after the game, Tijerina sat everyone
down on the outfield grass and started ripping us for not going after
one of their guys. For a good while, he just lit into the entire team.
It showed how much he cared.

I don't know if it's because I was a first-round pick or simply
because he took a liking to me, but Tijerina really took me under
his wing that season. Remember, I was nineteen years old at the
time, still accustomed to hammering high school pitchers who either didn't have good breaking balls or couldn't throw them over the
plate. That changed once I started playing professionally and experienced some of the typical trouble dealing with curveballs and
sliders. To help, Tijerina came to the ballpark early about once a
home stand. I'd step into the batter's box and he'd climb onto the
mound, throwing me breaking ball after breaking ball after breaking ball—probably about a hundred per session. It was always just
me and him, dripping sweat in the summer humidity. Tijerina put
in a lot of time for me that he didn't have to.

Although I was improving, I wasn't where I wanted to be, and
as I progressed through that grind, I often found myself feeling
homesick. That, for me, was the biggest adjustment from high

school to the pros. While my parents came to visit from time to time, they both had jobs back home that they couldn't just abandon. Plus, they were wary of the effect visiting would have on my routine, concerned that I'd feel like I needed to entertain them the entire time they were there. My dad, a history buff, loved visiting some of the old battlegrounds the year I played at Capital City Stadium in Columbia. So we'd go to one and have a good time, but he'd worry that walking around the battleground all morning would make me tired for the game at night. For those reasons, I think my parents purposely limited the number of visits they made.

My brothers were all younger than me, all still in school, and obviously couldn't drop everything to visit. Growing up, we had done everything together. They weren't just my brothers but my best friends. Being without them made me homesick to an extent that I hadn't anticipated.

Advancing to the Florida State League didn't help my little problem. Although the FSL is still technically Class A ball, it's a clear step up from the South Atlantic League, where I played at Capital City, and worlds away from the Appalachian League. It was my farthest stop yet from home, and, simply put, it was a slog. Not only was the competition better than at any other Class A level—pitchers didn't miss the strike zone as much with their breaking balls—but temperatures hovered over ninety degrees in the summer, with sweltering humidity. Rainouts were a common occurrence in the Florida State League, leading to lots of doubleheaders. The weather made everything more difficult. And there weren't all that many good places to eat in Port St. Lucie, Florida, which was only beginning to experience some of the development boom that would occur over the next decade.

For anyone who didn't really love baseball, life in the Florida State League could be both mentally and physically exhausting. I moved in with a couple of older teammates, Matt Galante and Joe Hietpas, and the three of us went to Outback Steakhouse or Friendly's too many times to count. Friendly's had this dessert called the Cyclone, filled with soft-serve ice cream, peanut butter cups, and peanut butter sauce. I may not have done much drinking or partying as a minor leaguer, but I never said I was perfect. The Cyclone was my vice. After games, the three of us often ate together, then drove back to our condominium in the nearby PGA Village to sleep, rinse, and repeat.

Those two helped make things feel more like home. Galante was the comic; Hietpas was more serious. One week that summer, one of my old Virginia Blasters teammates, Marshall Graves, gathered a group of friends together to drive down to Port St. Lucie. Graves got to talking with Hietpas, a sixteenth-round draft pick who would go on to have something of a Moonlight Graham moment, appearing in one career major league game without ever taking an at-bat. Hietpas had seen enough, and worked hard enough, to have a little baseball wisdom.

"You know your buddy is the real deal, right?" Hietpas told Graves.

"Well, yeah," Graves responded. "We've known he's been really good for a long time."

"No," Hietpas said. "He's something special. He's going to mean something to baseball. He's going to mean something to the New York Mets."

||||||||||||||

Those words may have been flattering, but I didn't entirely feel like I deserved such compliments at that time. On the field, I was struggling, unable to make a seamless adjustment from the lower minor league levels to the Florida State League. It's not that I was struggling to hit for power, or struggling to hit breaking balls, or anything specific like that. It's that I was struggling to hit, period. Things got bad enough that my roommates, Galante and Hietpas, sat me down one night at our kitchen table just to talk things out, to brainstorm ways to get me back on track. At that point in my life, it was probably the most significant dose of on-field adversity I had faced.

Luckily, I had some savvy people on my side. One day about halfway through the summer, Guy Conti, the Mets' minor league field coordinator and a longtime baseball man, called me into a meeting to look over my statistics. He asked me how I felt playing at home versus on the road.

"Fine," I responded. "The same."

Then Conti showed me the splits. I was hitting about .400 on the road but barely .200 in Port St. Lucie. He told me his hypothesis. At home, Galante and I had a routine of showing up to the ballpark around one P.M. to take dozens of swings in the afternoon heat before everyone else arrived two hours later. Then we stretched and took more batting practice with the rest of our teammates, all before the actual game. Compare that with my routine on road trips, when I hopped a bus to Vero Beach or Melbourne or wherever we happened to be playing, took regular BP, and that was that. As much as my intentions were in the right place with all the additional work, Conti believed I was doing more harm than good, so he banned me from taking extra swings at home.

This was an entirely new perspective for me. My whole life, I'd believed I could do nothing but good with all those extra swings, all those extra hours in the cage, all those extra reps at the field. Since I was young, my dad had taught me what it meant to work and work and work and work. That wasn't for show or for vanity. It wasn't because I wanted others to look at me and see how much I was doing. It was just programmed into my brain that the harder I worked, the greater my chances of success. One time when I was a kid, my dad bought tickets to an Old Dominion University event where former Giants first baseman Will Clark was speaking. I listened, rapt, as Clark talked about his routine of taking a hundred swings a day.

*All right,* I thought. *I'm going to take a hundred fifty.*

Summers, when my friends spent their afternoons at the beach, I always made a conscious effort to do something baseball related. Anything I could. I had this sick thought in my head that while they were hanging out, doing nothing productive with their days, they were giving me a chance to get that much better than them. Every Thanksgiving and Christmas, I made sure to do the same, because I knew I would be the only one working on those holidays. I looked at those moments as chances to widen the ability gap between myself and my peers. In my brain, every swing added up. I may not have been able to control my natural talent, but I could control my effort and dedication. Even if I didn't reach my goals in professional baseball, I wanted to be able to rest easy knowing I had done everything possible in my attempt to make the majors. Early batting practice was part of that.

But I did take it too far at times, with insecurity probably playing a role. As a supplemental first-round pick, I was under a microscope from the moment I arrived at Kingsport. I wanted badly to fit in with my older teammates. I didn't want people to think I was this eighteen-year-old hotshot who was going to show up in a Lamborghini, act entitled, and pretend he was a big leaguer before he had accomplished anything. I wanted to take the most blue-collar approach possible. While all the hard work helped me, there was a happy medium I hadn't yet discovered. My final game in Kingsport, we were trailing by a run, playing out the string for a last-place team. Could've fooled me. In trying to earn the respect of my teammates, I ran over the opposing catcher and accidentally broke his leg. I wanted to play the game hard all the time. I wanted to play the game to win.

Only slowly did I come to understand that while working hard is important, so is working smart. The benefits of work tend to dissipate when you're doing things like taking extra batting practice without necessarily understanding why. Years later, I had a chance to talk to Hall of Famer Tony Gwynn—one of the greatest hitters in baseball history—at an All-Star Game. He told me one of his famous pieces of advice: He never took additional swings when he was struggling because he didn't want to practice when he felt like something was wrong. Instead, Gwynn did all his extra work when he felt sharp, in an attempt to lock in positive muscle memory. It was a lesson I hadn't yet learned but one that Conti knew: That summer in St. Lucie, I was overworking to the point where it became detrimental.

On Conti's advice, I chilled out with my early work and finished strong enough to hit .270 with fifteen home runs and an .828 OPS at St. Lucie—a minor miracle, considering how poorly I started the season. We won the Florida State League championship and I had a great postseason to lead us, drawing praise from Conti when I hung myself up in a rundown long enough for a key rally to continue in one of those playoff games. Overcoming that summer's adversity was critical to my development.

It was also one of my favorite summers for a different reason. The manager of the 2003 St. Lucie Mets was Ken Oberkfell, an infielder—mostly a third baseman—for sixteen big league seasons, as well as a World Series champion with the Cardinals. The hitting coach was Howard Johnson, one of my idols. Back when I first started to follow the Mets in the late 1980s, HoJo was the man. He played nine years in New York, making All-Star teams in 1989 and 1991. He compiled three 30-30 seasons, with at least thirty home runs and thirty steals in each of them.

Along the way, HoJo won two World Series, including one with the Mets in 1986. Did I mention he was the man?

I was super-intimidated by HoJo at first because he was the guy who had done it all. I was just the new guy. When I arrived at Port St. Lucie, I walked onto a roster filled with players who had been there the previous year. They were always joking around with HoJo, and I thought to myself, *Man, I want that relationship. How do I get that relationship?*

It's something that happened over time. He and Oberkfell—"Obie," we called him—knew how to keep things light amid a Florida State League grind that could crack anyone. They had this great air about them where they were always joking in an affectionate way with each other, with my teammates, and eventually with me. It was typical minor league stuff—going out on the field and doing tarp slides during rain delays, for example. But it was effective.

We all knew we had jobs to do. We all knew minor league baseball was difficult. HoJo and Obie made it fun. So did Paul Taglieri and Traer Van Allen, who essentially ran the whole operation down in Port St. Lucie. Slowly, thoughts of homesickness and doubt began giving way to the realization that I was getting closer to the majors, closer to slipping on that uniform for the first time, closer to the biggest goal on my mind.

That September, the Mets sent me to the Arizona Fall League, an annual showcase for some of the game's best prospects. I was pumped to get that invitation—I mean *pumped*—for a few reasons. First, the AFL was largely a showcase for Double-A players at that time, and I was coming out of A ball, still just twenty years old. Second, I had formed a tight-knit group with some of my teammates moving up the minor league ladder, including Justin Huber, D. J. Mattox, and Matt Peterson, all of whom went to Arizona as well. Third, the AFL is legit. My team alone featured twenty-one future big leaguers, including guys like Adrián González, Mike Jacobs, and Rickie Weeks. We all received big league–style bats with our names etched onto them and were allowed to wear the major league uniforms of our various clubs. It was a huge deal for me when I slipped on that snow-white Mets jersey for the first time since draft day, and a bigger deal still when I hit .341 in those games on a national stage.

The AFL was, and still is, a great place to hit.

||||||||||

# FIVE

# GOING HOME AGAIN

When I was twenty-one years old, I moved back in with my parents.

A little backstory: Buoyed by my strong performance in the second half of 2003, I opened the following season at Double-A Binghamton, which featured an entirely different set of problems than St. Lucie. Instead of hot and humid, it was cold and sometimes snowy in upstate New York. Instead of doing tarp slides, we amused ourselves by taking the shards of broken bats, sticking them into a big dugout space heater, then spraying the wood with bat grip from an aerosol can. They made for great blowtorches, and great fun.

Probably the best part about Binghamton was that both Obie and HoJo made the trip with me, as the Mets promoted them a rung up the minor league coaching ladder. Under their guidance, everything continued clicking. I hit .363 with a 1.086 OPS in sixty games, and it wasn't long before I was due for another promotion.

The question was where. Some of the organization's decision-makers believed Triple-A Norfolk's culture might be toxic for me, surrounding me with a bunch of veterans bitter that they weren't in the majors. Among those in that camp were Obie and HoJo, who argued for me to stay at Binghamton awhile longer, then jump straight to the big leagues. But they weren't adamant about it, asking me what I thought was best. I could honestly see it both ways. On one hand, I felt confident I could leap two levels to the majors. On the other, Norfolk was home. Missing a chance to play there seemed like an opportunity lost.

Ultimately, general manager Jim Duquette got on a conference call with Obie, HoJo, Norfolk manager John Stearns, and others, and they decided to send me to Triple-A.

Coming full circle back to Norfolk legitimately felt like getting called up to the big leagues. This was home. All those nights going to see the Tides with my family, trying to get autographs and pictures—suddenly I was on the other side of it all. In a way, that experience prepared me for the big leagues, because I had to learn to deal with the distractions—the dozens of ticket requests, the scores of interviews, the countless friends wanting to go out after games. I was getting pulled in every direction, but my mind was on baseball, not on being a local celebrity, so I decided to move back in with my parents.

Once again, I found myself fighting with my brothers over the last cookie in the cookie jar, arguing over who could run the fastest, who could throw the hardest, who was best at Mario Kart. It was just a great reunion.

All told, I was in Norfolk for barely a month, but that experience did help immensely when I made it to the majors. I proved in that short stint that I could balance the requests, the appearances, the demands on my time, the distractions that could have prevented me from playing good baseball. Rather than get sucked into all of it, I hit .298 at Norfolk, with eight home runs in thirty-one games, performing in front of friends and family every night.

If we hadn't received comped tickets to the games back then, I might have needed to dip into my draft bonus check. Each night, I requested twenty or thirty tickets. Each night, I signed autographs until there were no more left to sign, sometimes for forty-five minutes to an hour after games. It was easy to remember being that kid in the stands, hoping for any sort of attention from a player; I realized this was my chance to repay that kindness. When I read in the papers that the Tides were selling more tickets than usual, I felt obligated to say thank you to everyone who came out to support me. Signing autographs was the least I could do.

My first day at Norfolk, it seemed like every media member from miles around wanted to do a segment on me. I wound up being late to stretch and taking some heat for that. The veteran guys just wore me out, joking about how big a celebrity I was. Like so much of the Norfolk experience, it wound up being a small foreshadowing of what it would be like to join the Mets in the country's biggest media market. But I never considered that a burden. I learned to prioritize, to take time out of my day for both the fans and the media. When the opportunity came to do all that stuff on a daily basis in New York, I was ready.

IIIIIIIIIIIIIII

Who am I kidding? I'd be lying if I said some doubts didn't linger.

Outwardly, I'm a pretty confident guy, especially in matters related to baseball. But for as long as I can remember, I've always had a voice in the back of my head questioning my abilities. I've never seen myself as a star.

When I was a kid playing Little League, I knew that I was good for my town but had no idea how I stacked up beyond that. When I started playing travel ball for the Blasters, I learned that I was good for my area but didn't know what it meant compared to kids from Texas or California—much less from Japan or the Dominican Republic. On draft day, I genuinely didn't know where I would land; when I went thirty-eighth overall, part of me felt that maybe I was lucky, that the Mets' scouts had happened to see me on good days. In rookie ball, I posted solid numbers, but that was just rookie ball. In Single-A and Double-A, when my success continued, that voice in my head said, *Yeah, but you still haven't faced any big league pitching.* Even once I reached Triple-A, I thought, *I'm having success, but against guys who are in Triple-A for a reason.*

I convinced myself that I didn't belong. In a twisted way, I always feared failing more than I enjoyed succeeding. I always berated myself when I played poorly more than I patted myself on the back when I played well. Mentally, that probably wasn't the healthiest way to go about my business, but it was one of the driving factors that motivated me.

It wasn't as if I had a chorus of other voices telling me otherwise. The minor league landscape was different back then. Social media didn't exist. You couldn't just Google prospects to find detailed scouting reports and rankings, and I was never a can't-miss prospect anyway. During a game in Norfolk, my mom got to chatting with Marshall Graves, one of my childhood friends. She asked him if I still had a good head on my shoulders. Given all my doubts about my own abilities, how could anything have changed? Sure, I knew I was on the right path, but for a long, long time, I harbored insecurities about my ability to succeed at the highest level. I needed to do it to believe it.

At Triple-A, those doubts manifested themselves in the form of defensive struggles, which began with my very first throw from third base. Up until that level, I thought I was nails defensively. I don't know what happened, but I'll never forget, during pregame warmups on my first day with the Tides, taking a ground ball from Craig Brazell and three- or four-hopping it back to him at first. He gave me a funny look and a good-natured jape.

"Throw the damn ball," Brazell told me.

It might have been easy to chalk that up to nerves, but it started happening often. The more I made mistakes, the stiffer I became at third. Once I began worrying about my footwork, the whole thing wormed its way into my head. Every motion felt mechanical. I tended to throw the ball on target but was always short-hopping it. Things grew bad enough quick enough that the Mets sent out Edgar

Alfonzo—the organization's infield coordinator and the older brother of former Met Edgardo Alfonzo—to work with me, and he spent so much time in Norfolk that I started to feel self-conscious about his being there. I tinkered with stuff that I probably shouldn't have, which carried over into my early days in the big leagues. Even when I made plays, I felt uncomfortable both physically and mentally. Edgar and others wanted me to stop double-tapping the ball in my glove before I threw, which was a tough habit to break.

Through it all, I tried to be coachable, but I learned I had to stop thinking so much out on the field. Spring training was the time for mechanical work. The season was the time to see the ball, catch the ball, throw the ball. Oftentimes, the less I thought about what was going on around me, the better I played.

|||||||||||||||

My hitting, at least, was never in question, and I performed well enough at Triple-A to earn a trip to the Futures Game during All-Star week in Houston.

If I thought the Arizona Fall League was cool, this was even cooler. Like the AFL, the Futures Game brought together some of baseball's top prospects—mostly guys in Double-A and Triple-A. This time, though, there were only two teams instead of six, making it even more of an elite showcase. In front of a national television audience, ESPN mic'd up me and B. J. Upton, my old Virginia Blasters teammate, who had also received an invite. Being together on such a big stage with Upton, the second overall pick in the 2002 draft, was an amazing experience.

The real highlight, though, occurred two days later. I stuck around for the major league All-Star Game because my agents let me shadow Cardinals third baseman Scott Rolen for the day. At that point, Rolen was a former Rookie of the Year and a four-time Gold Glover who would go on to receive regular support on the Hall of Fame ballot. As far as baseball players go, he was the guy I wanted to be because he could do it all—play rock-solid defense, hit for average, hit for power. Before the game, Rolen told me to sit down at his locker, then talked to me for fifteen or twenty minutes about pregame preparation, off-season work, playing third base in the big leagues, all of it. He was awesome. He signed a Cardinals hat for me, which I still have, and introduced me to a couple other players. It could not have been a better experience—except for one thing.

When Rolen went to take batting practice, I walked with him, bringing the hat to try to get a few more signatures. The guy I wanted to meet most was Derek Jeter, and there he was out on the field, stretching and taking BP as well. I won't bore you with Jeter's credentials—a fourteen-time All-Star, a five-time World Series champion, a one-way ticket to Cooperstown by the time he turned thirty. I tried to approach Jeter on the field to shake his hand and ask for an autograph but totally chickened out. Instead, I just stood there, taking in his presence on the field, watching him in awe.

|||||||||||||||

One other pretty amazing thing happened at the All-Star Game in Houston. The Mets' general manager, Jim Duquette, pulled aside one of my agents, Keith Miller, to tell him I was weeks—if not days—away from getting called up to the majors. When Miller approached me all giddy to deliver the news, it hit me right in the gut. I had figured I was close, but this was real. This was hard information, coming straight from the source. It felt like all my hard work was about to pay off.

Early that summer, we played a game against the Durham Bulls, which was a big deal because, once again, I found myself crossing paths with Upton. It was a busy week in town, with lots of adrenaline, lots of excitement, and even more friends and family than usual at the games. After one of them, I went through my typical routine, lingering a long time to sign autographs before showering and changing. I could have slipped out of the stadium pretty easily any time after the game ended, but it wasn't until right as I was about to leave that John Stearns, the Tides' manager, called me into his office to talk. This wasn't normal. I searched my memory for evidence of something I might have done wrong.

I was concerned, but instead of chewing me out, Stearns had good news. Fantastic news. That night, in his office, I learned I was heading to the big leagues.

The ensuing hours were a blur. I packed up everything at the stadium, headed home, grabbed the only suit I owned, and slept for maybe an hour or two. The next morning, my parents drove me to the airport, where Edgar Alfonzo and I met for a nine A.M. flight on a propeller plane bound for Queens. I remember flying over New York for just the second time in my life, having only been there previously to sign my first professional contract. I saw the city come into focus down below and, just as I had on that initial car ride to Kingsport three years earlier, thought: *Here we go.*

Even though I felt like I had accomplished such a tremendous goal, I knew this was just another beginning. Now I had to prove myself, again, and stay. Nothing I had achieved over the previous twenty-one years mattered anymore as I walked into a clubhouse with longtime big leaguers, All-Stars, even a couple of future Hall of Famers.

The Mets' starting third baseman at the time was Ty Wigginton, who was batting .343, but he was turning into a prime trade candidate because the Mets considered me the long-term answer at the position. When news of my call-up broke, Wigginton requested a meeting with Duquette and manager Art Howe to discuss his status. Needless to say, he wasn't happy, giving me reason for concern. As I sat on that prop plane, bleary-eyed from lack of sleep, a thousand scenarios flitted through my mind. What if Wigginton refused to talk to me? What if the whole room resented me for taking his spot or even driving him out of town? All sorts of dark thoughts clogged my brain. I started psyching myself out a little bit. But when I walked into the clubhouse, Ty was the first one to greet me.

"Look, whatever you've read, whatever you've heard, this has nothing to do with you personally," he said. "I'm certainly upset at the situation, but I'm not upset with you and I'm rooting for your success. I'm going to do everything I can to help you."

Hearing that put me at ease, and in the days that followed, Wigginton backed up those words 100 percent.

I dropped off my bags at the Holiday Inn across the highway from Shea Stadium, then went straight to the ballpark because I had no idea what time I was supposed to report. I wasn't about to repeat my embarrassing first day at Kingsport, and a busy agenda awaited me anyway. From the moment I arrived at Shea, longtime Mets public relations director Jay Horwitz was in my ear about meeting the media, doing this, doing that. It was hard to concentrate on any one thing. I had to try on my uniform and spikes to make sure they fit. I grew panicked trying to find Charlie Samuels, the equipment manager, because I'd forgotten my wristbands and needed them to play well. (Yeah, I'm not superstitious at all.)

At some point during that scramble, I realized Samuels had given me uniform number 5, the same number I had been assigned in Norfolk. I hadn't chosen it. That spring in major league camp, I had been number 72. Growing up with the Blasters, I wore number 4, which I used whenever possible in the minors. When that number wasn't available at Binghamton, I picked number 44.

Going into my Mets debut, I knew number 4 was off-limits because it belonged to third-base coach Matt Galante Sr. (the father of my minor league roommate Matt Galante Jr.), but I wasn't sure which number I would get instead. I learned later that when the Mets assigned me number 5 for the first time at Norfolk, that was no accident. Samuels—a big history buff—told me he gave me it because two of the greatest third basemen of all time, George Brett and Brooks Robinson, wore number 5. That was cool. Years later, I met Brett at the 2012 All-Star Game in Kansas City and he signed my jersey, writing on it: "From one No. 5 to another."

Seeing that number 5 Mets jersey hanging in my locker for the first time on July 21, 2004, floored me. I realized they must have thought I was at least halfway decent, because they don't give out those single-digit numbers very often.

The entire afternoon raced along until game time. At that moment, part of me relaxed, the stress of the previous twenty hours melting away. The other part tried to stop my heart from beating through my chest, especially on defense, given my recent struggles. I was starting at third base and batting seventh and, before stepping into the batter's box for the first time, I made it a point to find Shea Stadium's big scoreboard in right-center field and gaze at my name in lights. The moment felt like a dream. I didn't mind too much that I finished 0-for-4, including a foul pop in my first at-bat that Expos catcher Brian Schneider made an incredible play to snag. (Years later, Schneider would become a teammate and friend, and eventually a coach on the Mets' big league staff, so I couldn't hold the grudge for too long.)

Even though I was disappointed at the result, I had made it. The entire day was one big exhausting dream; worries about staying in the majors could wait until tomorrow.

As I prepared to leave Shea Stadium that night, my teammate Joe McEwing came up and invited me to go grab a bite. I was a bit confused, knowing we had plenty to eat in the Shea Stadium clubhouse.

"No, no, no," McEwing said. "Let's go get some food and celebrate."

He explained that this was my big league debut, a once-in-a-lifetime event deserving of some recognition. So, despite being on about two hours' sleep, I dragged myself to midtown Manhattan, where Joe and I went to a baseball bar called Foley's. We had something to eat and walked around the restaurant, looking at the cases stacked with balls that players, coaches, umpires, and sportswriters had signed over the decades. Giving me a celebratory cigar, Joe told me to enjoy my time in the big leagues as best I could, because I had no way of knowing how long the journey might last.

From there, I headed back to the Holiday Inn and collapsed. I'm not sure I had ever slept so well in my life.

## SIX

||||||||||

# FLIP-FLOPS AND KARAOKE

On my first road trip as a big leaguer, I showed up at Olympic Stadium in Montreal wearing jeans and flip-flops. I cannot stress enough what a mistake this was.

While I was finally in the majors, I still had plenty to learn about how to be a major leaguer—what time to arrive at the ballpark, what to wear, how to behave, how not to embarrass myself. Luckily, the clubhouse had a significant veteran presence to help me figure it all out. That meant ribbing me every time I did something wrong, like wearing flip-flops to and from the team hotel when I was supposed to put on jeans, a nice shirt, and dress shoes. Message received, loud and clear.

In more ways than just beachwear, my initiation to big league life began with fashion school. At twenty-one years old, I owned a single suit—an ill-fitting thing that I wore not only on my flight from Norfolk to New York City but also to every wedding, funeral, and special occasion I attended. One of my teammates, Cliff Floyd, quickly worked to change that, carrying on baseball's decades-old tradition of veterans' buying suits for rookies. An outgoing outfielder of a dozen big league seasons, Cliff occasionally hired tailors to measure him for custom-fit suits and shirts, right there in the clubhouse. For someone accustomed to buying all his clothes off the rack at the mall, this was a foreign concept. Cliffy style wasn't exactly my style—he liked his suits big and baggy—but the materials were nice and, more important, they were free. I didn't say no.

What I came to realize is that nothing is ever truly free. Because I was the rookie on the team, Cliff required me to wake up early before the final game of each road series, come to his room, and carry his Louis Vuitton luggage down to the lobby. It was a task· I gladly bore, considering how much more comfortable he and others made my assimilation to the majors. Joe McEwing, bought me a nice pair of shoes to replace the sneakers I wore pretty much everywhere I went. A third teammate, John Franco, offered a different sort of fashion advice. Franco told me that although I always needed to have a jacket when I traveled, it didn't have to match my pants so long as I walked around with it slung over my shoulder. I spent my early days as a big leaguer soaking in lots of important life lessons like that.

More than anything, I tried to show the guys that I could be one of them—that they could rib me or try to embarrass me, and I could take it all in stride. I felt like I was back in the minor leagues, watching established players joke around with Howard Johnson and wanting desperately to be part of that camaraderie. So I said yes to everything the veterans asked me to do ... and it wasn't all ordinary. Beginning with that first road trip to Montreal, the older players started making me go to the front of the bus and sing to them—stuff like the national anthem, or songs from a movie soundtrack, or whatever else they wanted to hear that particular day. It was all in good fun, but that didn't make it any less intimidating. Mike Piazza always sat in the first seat with his big, hulking frame, meaning I'd have to brush his shoulder to get by him. As I sang, he would stare at me with that Piazza scowl I was used to seeing on television.

The words coming out of my mouth might have been Whitney Houston lyrics, but inside, I was thinking: *Man, I'm serenading Mike Piazza right now.*

While it may not have been the most comfortable experience in the world, it was also a pretty cool feeling to make those guys laugh. During that same trip to Montreal, a group of veterans brought me and another rookie, Tyler Yates, to a local karaoke joint. They pushed us one at a time to the front of the room, making me belt out "You've Lost That Lovin' Feeling," *Top Gun*–style. I was terrified. With the possible exception of Tom Cruise, what person would enjoy getting up there and singing in front of Hall of Famers? I felt far less pressure going into a big at-bat in the ninth inning than climbing onto a karaoke stage, not knowing what the veterans would ask me to sing. As I belted out my best Righteous Brothers impression that night, my anxiety level was through the roof. (But to this day, I maintain that I did nail the song.)

In the worst way, I just wanted to be one of the guys. If that meant future Hall of Famers howling at me at some Montreal karaoke bar, so be it.

Singing wasn't the only activity that brought us together. My rookie status meant the veterans were constantly singling me out for various reasons, which was fine by me. I didn't want these successful baseball stars to think of me as some hotshot who felt like he deserved special treatment. I just wanted to be one of the guys, and they made it worth my while by inviting me to dinners and other events I didn't feel like I deserved to attend. Often, I was the only rookie present at these things, which I think had a lot to do with the fact that I kept my sense of humor about me.

One day early in my career, Tom Glavine pulled me aside to tell me he wanted to help me out as much as possible because, in his words, "you get it." That was one of the biggest compliments I could receive from a guy like that; it meant that I listened more than I talked, that I was respectful to both the clubhouse veterans and the game itself, that I understood baseball history and had a desire to play the game the right way. For him to say those few words—"You get it"—meant a lot to me. In the years that followed, I spent time around plenty of younger players who didn't react well to the type of clubhouse culture that brought teams together. I'm so glad the veterans saw me as the type of guy who did.

I tried to pick my spots in giving that sort of treatment back to them. As I mentioned, I had a lot to learn. One afternoon that first summer, I saw Piazza sitting alone at his locker, staring at the ground with a dejected look on his face. It was like he had a force field around him; no one wanted to go remotely close. But because I was brave, or maybe a little stupid, I went up to him in a joking manner and started massaging his shoulders.

"Mike, you all right, buddy?" I said to him.

No response. I kept rubbing his shoulders.

"Mike, what's wrong?"

No response.

"Mike, everything okay?"

After a few minutes of this, I gave up. I never found out what was wrong with Piazza that day. I was just a happy-go-lucky twenty-one-year-old pestering Mike Piazza, when all he wanted was a few minutes of alone time. Looking back, I'm just fortunate he didn't punch me in the face.

Thankfully, those cringe-worthy moments were few and far between as I assimilated into clubhouse life. I've always been appreciative of the era when I got called up to the majors and the Mets. If I had debuted on a younger team, I wouldn't have had those types of veterans there to teach me the proper way to handle myself, to show me the ropes. Maybe it wouldn't have affected my success, but it certainly would have impacted my knowledge of how to be a leader. I can't say enough about what those guys did for me and my development, in both light moments and serious ones.

None of them were as helpful as McEwing, a thirty-one-year-old utility man who had built a successful career despite never being the biggest, fastest, strongest. My rookie year, I rented an apartment in the Avalon Riverview building in Long Island City, where McEwing lived. It was a beautiful new high-rise overlooking Gantry Plaza State Park and the East River, about a twenty-minute ride from Shea Stadium in the early afternoons. Every day, I rode to the ballpark with McEwing, scribbling down directions in a notebook so I could learn how to get there myself.

Eventually, our conversations pivoted from how to navigate the

Grand Central Parkway in traffic to how to succeed in baseball and life. We constantly talked about routines, with McEwing's shaping mine. We talked about situations on the diamond and how to react to them. We discussed things as simple as how much to tip clubhouse attendants or where to find taxicabs outside various stadiums, and as weighty as our careers and futures. I felt like I had so much to learn. Looking back, I realize how difficult my rookie season could have been had McEwing not been there to mentor me.

Perhaps it's not surprising that McEwing, a former twenty-eighth-round draft pick who managed to carve out a nine-year career in the big leagues, was such an excellent role model. Standing five foot ten, McEwing was not the most physically gifted baseball player. But he ground it out every day, becoming a fan favorite for that reason. He learned to play every position except pitcher and catcher. He was meticulous in everything that he did. He tried to instill those qualities in me as well, teaching me how to set a daily routine, how to prepare for games, how to stay fresh over a six-month regular season. Along the way, McEwing wound up turning into more than just a mentor. He became a big brother. In Long Island City that summer, McEwing and his wife cooked for me constantly, inviting me over to their apartment for meals. The following spring, I ate with the McEwings almost every day.

At a time when my transition to the big leagues could have been very, very difficult, Joe made it easy. Cliff made it easy. Franco made it easy. All those guys played such important roles at a critical juncture of my career.

If I wanted to earn the same sort of respect those guys commanded in the clubhouse, I had to conduct myself in a similar way.

For me, that was the easy part. The hard part was learning how to produce at a major league level, facing the world's best pitchers on a daily basis. The feeling was similar to when I signed my first contract after the 2001 draft. Back then, despite accomplishing my lifelong goal of playing professionally, I harbored doubts about my ability to work my way up the major league ladder. When I overcame them and finally put on a big league uniform, I knew the real challenge would be having enough success to stick—not just for a day, but ideally for a week, then a month, then a year, then more. The weight of that responsibility hit me all at once. I wanted to celebrate the achievement of reaching the majors. At the same time, I couldn't rest for a second. I knew the Mets could send me back down to Norfolk in short order if I didn't do what I was capable of doing.

So I put in the time. In my second career game, I grounded my first hit down the left-field line, a double off Expos pitcher Zach Day. On my way to first, Brad Wilkerson pretended to stretch for a throw, trying to deke me into thinking the third baseman had caught the ball. There was no fooling this rookie. I rounded first anyway and sprinted to second, feeling like I had checked another box off my lifetime bucket list. As I stood there catching my breath, Expos shortstop Orlando Cabrera caught the relay throw and flipped it to Matt Galante Sr., our third-base coach. A couple years earlier, when I was playing in Port St. Lucie, both Galantes had become friends of mine, sometimes taking me on little road trips to see the big league team play in Miami. It was cool to have the older Galante be the one to collect that ball for safekeeping. It still has a place of honor in my home today.

Every major league "first" was enjoyable, including my first home run, which I hit hours after showing up at Olympic Stadium wearing flip-flops. (Maybe that wasn't such a bad idea after all.) But initially, those moments came few and far between. My first six games, I batted .167. Looking back, that "slump" was nothing more than a one-week adjustment period to the majors. At the time, it seemed like it dragged on forever.

In the midst of it, Mets manager Art Howe kept me out of the lineup for a game in Montreal because he wanted to prevent me from pressing. I was upset. It felt like a punishment, when in reality Howe was just trying to help me shake off a rough patch at the plate. As it happened, José Reyes suffered a minor injury later that night and I came off the bench to replace him. In my second at-bat, I singled and scored; just like that, my little slump was over. From that day until the end of the season, I batted .305 with thirteen homers in sixty-three games.

During those first few weeks of my career, I generally batted sixth or seventh in Howe's lineup. By the end of it, I regularly hit third, which was no accident. One day late that season, Howe pulled me aside and told me that he wanted me to be not only a middle-of-the-lineup type of guy but also a clubhouse leader. Once again, a small conversation like that meant the world to me. That always stuck with me even as I moved forward in my career. In a clubhouse full of All-Stars and future Hall of Famers and high-character humans, Art Howe was asking a twenty-one-year-old kid to be a leader.

||||||||||

# SEVEN

# BIGGER, FASTER, STRONGER

Once my rookie season ended, I felt in some respects like I was a big leaguer—and, believe me, that's an incredible feeling. But I also had plenty of old doubts creeping in. Even as success began to come more regularly at the plate, I told myself that anybody could do it for half a year, then join the long list of players to sink into sophomore slumps. To convince myself I belonged, I would need to have success for at least a full season.

My teammate, mentor, and confidant Joe McEwing told me to take some time off and get back into my workout routine around the holidays, which seemed to me like a long time to be idle. It felt that way to my father, too. Once I traveled back home to Virginia, living again at my parents' house, that sort of schedule just wasn't going to fly. Early that off-season, Rhon asked me one morning what my plans were for the day.

"Nothing," I replied.

"You're not going to hit or anything?"

It was a rhetorical question. Later that day, I was right back in the batting cage working out again.

Baseball, my dad explained, was my craft; I needed to treat it no differently than a policeman or a lawyer or a doctor would treat his work. When Rhon clocked in at the precinct, he spent eight or nine hours there on a regular schedule. In his mind, I needed to do the same, blocking off a chunk of time each day to settle into a routine. That made sense to me. If I was going to enjoy the financial perks and fame that came along with being a baseball player in New York, then I owed it to myself and to the fans to work hard enough to maintain that level of success. In truth, given my insecurities about belonging in the majors, working hard always put me a little more at ease.

To help, I hired a trainer named Robert "Piney" Reyes, who'd spent his early life as a carpenter and superintendent at a local Virginia shipyard. Piney had also been working part-time at a local gym called New Fitness when he met Michael Cuddyer, who didn't know a lot about weight lifting at that time. This was a tiny, two-room gym with zero frills. When Cuddyer asked Piney for some help with his form, the two of them got to talking and developed a relationship, and eventually, Piney became his personal trainer. Although he didn't have much experience with baseball, Piney hit the books and earned some extra certifications. This was right around the time I was becoming close to Cuddyer, mostly due to our spending winters together in the same area. My respect for him made me want to use his off-season routine as my blueprint. It wasn't long before I hired Piney as well.

These were old-school strength workouts with a twist. Piney took what he knew about football and soccer training methods, then made them functional for baseball players. For a guy like me who enjoyed sleeping late, Piney was also my alarm clock. One of his most important jobs was simply to tell me a time when I had to be at the gym, which helped me keep the routine that I needed. Even if I didn't feel like working out, I had to show up because Piney was counting on me to be there.

So was Cuddyer. Although I'd idolized Cuddyer in high school, I never played against him or knew him well because of the four-year gap between us. That all changed once I turned pro. I certainly didn't consider myself on the same level as Cuddyer, who had been establishing himself as a major leaguer around the same time I was a wide-eyed teenager in Kingsport. In a way, I still very much looked up to him. But we grew close because of our off-season workouts with Piney, who eventually added B.J. and Justin Upton, Ryan Zimmerman, and Mark Reynolds to his training roster. One after another, all these professional baseball players started rolling into this little local gym. It was like a secret club that we had, with Piney running the show.

Cuddyer in particular became not only a workout buddy but a close, close friend. During both good times and bad, he knew exactly what I was going through because he had gone through it all as well. Our work ethics were the same. One winter, Cuddyer got really into interval training, often running a three-and-a-half-mile circuit over the course of twenty-six minutes. Because I had to prove I was in top shape, too, I challenged him to repeat the entire workout while I did it for the first time. Of course he said yes. We both burned to succeed, which manifested itself in how hard we worked in that small Virginia gym.

However, Piney was not my only personal trainer. That winter, the Mets made a series of splashy moves, starting with three-time Cy Young Award winner and Red Sox legend Pedro Martínez. A month later, they agreed on a seven-year, $119 million contract with Carlos Beltrán, the 1999 American League Rookie of the Year in Kansas City. Following a midseason trade to Houston in 2004, Beltrán had become one of the most productive trade deadline acquisitions in major league history, hitting twenty-three home runs in ninety games for the Astros. Then he hit eight more in twelve post-season games, batting .435 and almost singlehandedly leading Houston to within a game of the World Series.

Shortly after Beltrán signed, I was at a mini-camp in Port St. Lucie when the Mets flew him down to tour the facility. He didn't recognize me at first, but when I went up and introduced myself, I saw something click in his eyes.

"You're going to train with me," he said.

Beltrán didn't speak those words like a question or an invitation. This was a requirement, and I arrived in Florida that spring to find out he was serious. Each morning, Beltrán instructed me to come to the complex for early hitting before we stretched on the field with the rest of the team. We hit again in the afternoon, and once the Mets' organized workouts were done for the day, Beltrán and I drove to a Gold's Gym down the street to lift weights together. At first, I didn't totally understand his reasoning. Not only did we have a perfectly good gym right there at the stadium, but I also didn't want to offend our strength coach, Rick Slate, who organized weight-lifting sessions at the ballpark. Beltrán was insistent, though, so I cleared it with Slate. He encouraged me to go with Carlos.

That's how I came to spend most afternoons with Beltrán and his personal trainer, both of us exhausting ourselves with max-effort, sweaty workouts.

Immediately, I learned how working with Beltrán would be different. He showed me what went into being the type of five-tool, all-around superstar that he was.

Before training with Beltrán, my workouts away from the team revolved around basic beach-style strength training—hop on a bench press, do some bicep curls, do some triceps push-downs, things like that. With Beltrán, each exercise was related to baseball in some way. If we were working our biceps or our triceps, for example, our movements would mirror those we used on the field. There wasn't any slacking off during these workouts. We weren't completing a set of exercises, goofing off for a minute, and then doing another. We were there to accomplish a series of goals, and we weren't going to leave until we achieved all of them. Every aspect of the sessions had a purpose, including the most eye-opening feature of them: stretching.

As it is to most twenty-three-year-olds, stretching was a foreign concept to me outside of the half-hearted warmups I did on the field. That changed quickly with Beltrán. We stretched before and after every workout, and, man, it was intense. There were times Beltrán's trainer would pull my legs to the point that I thought the muscles inside them might pop.

Combined with what I learned from Piney, Beltrán's sessions took my workouts to a new level. I don't know what went on in Houston in 2017 as far as the sign-stealing scandal that cost Beltrán a chance to manage the Mets, but I do know that as a player in New York, he was a pro. In some ways, that made working with him intimidating. In most ways, it was educational to see how a guy who had just signed one of the largest free-agent deals in major league history—and who had just produced one of the most dynamic seasons the sport had ever seen—went about his business. I was working out alongside one of the best players in baseball, which only added to my comfort level heading into my second season.

|||||||||||||||

That spring, I lockered next to McEwing, which gave us an opportunity to extend our mentor-mentee relationship. Throughout the winter, Joe and I spoke on the phone two or three times a week. When we arrived back in Port St. Lucie, I resumed the tradition of joining him and his wife for meals.

As someone who shared my values both on and off the field, Joe continued to be a wonderful source of advice and companionship for me. We both worked hard. We both took things seriously. We both just wanted to be the best baseball players we could be. To have such a like-minded individual next to me in the clubhouse was hugely helpful. What I didn't realize (or at least, didn't want to believe) was that McEwing entered the spring of 2005 in a perilous position. The previous August, Joe had broken his leg and missed the final six weeks of the season. He reported to spring training on the back end of a two-year contract and—unbeknownst to me—had already had an uncomfortable conversation with general manager Omar Minaya about his future. Minaya had told Joe that he probably wouldn't be part of the mix going forward but that he would try to trade or release him to give him a chance to play elsewhere.

As a young player, I could be pretty naïve, particularly about the business side of baseball. I assumed nobody I liked would ever get released, that all my clubhouse friends would stick around forever. One day in Port St. Lucie, after I overheard an exchange between Joe and a reporter, Joe finally told me he wasn't a lock to make the team.

"What do you mean you're not going to make the team?" I responded.

At the time, it seemed shocking to me that Joe would think he was in danger. Looking back, my reaction was one of denial. Joe was my guy. He was in trouble, but most of the thoughts racing through my head were selfish. *Who's going to live in the same apartment building as me? Who's going to cook dinner for me every Sunday? Who am I going to drive with to the ballpark? How am I going to get through a full season without Joe's help?*

When the Mets finally released Joe shortly before the start of the regular season, he broke the news to me at night, before any of our other teammates knew what had happened. That was an emotional conversation. The next day, I steeled myself entering the clubhouse, but it didn't work. When I saw Joe's empty locker next to mine, I teared up. My grief was so obvious that one of my team-mates, Jason Phillips, even said: "I'm not concerned for Joe. He'll get a job. Everyone knows he's pro. I'm concerned for David Wright."

Jason was right on all accounts. Joe did get a job, hooking on with the Royals and spending parts of two more seasons in the ma-jors before becoming a successful minor league manager and big league coach in the White Sox organization. And I did take his re-lease hard. I felt like I'd let Joe down after the way he had helped me, like I could have done more to protect him. I thought about all the times I had failed to advance him on the basepaths. I thought about the times Joe was playing second base, I was at third, and I screwed up a double-play feed. Maybe if some of those throws had been more accurate, Joe would have handled them better, impressed the front office, and extended his career with the Mets.

For me, it was a reality check. McEwing's daily mentorship and companionship had come to an end.

On Joe's final day as a member of the team, a line of players came over to shake his hand. I never forgot that because it doesn't happen for just anyone. I could only hope that when the end came for me, I'd have done enough to garner even a fraction of that respect.

||||||||||||||

It helped that things were moving fast for me entering my first full big league season, taking my mind at least a little bit off McEwing's release. On the field, I was experiencing success and feeling increas-ingly comfortable. Unlike Art Howe, who had bumped me to third in the lineup toward the end of my rookie season, new manager

Willie Randolph slotted me fifth, sixth, and even seventh for much of the year. He wanted to ease pressure off me as I became accustomed to the ebbs and flows of the major league grind; I certainly couldn't argue, considering the guys hitting above me were stars like Reyes, Beltrán, and Piazza. I also couldn't argue with the results. That summer, despite my low lineup spot, I batted .306, with 27 home runs and 17 stolen bases in 160 games. As the 2005 season progressed, I shed some more of my nagging doubts that I belonged in the majors.

Just as important, my defense—the target of so much hard work throughout my amateur and minor league careers—began showing tangible signs of improvement. While it would be another two years before my metrics at third base really started ticking upward, two plays in particular stood out from that 2005 season.

The first was one of my absolute career highlights. Ever since I was a kid, I'd wanted to scale a stadium wall to make a catch. Even after I made the majors, I occasionally spent time during batting practice trying to rob home runs. I loved the scene in *Major League II* when Isuro Tanaka climbed the left-field fence, balancing on top of it to rob a homer and send the fictional Indians to the fictional playoffs. I thought way too much about when I might get a chance to make a play like that.

Third basemen don't often get to rob homers, but we do get our share of opportunities in foul ground. I had to make mine count. During a game against the Yankees early in 2005, Jason Giambi hit a ball down the third-base line, but I shied away from the wall and missed it.

*If that ever happens again,* I thought, *I'm just going to go for it.*

I didn't have to wait long. Another chance came June 18 in Seattle, with Martínez pitching for the Mets. Raul Ibañez flared a little fly ball into foul ground, and as soon as it went up, I realized it could be my chance to fly into the stands. Timing my steps, I saw the ball falling right near the wall, and extended my glove high enough to clear a group of fans reaching for it. The distance was perfect for me to jump and make the play. As the ball fell into my glove, I felt a split second of triumph, which lasted only until gravity pulled me onto a little ledge where people were resting their drinks. Reality hit next in the form of a painful bruise and a temporary limp. Although I didn't miss any time, my leg was black-and-blue for months. Even today, just thinking about it makes me shiver with pain.

After that play, people tried to tell me to dial back my style of defense or I'd wind up on the disabled list. I was hardheaded about it, vowing to pursue balls no matter where they might land. That was just my mindset. It didn't matter what anybody told me. I was young, my body was strong, and it was not in my DNA to back away from a challenge. My philosophy was to dive first, worry about the consequences later.

Two months after the Seattle catch, I made a play in San Diego that people often lump together with it. To me, it felt quite different. Dae-Sung Koo, a Korean pitcher who had made headlines earlier in the season for recording his only career hit off Hall of Famer Randy Johnson, threw a slider down and away to Brian Giles. The pitch broke Giles's bat, resulting in a little flare over my shoulder. Because I was playing shallow, I had to turn and sprint after the ball, taking my focus off it as I tried to cover as much distance as possible

in just a few seconds. When I turned back to find the ball, I realized
it was over my right shoulder, not my left. I'd have no chance to
catch it if I tried to thrust my glove across my body.

*Here goes nothing,* I thought, forgetting my glove and sticking out
my right hand instead. As I fell to the ground in shallow left field,
the ball landed smack in the middle of my palm. My teammates
loved it. I couldn't help but grin as Floyd jogged over from his position to give me a pat and a high five, then Reyes took the ball and
playfully smacked me on the head. Inside, though, I was almost
embarrassed. I didn't want people to think I was showboating. I
honestly thought catching the ball with my bare hand was the only
way I was going to make that play.

I often worried about the effects of my actions because, from
the time I was young, my parents and coaches had drilled into me
the importance of playing the game with respect. That meant not
showing up opponents, umpires, or anyone else on the field. It meant
not making an acrobatic catch when a simple one would do. Earlier
that season in Atlanta, I had gotten into a shouting match with umpire Jeff Nelson when he ruled that I slid out of the baseline to break
up a double play. The call cost us two runs and, ultimately, a game.
For the first time as a big leaguer, I completely lost my cool, forcing
Nelson to eject me due to the way I was screaming at him. The next
day, I went over to him to apologize—not for my argument, because
I still felt I was correct, but for the way I had expressed it in that
moment. I never intended to show Nelson up or make the game
about me. It's a lesson I'd learned a long time ago when I threw my
helmet during a Blasters game and Coach Erbe asked me if I was

planning to tell my dad or if he should. Sometimes the heat of a game could make me forget those lessons. I never wanted to make anyone uncomfortable, especially in the public eye.

Looking back, though, I probably shouldn't have worried too much about that catch in San Diego. That one was all instinct. It made me think about a baseball card I owned of former Mets outfielder Kevin Mitchell, who once caught a deep fly ball with his bare hand. His bare hand! I wasn't nearly that talented—a fact that my brothers underscored with a voice mail following the game.

"It's a good thing you didn't try to use your glove," one of them said over the recording, "or you probably would have dropped it."

||||||||||||||

One of the people who helped me establish the line between competitiveness and respect was Willie Randolph, whose old-school style jibed with the type of player I wanted to be. One night early in our time together, I slid hard into second base to break up a double play, then helped up the middle infielder and asked if he was okay before jogging back to our bench. When I returned to the dugout, Willie was there waiting for me.

"Why don't you kiss him?" he asked me.

I shot him a funny look. *What?*

"Why don't you kiss him?" he repeated. Then Willie explained that I could play the game the right way without being too chummy with the opposing players. "Just play the way you're going to play," Willie said, "and don't apologize."

Straddling that line could be difficult, Willie knew, especially in the modern era of free agency—most of us had friends or former teammates dispersed throughout the league. Willie wanted me to retain a high level of respect for my opponents, but not at the cost of a killer instinct on the field. He knew that if my teammates saw me playing with an edge, they would follow suit, which would become increasingly important as my clubhouse influence swelled.

As the 2005 season progressed, I grew close with Randolph, a first-time manager who brought a championship pedigree to Flushing. Given that I was still new to the big leagues, I probably would have been excited no matter whom we hired. But I was particularly excited about Willie for a couple of reasons. To start, he was a proven winner. Randolph spent thirteen of his eighteen big league seasons with the Yankees, serving as captain for three of them, then another eleven as a coach. During that time, he won six World Series rings—two as a player and four as a coach.

When he signed a three-year contract to join the Mets, Willie was still just fifty years old, which is relatively young for a manager. I was twenty-two and under team control for six more seasons, giving me a great opportunity to bond with someone I hoped would be my manager for a long, long time. Willie must have felt the same, because he took me under his wing from his first day on the job, looking at the big picture of my career at a time when I was focused mostly on what was right in front of me. Even though I was young, Willie wanted to mold me into one of the leaders on the team. He often called me into his office to chat. Sometimes, when we were playing away games, we'd walk from the various ballparks to the hotel we were staying at.

With limited experience and plenty of older players around me,

I wasn't yet comfortable with the idea of being a vocal clubhouse presence. But I did understand the value of leading by example, of going about my business the right way. So I picked Willie's brain constantly, asking how Derek Jeter and some of the other veterans across town ran things. Willie had been a Yankees coach when Jeter established himself as one of baseball's best players and most influential leaders. Before that, he'd spent years playing alongside Don Mattingly, who went on to become a Yankees captain and major league manager. Given Willie's experiences with those types of players, I was very interested in learning what he had to share. And he was very interested in teaching.

It was during one of our late-night walks that I enjoyed one of my most poignant moments with Willie. Thanks in large part to our off-season additions, the Mets were clearly improving, transforming from a seventy-one-win club in 2004 to a playoff contender as we entered September 2005. But we lost six straight games early that month to fall out of wild card contention, including three in a row to open a four-game series in St. Louis. As Willie and I walked back to our hotel from Busch Stadium, he put his arm around me and told me to remember exactly how I was feeling.

Willie often alluded to his experiences as a twenty-two-year-old playing for the 1976 Yankees, whom the Cincinnati Reds "totally embarrassed" in a World Series sweep. The next year, he used that loss as motivation to work even harder and win his first World Series ring. Willie also talked frequently about coaching for the 1995 Yankees, who lost American League Division Series Game 5 to the Mariners despite leading in the eleventh inning. He watched Jeter and Jorge Posada stay in their dugout to observe the Mariners' celebration, searing the memory of it into their brains. Just like Willie had two decades earlier, those players used their defeat as fuel to improve, going on to win four World Series in five years beginning the following October.

The Mets, Willie said as we walked back to our hotel that night in St. Louis, could do that same sort of thing. Winning was on the horizon. We all understood that. Willie wanted to make sure I was prepared to embrace it.

Losses, he said, even tough losses, could be blessings in disguise. He told me to remember how much losing sucks, because it would make winning taste that much sweeter.

# EIGHT

# FAME

On May 19, 2006, my parents flew up from Virginia to watch the Mets play the Yankees at Shea Stadium. Not that the Subway Series is insignificant now, but back then, it was still novel enough to come with big-time bragging rights. Tack on the fact that the Mets were off to a hot start with lots of hype going into that week, and the atmosphere in Queens was electric.

That off-season, general manager Omar Minaya stayed aggressive, acquiring multi-time All-Stars Carlos Delgado, Paul Lo Duca, and Billy Wagner to fill in gaps at first base, catcher, and closer. Those players joined me, José Reyes, Carlos Beltrán, and so many others on what I considered a truly stacked roster. At the start of each season, players tend to look around their clubhouses and consider what needs to go right for them to make the playoffs. That spring, I distinctly remember looking at the nameplates above each locker and thinking, *He's an All-Star. He's an All-Star. He's a Hall of Famer.*

There were no ifs about it. We were going to be good.

The next step was to prove we were for real, with a Friday night Subway Series game providing the perfect forum.

Because my parents' flight was delayed, they didn't slip into their seats until the later innings, with the score knotted, 6–6. My seventh-inning strikeout was still fresh on my mind when Mariano Rivera intentionally walked Delgado to face me with a man on second base and two outs in the ninth.

That's future unanimous first-ballot Hall of Famer Mariano Rivera, barely halfway through his career but already one of the greatest closers in baseball history. With less than two years' major league experience myself, I couldn't help but feel intimidated facing a guy whose baseball cards I grew up collecting. I also couldn't help but see it as an opportunity. Beating Rivera would mean proving that arguably the best closer of all time couldn't overmatch me. Doing it with a Subway Series game on the line would mean even more. As a crowd of more than fifty-six thousand people went nuts around me, I dug into the box with as much confidence as I could muster.

Rivera may have been Rivera, but he was still mortal, which he proved by grooving a 1-1 cutter to me in the middle of the strike zone. When he did, I snapped into motion, putting my best swing on Rivera's best pitch.

Foul ball. He'd made a mistake and I'd flat-out missed it.

*You've still got this,* I told myself, trying to stay optimistic even though I didn't really believe my own words. The idea of Rivera slipping up twice in an at-bat seemed unrealistic. He'd done it once and I hadn't made him pay for it. There was no way he was going to give me another chance to beat him.

As it turned out, I wasn't entirely wrong. Rivera's next cutter was a good one, a pitcher's pitch down below the zone. But I saw it well enough out of his hand to get my barrel on it, then looked up to notice how shallow Johnny Damon was playing in center field. The ball had some carry to it. It actually had a chance—either Damon was going to make a spectacular catch, or my hit was going to fall behind him for a walk-off.

Those seconds seemed to freeze in time. Yelling out loud at the baseball, I tried to coax it over Damon's head as I jumped up and down between home plate and first base. My eyes locked on the ball until I saw it bounce down on the warning track, ricocheting off the outfield fence for a hit.

The crowd erupted. All these powerful emotions washed over me. It was bedlam. I looked to my left to see Paul Lo Duca score the winning run, his arms raised in celebration. The rest of my teammates stormed out of the dugout to greet me on the field. As "New York Groove" blared from the Shea Stadium loudspeakers, fireworks shot off beyond the outfield fence. Somewhere within the mosh pit of Mets players on the infield grass, I lost my helmet. I couldn't stop grinning like an idiot.

Especially in that moment, it was difficult to register what I had just accomplished. I had become the thirteenth player to walk off against a dude who almost never lost in that fashion—just 24 times in 1,211 regular-season and playoff games across his entire career, for a 98 percent success rate. Rivera had this unbeatable aura about

him, yet somehow, on that night, I beat him. I can't understate what
that did for my confidence. In a lot of ways, it felt like I had
arrived.

On a team level, winning that game and going on to win the
series on such a big stage, in such a lively atmosphere, felt enormous.
In terms of the playoff chase, those Subway Series matchups may not
have been quite as impactful as games against our National League
East rivals, but you wouldn't have known it by looking up to see all
those people screaming their faces off at Shea Stadium. These were
bragging rights in a town where bragging rights really meant something. I soaked in that moment as much as I could, because in a lot of
ways, it felt like the Mets, as a team, had also arrived.

|||||||||||||||

I'll always remember 2006 as the year in which everything seemed
to click. Coming off a successful first full big league season, I spent
the winter months training with Piney in Virginia, then the spring
working out with Beltrán in Florida. By Opening Day, I was feeling
stronger and more confident than ever. The results followed, and
not just against Rivera. That April, I hit five home runs and stole six
bases as the Mets jumped out to the best record in the NL East. In
May, I hit .336 as we built our division lead, highlighted by my Subway Series walk-off. By the end of June, we had the best record in
the majors, and with All-Star voting in full swing, I hit ten home
runs that month to seal my spot on the National League roster in
Pittsburgh.

By the time Major League Baseball revealed the ballot results, my first All-Star selection wasn't a big surprise. What I wasn't expecting was for MLB to call my agent, Keith Miller, and ask me to participate in the Home Run Derby. Millsy was pumped to tell me about the opportunity. He was less excited when I told him I didn't really want to do it.

The idea of participating in a derby made me anxious because I never really considered myself a home run hitter. Sure, I hit my share during games, but in general, my batting practice sessions tended to be pedestrian. I didn't pull the ball much. I wasn't the type of guy who made people's jaws drop with gargantuan homers. I'd hit a few average ones during BP each day and that was about the extent of it. The idea of embarrassing myself on a national stage made me nervous enough about the whole enterprise that, had Millsy not been so adamant, I probably would have said no.

"Dude, you've got to do it," he said to me. "You'll always regret it if you don't."

I certainly didn't feel that way, but Millsy was persuasive. He had my best interests at heart, and, truthfully, it did seem like a once-in-a-lifetime opportunity. How bad could it be?

With all that swirling through my mind, I reluctantly agreed to attend. The day of the derby, MLB gathered the participants at PNC Park for a meeting to go over the ground rules, which didn't exactly increase my confidence. As I looked around, I saw superstars and living legends like Miguel Cabrera, David Ortiz, and Ryan Howard. All I could think was *Why am I here? This doesn't make sense.* During that meeting, 2004 Home Run Derby runner-up Lance Berkman took it upon himself to offer the other contestants advice, telling us to take our time and not be afraid to take pitches. I felt like he was speaking directly to me, like he and everyone else knew I didn't belong in that room.

Recognizing my nervousness, my Mets pals Cliff Floyd and Mike Cameron wouldn't leave me alone, imploring me to hit at least one homer so I wouldn't completely humiliate myself. They tried to get other teammates to bet on my performance, setting the over-under at two or three home runs. Even B. J. Upton texted a message from Virginia that read: "Don't embarrass the area." I felt like I might.

Unlike most derby participants, I barely practiced beforehand, dedicating maybe half a round of BP each afternoon to hitting home runs. Those efforts didn't bear much fruit, which only added to my unease; by the time I arrived in Pittsburgh, I felt like the pressure level was off the charts.

Just before the derby, each contestant took one final round of BP, which was designed to help us to grow comfortable at PNC Park. For me, it had the opposite effect. Midway through, the grounds crew wheeled the cage away so we could get a feel for what we would experience later that night. I was so accustomed to taking BP from inside a cage that it was jarring to see that safety net gone. Cameramen started swarming around as I tried to ignore the fact that I had no business being there. It was just me, the pitcher, and about forty thousand of my closest friends.

At least I had a familiar face nearby. I had chosen Lo Duca, our starting catcher and one of six Mets All-Stars that year, to pitch to me, which proved to be a good decision for a couple of reasons. For starters, he had a big personality. He knew how to make me laugh in those pressure-filled moments. He also threw extremely slow, which was perfect for my bat speed. On my second swing of the derby, I pulled a ball 419 feet into the second deck in left.

*Okay,* I told myself. *I can go home happy.*

I meant it. That first home run really, truly calmed my nerves, allowing me to block out the crowd and the announcer providing play-by-play over the stadium speakers. I settled into a zone. I still didn't expect to win, or frankly even advance very far. I certainly wasn't going to put on the type of show that Josh Hamilton did in a record-setting performance two years later at Yankee Stadium, or that Pete Alonso did during the 2019 event in Cleveland. Much of my power was to right-center field, meaning my home runs tended to land in the third or fourth row rather than the upper deck. But as I grew a bit more comfortable, I performed well enough to hit sixteen over the fence in the first round, including fourteen over the course of seventeen swings.

The format was simple: ten outs per player per round, with every swing counting as either a home run or an out. Given those rules, sixteen homers was a big deal, surprising me as much as anyone. Not only did I avoid embarrassment, I actually found myself leading the derby after one round. More than that, our first-round scores carried over to the second round, which gave me a real chance to qualify for the finals.

That rule came into play when, after hitting homers on my first two swings of the second round, I went ten in a row without one. Thanks to my early performance, it didn't matter. Somehow, some way, I was through to the finals.

Gone were Cabrera, Ortiz, Berkman, and the roomful of others. Suddenly, it was just me and Howard, who had gone deep twenty-eight times during the first half of the season. A fellow first-time All-Star, Howard would go on to lead the league with fifty-eight homers, following up his 2005 Rookie of the Year campaign with an MVP season in 2006. He had four inches and about fifty pounds on me and, unlike me, seemed to be getting stronger as the derby progressed. When I saw I would be matched up against him in the finals, my immediate thought was just to forfeit. Not only was Howard an elite home run hitter, but I was clearly gassed. It felt like the varsity against the JV.

Still, my competitive juices were flowing. I felt more confident than when I had started. A small part of me figured if I'd made it this far, maybe I could pull off one last upset.

Or not. Batting first in the finals, I mustered only four home runs, crashing back down to earth after my great first round. Howard, who hit a couple homers into the nearby Allegheny River on the fly, followed with five, and probably could have crushed a bunch more if he'd needed to. As a giant scrum of people surrounded Howard on the field, I rushed over to congratulate him. Silently, I congratulated myself as well.

Considering my hesitation leading up to the event, I couldn't be too upset with the loss. If you had told me at the beginning of the derby that I'd finish second to Ryan Howard, I'd have signed up for that in a heartbeat. Millsy was right. I loved the experience.

|||||||||||||||

Following the pressure of the Home Run Derby, the All-Star Game itself seemed like a breeze. Having five of my Mets teammates there relaxed me in a way that simply hadn't been possible the previous night. I also had my parents and brothers in attendance, which turned the entire week into a hectic, fun whirlwind. After carving out time for my family, my agents, the media, and the derby, there wasn't much left to soak in the experience. I was finally able to do that on All-Star night. Heading out to my usual spot at third base allowed me to take a deep breath and relax. I wouldn't say I was carefree, considering the millions of people watching around the world, but I definitely felt looser than I'd expected.

In a cool little reunion before my first at-bat, I chatted with American League third-base coach John Gibbons, who had been the Norfolk Tides manager when I visited the team shortly after the Mets drafted me. I joked to him that I hoped to see a first-pitch strike, because I planned to swing no matter what. Sure enough, Tigers lefty Kenny Rogers hung a breaking ball high enough in the strike zone for me to pull it over the left-field fence. As I crossed home plate, Lo Duca was waiting in the on-deck circle with a huge grin on his face.

Even though the National League wound up losing the game in the ninth inning, that home run felt big. In the midst of a breakout season, it provided even more evidence that I belonged on that stage. I had been in the big leagues less than two years and hadn't actually accomplished much in my career. But in that moment, I didn't feel totally out of place sharing a clubhouse with Howard and Cabrera and Albert Pujols and Scott Rolen. Like my hit off Rivera, the All-Star Game homer gave me a sense of pride and validation that I belonged.

Only two years had passed since my experience as a scared kid at the All-Star Game in Houston, asking Rolen for an autograph and feeling too intimidated to talk to Derek Jeter. Suddenly, I was one of them, starting ahead of Rolen at third base and passing Jeter each inning on the field. As I descended back into the dugout following my homer, I found some of the greatest baseball players of my lifetime waiting there to congratulate me. *Oh my God,* I thought. *I'm high-fiving Albert Pujols right now. I'm high-fiving Scott Rolen right now. I'm celebrating with guys I've looked up to for years.*

|||||||||||||||

With success on the baseball field came fame away from it, especially in the fishbowl of New York City. In 2005, I moved my in-season residence from Long Island City to Manhattan, where I would spend summers for the rest of my career. Searching for apartments, I had two requirements: My new home needed to be on a high floor, and it needed to have a gigantic television. The place I found was on Fifty-Fifth Street between Second and Third Avenues with a view over Manhattan, high enough that I could see beyond the rooftops of nearby buildings. Perfect. I bought a TV to pair with it and rented some furniture. My old crew from Virginia loved the place, because they could use it as a crash pad each winter when I went home to spend time with my family.

Those lifelong friends, like my hometown buddies Matt Smith, Pete Aitken, and Rob Robinson, were huge for me. I kept them close, creating a tight circle that was admittedly tough for new people to crack. As I gained fame, I became wary of others' intentions. More and more folks wanted pieces of my time, which caused me to surround myself with people I trusted—those who I knew had my best interests at heart. I didn't want people hanging around me just because I was some pseudo-famous baseball player. I never wanted to do anything to embarrass myself, my parents, the Mets, or anyone else.

As a result, my new friends tended to be older guys with good heads on their shoulders, like Joe McEwing or the Mets' bullpen catcher, Dave Racaniello. I could relate to people like that—guys who worked hard to grind out livings in baseball—far more than I could to flashy superstars. Throughout my life, my inner circle has mostly consisted of people I became friends with before baseball or who never really cared about my fame and fortune. I just wanted those I interacted with to treat me like a normal human being, not above or below anyone else.

Despite New York's temptations, I wasn't much of a partier or a drinker. I didn't spend my nights seeking out hot clubs or dates with celebrities or anything like that. I was never going to get caught doing something unsavory on *TMZ* or "Page Six" in the *New York Post*. A lot of what some people enjoy about the city was lost on me.

I loved my little corner of Manhattan regardless. My apartment was steps away from P. J. Clarke's, the iconic burger joint, and a few blocks from the steakhouse Smith & Wollensky. Both served good food and stayed open late after games. Despite still being pretty new to midtown at that point, I knew all the best spots to find a solid meal. Any time my agents or my parents were in town, we'd head someplace in the area.

That was, essentially, my social life. My brother Steve liked to joke that I was twenty-three going on fifty. Cliff Floyd, my teammate,

told reporters I was so wholesome, I drank milk instead of beer after games. (It happened, like, one time, Cliff.) I don't want to make
myself out to be some saint; it's just that baseball was my top prior-
ity at all times. The grind of the schedule always felt nonstop. Most
days, I slept until late in the morning, drove to Shea Stadium, played
nine innings, and drove back home. As much as I might have loved
my apartment, I didn't spend a ton of my waking hours there. If I felt
like I needed to unwind, I grabbed a low-key meal at one of my
neighborhood spots. The staff at those restaurants were always excited to see me and talk about the games. They took good care of me.

Once the Mets began winning consistently in 2006, anonymity
became tougher to maintain, which wasn't always a bad thing, because it gave me a chance to share my success with others. The atmosphere at any restaurant I walked into in Manhattan or Queens
felt electric. Places flew Mets flags outside their doors. Sometimes
when people saw me enter, they started cheering from their tables,
reaching out to shake my hand or slap my back. I felt like a contestant on *The Price Is Right*. Random strangers paid for my dinners no
matter how much I protested. Kids came up to me seeking pictures
or autographs. Waiters and waitresses asked about the team's playoff
prospects. All that most people wanted in return was a high five or
a quick conversation, or just to say good luck. For someone who
never loved being the center of attention, that sort of thing could
always be a bit uncomfortable. I tried never to lose sight of the fact
that it was also very, very cool.

Even though dealing with fame didn't come naturally to me, I
tried to enjoy the perks of people's recognizing me more frequently

around town. One day early in my career, Millsy and I were riding in a taxi when a pedestrian glanced in the window, stopped short in the middle of the crosswalk, and started pointing and shouting at the top of his lungs.

"That's David Wright!" the guy exclaimed as traffic flowed around him.

What? Me? I was so surprised I didn't know how to react. Millsy was loving it.

"That's the coolest thing I've ever seen!" he said. "This guy's about to get hit by a car and he's stopping just because he wants to say hi to you!"

That interaction made a lightbulb go on for me about just how passionate fans are in New York. Millsy was right: It was very, very cool. At the outset of my career, I didn't really get how hugely different the New York experience was going to be from what I was accustomed to in Virginia and across the minor leagues. Those early interactions made it clear. Fans in New York wanted to get to know me as a person. They wanted to talk. I never minded stopping on the street to sign an autograph, take a picture, or have a quick conversation, even if that crush of attention was something that took a bit of getting used to.

Millsy understood my personality, so he didn't push me too much on the promotional side of things. Generally, I did what appealed to me. One of the lawyers at my agency, Peter Pedalino, was childhood friends with Mike Repole—the guy who founded the beverage company Glacéau. Through that connection, I became a spokesman for Vitaminwater, which I had tried a few times and considered a healthier alternative to other sports drinks. The catch? Glacéau wanted to pay me in equity rather than cash, which worked out pretty well when Coca-Cola bought the company a year later for $4.2 billion. Talk about being in the right place at the right time. After the sale, I sat there trying to do the math on the percentage of a percentage of the company that I owned. It blew me away. Since then, I've always tried to have a vested interest in the products I endorse—for example, Beyond Meat, a company I took equity in when I began endorsing them years later. I've never wanted to vouch for something I don't use myself.

Glacéau especially loved me because of what happened during the Home Run Derby. After every round, MLB sent a kid out to greet each hitter with a sweat towel and a bottle of Gatorade. When it was my turn, I took the towel but rejected the drink. Glacéau paid my brothers to go onto the field with some Vitaminwater instead, irking MLB, because Gatorade was one of their biggest sponsors. My brothers got kicked off the field, which gave me a pretty good laugh. It was worth it. I was a Vitaminwater guy through and through.

For the most part, I declined other endorsement opportunities, except on the few occasions Millsy refused to take no for an answer. He knew me well enough to understand the fine line between promotions that would make me uncomfortable and those I would regret passing on later in my life. After the 2006 All-Star Game, for example, I went to CBS studios for a spot on the *Late Show with David Letterman*. What an amazing experience.

"Things are going pretty well for you, aren't they?" Letterman asked me as I took a seat in his iconic studio.

"Very well," I replied. "Busy, but very well."

I went on *Letterman* again two years later, reprising my Home Run Derby performance in the middle of a street outside the studio. I also made appearances on *The Daily Show* with Jon Stewart, a big Mets fan, and *The Celebrity Apprentice*. Later in my career, I appeared on *Jimmy Kimmel Live!* in Brooklyn with three of my teammates. One week in 2006, *Sports Illustrated* featured me, Beltrán, Reyes, Delgado, and Lo Duca on its cover. Early the next year, I graced the cover of *MLB 07: The Show* for PlayStation. My ugly mug was everywhere. *The New York Times* and *New York* magazine made me the subject of feature stories. Delta Air Lines named a plane after me.

Even though those sorts of things could make my anxiety level go through the roof, they became scrapbook items that I could treasure for the rest of my life. At the time, I didn't really want to do any of it. Looking back, I'm so glad I did.

Most of it, anyway. One of the opportunities Millsy brought to my attention late in 2006 was a fashion shoot with the magazine *GQ*, which was a big, big deal at that time. As usual, my gut reaction was to say no, but even I was impressed by the cachet of *GQ*.

Reyes, who had also been invited to the shoot, kept pestering me about accepting the offer. I was skeptical. He was all in. I had a feeling he was going to win the argument.

Reyes and I first met as teenagers in 2001 during instructional ball in Port St. Lucie. Half a year younger than me, Reyes signed with the Mets as an international free agent at age sixteen, flying through the farm system as one of the best prospects in baseball. He was a true five-tool player, with incredible bat speed, a rocket arm, and some of the best wheels in the minors. Whenever I picked up *Baseball America*, I saw his name. When Reyes cracked the majors a year before I did, I paid attention. The idea that he and I would man the left side of the Mets' infield for years to come always stuck in my mind, and when the two of us began hanging every day in the majors late in 2004, we struck up something of an unlikely friendship.

Taking baseball out of the equation, Reyes and I could not have had less in common. He was a kid from the Dominican Republic who loved reggaeton music, ate Latin food, and spoke very little English. I was a kid from Chesapeake, Virginia, who listened to rock and country, ate hamburgers, and spoke very little Spanish. Sometimes, we could barely communicate with each other. And yet, because we spent most of our days standing a few feet apart, we formed such a strong bond that we became like brothers. It was really cool to grow up with him.

Baseball was our common thread, and the league seemed to take notice. Everything was always "Wright and Reyes" or "Reyes and Wright." I was the slugger, he was the speedster, even though he enjoyed putting on shows in batting practice and I liked to think I could beat anyone in a race. The Mets considered the two of us cornerstones of the future. That August, the team signed Reyes to a four-year, $23.25 million extension that would keep him in Flushing through at least 2010. As soon as they agreed on that, Minaya called my agents and said he wanted to negotiate a similar deal with me. He wanted to get it done within twenty-four hours. Sure enough, a day later, I received a six-year, $55 million extension through 2012.

I was ecstatic. Obviously, as someone who had never spent a cent of his draft signing bonus, the long-term financial security meant a lot to me. But so did the idea that I could really build a life in New York, with the team I'd grown up rooting for. As I said that day, it was a special feeling to be drafted by my favorite team and a special feeling to know I would stay put for at least the next six years. I also loved the idea of continuing to grow alongside Reyes, my friend. We were in our primes, playing good baseball and bonding in such a unique and cool way.

Still, we were very different people. From time to time, Reyes tried to get me to branch out into other areas. He was always pestering me to be an extra in the music videos he liked to make, which became the foundation of his career after baseball. I said no to all of it, thank God, except for the GQ shoot. I probably should have said no to that, too.

When we showed up, the staffers put us in headbands, tight shirts, and sweatpants, going for that athletic chic vibe. José, who was in much better shape than me, looked fantastic. He had a lot of things I didn't, including six-pack abs that you could see through his shirt. The only thing visible through mine was my gut. José also had that type of swag where he felt confident wearing those kinds of clothes. I certainly did not, which I think came through in the pictures. We took photos in the clubhouse tunnel at Shea Stadium and out on the field wearing half-zipped jackets and designer jeans. For one set of photos, I wore a white leather jacket with a Mets T-shirt underneath. In almost all of them, I wore a goofy grin on my face. When I look back on them now, only one thought pops into my mind:

*What the hell was I thinking?*

The shoot did force me out of my comfort zone and strengthened my friendship with José, but the clothes were so far from my usual style that it was comical. To this day, I'll pick up my phone and see a text flash across from a friend or one of my brothers. It'll be a picture of me from the GQ shoot, smiling like the huge dork that I am.

So maybe GQ wasn't my finest decision. Even so, the more I did those types of things, the more my little slice of fame grew. I started realizing that, whether I was ready for it or not, I was becoming a role model for people who didn't really know me at all. People bought those magazines with my face on the cover. Kids started wearing number 5 in Little League because of me. People who weren't even Mets fans looked up to me. As a result, I knew I had to be even more cognizant of my behavior and actions.

Off the field, that meant being accountable and staying out of trouble. On the field, it meant playing by the rules at all times. No exceptions. I'm well aware I played during an era, especially toward the beginning of my career, when steroids and other performance-enhancing drugs were prevalent throughout Major League Base-ball. That didn't make it right. It certainly didn't make it acceptable for me or anyone else to use them. In my eyes, that sort of thing was never an option.

Even if I'd felt tempted, which I never did, I feared my father killing me far more than I worried about anything else. I grew up with great respect for the work my dad did, flushing out criminals in the vice and narcotics wing of the Norfolk Police Department. To take illegal substances would have meant not only disrespecting my own body and sensibilities but also disrespecting my parents. For those reasons, over my fourteen-year career, steroids were never a topic that entered the depths of my brain.

More than that, I always felt strongly that those who break the rules should be punished. Whether it's a complete stranger or one of my best friends, rules are rules. Players should follow them. People should obey laws. If that's an unpopular opinion, so be it, but I'll always root for people who break the rules to get caught. And I'll always hope the punishments for rule breakers continue to increase, because those players are probably taking the spots of people working harder than them. It's difficult enough to make the major leagues, let alone stay there, let alone do all that while battling people who aren't playing fairly. I will never, ever have sympathy for performance-enhancing-drug users. I advise people of all ages to stay away from them. That's not what sportsmanship is about, and it's certainly not how I was raised.

One of my minor league instructors, Guy Conti, used to say all the time, "You've got choices, decisions, consequences." Those words always stuck with me, probably because they encapsulated so much of what my parents instilled in me when I was younger. No amount of major league success or New York fame was going to make me forget the lessons that they'd taught me. Considering how many people were following my career with big expectations, I made it my mission to live and act accordingly.

# NINE

||||||||||

# OCTOBER

As my comfort level in New York City grew, things continued falling into place for both me and the Mets in 2006. By the end of July, our NL East lead had stretched to double digits, making the division ours to lose. Beltrán was putting together an MVP-caliber season that would finish with a .275 average, 41 home runs, and 18 stolen bases. Delgado was on his way to a 38-homer, 114-RBI campaign. Reyes and I were both thriving as we entered the primes of our careers.

Because the Braves had won eleven consecutive NL East titles, we never publicly boasted about how good we were. Nonetheless, we were young and hungry, with an edge about us. During a July 8 game at Shea, Marlins pitchers hit two of our batters, injuring Carlos Delgado in the process. One of the relievers we'd acquired over the winter, Duaner Sanchez, came to the mound after the second hit batsman and, despite holding only a one-run lead, fired a first-pitch fastball right at leadoff hitter Miguel Cabrera's leg. That's the kind of mentality we had on that team. Nobody had to say anything. We played for each other.

Sanchez was one of the leaders of a bullpen that led the National League in ERA. Each night, it seemed like if our starters could get through five or six innings, we could hand the ball off to our bullpen and that would be that. But our great bullpen downgraded to a merely very good one on the night of July 30 when Sanchez, who had opened the season with a twenty-one-inning scoreless streak, separated his pitching shoulder in a taxicab accident on I-95 in Miami. I learned quickly how important one piece can be. Even though we still featured a deep relief corps, losing a pitcher like Sanchez had ripple effects up and down the roster. It not only forced the front office to go out and make a trade, acquiring Roberto Hernández and Oliver Pérez hours later from the Pirates, but it also thrust other relievers into unfamiliar roles and situations. While we were confident we could overcome the injury, it still stung.

At least we didn't have much time to harp on it, knowing we needed to play two more months of focused, solid baseball to make the playoffs. Even though the Braves were struggling, sitting in fourth place well below .500, Hall of Famers John Smoltz and Chipper Jones, among other threats, were still on that team. In addition to their talent, the Braves always played the game the right way, with constant effort and professionalism, which impressed me as a young player. Until they were mathematically eliminated, I wasn't going to count them out.

An even more potent rival loomed in Philadelphia, where the Phillies were coming off consecutive second-place finishes and, like us, appeared to be a team on the rise. In addition to Ryan Howard, the Phillies had graduated a wave of talented young players, including Jimmy Rollins, Chase Utley, and Cole Hamels, to the majors. We knew they were eventually going to be an issue.

Thankfully, we stayed hot enough to keep them at arm's length, locking up the division with a late-August surge. About two weeks later, when the Phillies lost during our September 14 off day, our magic number fell to one—we needed just one more win, or one more Phillies loss, to celebrate. All the real pressure had vanished, because with two weeks left in the season, we had effectively clinched the NL East. But we were still eager to party.

That Friday, we lost in Pittsburgh and the Phillies won. The next day, we lost again and the Phillies won again. Then we lost on Sunday and the Phillies won a third game in a row. In the later innings of one of those games, when I walked into the PNC Park clubhouse to grab some water, I saw plastic sheets covering all the lockers. Even the Pittsburgh clubhouse staff was anticipating a messy celebration. Each night, we stuck around to watch the end of the Phillies game as a team, preparing to party if they lost. They never did, prompting one of our beat writers, MLB.com's Marty Noble, to dub the stadium "Pour No Champagne Park."

As frustrating as that weekend may have seemed, it wound up being a blessing, because it allowed us to clinch on our own field. Back in New York that Monday, we beat the Marlins, 4–0, at Shea Stadium. Everyone rushed the pitcher's mound, hugging and hollering, then we popped champagne in the clubhouse before spilling back out of the dugout to celebrate with everyone who stuck around. I was high-fiving a group of fans when one of them grabbed the NL East championship hat right off my head. Another swiped a champagne bottle out of my hand. It was chaos, but the best kind of chaos. Somebody handed me a banner that read, "2006 N.L. EAST CHAMPS!" which—with a victory cigar hanging out of my mouth—I held up high for everyone to see.

At twenty-three years old, I was heading to the playoffs. A lot of the fans who stuck around that night were about my age; they were also enjoying a winning team for the first time in their adult lives. Celebrating with them resonated for me and Reyes in particular, because as two young players who came up through the minor league system together, we considered ourselves key pieces of the Mets' foundation. We understood how important this was to people. We knew how badly everyone in Flushing wanted a winner. I was happy to let those guys keep the hat and the champagne bottle and whatever else they could grab. Slapping high fives and hanging out on the field with that group of Mets fans was as special for us as it was for them.

||||||||||||||||

Unfortunately, the good vibes of that night couldn't last forever. The first real significant blow we absorbed that season was Sanchez's taxicab accident. The second and third came in rapid succession in the week leading up to the playoffs. First Pedro Martínez, who had thrown only thirty-one innings in the second half due to various injuries, suffered a season-ending torn left calf tendon.

Then, on the eve of his National League Division Series Game 1 start, Orlando Hernández strained his right calf while jogging on the outfield grass. Just like that, we were missing two pitchers who had started more than a quarter of our regular-season games.

We still entered the first round confident, finishing the regular season tied for the best record in MLB, but we understood how much the degree of difficulty had increased. Game 1 of the NLDS started at 4:09 p.m., creating shadows at Shea Stadium that made it tough to hit. Tack on the fact that my anxiousness had reached an all-time high, and I felt like I would have swung at the rosin bag had Dodgers starter Derek Lowe chosen to throw it.

My mind was racing. My heart was racing. I couldn't calm down for even a second, which caused me to press badly at the plate. The intensity level just struck me as so different from that of a regular-season game. In the second inning, Shawn Green and José Valentín teamed up to throw out Jeff Kent on a play at the plate. As Lo Duca made the tag, he realized just in time that a second runner, J. D. Drew, was also trying to score. Whirling, Lo Duca tagged Drew as well to keep the game scoreless in one of the more bizarre and sensational plays you'll ever see. The crowd went nuts, which fired me up even more—as if I needed an extra jolt of emotion.

Eventually, my adrenaline eased up enough to let me fall into the rhythm of the game. After letting Lowe have his way with me my first two at-bats, I came to the plate with men on first and third in the sixth inning, one out, and a one-run lead. I stayed aggressive, but this time by swinging at the pitches I wanted to, fouling off a pair of hittable sinkers to fall behind in the count. When Lowe threw me another sinker in the strike zone, I was ready, shooting it into the right-field corner for a two-run double. I took third base on the throw, then almost took off third-base coach Manny Acta's hand with an overly aggressive high five. All the emotion I had bottled up for six innings poured out of me, allowing me to relax and just play my game from there. I started to feel comfortable playing October baseball.

The next step was to win the damn thing.

|||||||||||||||

Tom Glavine pitched six shutout innings in Game 2 and we put up nine runs in Game 3. It was a sweep, giving us cause for another champagne celebration at Dodger Stadium. We took turns running over to spray Cliff Floyd, who'd rolled his ankle during the game and was lying low in one corner of the clubhouse. We reveled in our accomplishment for a night, all while knowing we couldn't party long.

Our next opponent was St. Louis, which had won the National League pennant in 2004 and posted consecutive hundred-win seasons in '04 and '05. Even though they'd had a relatively down year in 2006, winning the NL Central despite an 83-78 record, the Cardinals were never a team that was easy to face. Led by longtime manager Tony La Russa, they embodied what came to be known as "the Cardinal Way." I had tremendous respect for their entire operation.

Heading into the series, much of the talk revolved around Chris Carpenter, the reigning NL Cy Young winner. Carpenter had put together another great season in 2006, going 15-8 with a 3.09 ERA, but we actually managed to knock him around a bit in Games 2 and 6. The pitcher we couldn't touch was Jeff Suppan, a much softer thrower who didn't strike out many batters. That didn't stop him from holding us to three hits over eight innings in Game 3.

By that point in the series, I was pressing. I mean really, really pressing. My first NLCS at-bat, I hit a hard shot up the middle that struck pitcher Jeff Weaver's foot, skipping right to the shortstop for an easy out. Those are the types of things that happen during slumps. I wound up going 0-for-9 over the first three games of the series, spiraling into the same sort of mindset that overtook me early in the Dodgers series. The game sped up. I began swinging at pitcher's pitches, which is exactly what the Cardinals wanted me to do. Everything felt like it was moving so fast. Every time I came to the plate, I tried to make a major impact instead of just worrying about taking pitches, staying patient, drawing walks, getting on base.

Guys like Suppan, who might not have had the best stuff but who really knew how to pitch, could take advantage of that. The entire Cardinals team, with La Russa at the helm and defensive wizard Yadier Molina behind the plate, were tremendous at discovering and exploiting weaknesses. They kept pitching me farther and farther outside the strike zone, knowing I would continue to hack away.

You know that cliché players like to use, "trying to do too much"? I was trying to do way, way too much.

Finally, in Game 4, I hit a solo homer off Anthony Reyes to ease some of the pressure off my shoulders. That home run was significant in terms of helping me regain the confidence I had lost. I learned during that NLCS how to control my emotions a little bit better, how to control my heart rate, how to take a deep breath and relax when the moment called for it. Baseball isn't like football, where getting all amped up helps. I was always a much better hitter when I was relaxed at the plate without a hundred things buzzing through my mind. When I was at my best, my swings felt effortless, like I was barely trying. I needed to figure out how to bottle that feeling, and that home run off Reyes was a start.

It was important for the Mets as well, giving us a 2–1 lead in a game where we never trailed again. We tied up the series that night, then dropped Game 5 in St. Louis but staved off elimination against Carpenter in Game 6.

The following night was a winner-take-all Game 7 at Shea Stadium, which turned out to be one of the most electric, heart-wrenching affairs of my career. I had given us a 1–0 lead in the first inning off Suppan with an RBI single, and was manning my usual position at third base in a tie game in the sixth when Rolen—my childhood idol and All-Star Game mentor—lifted a long fly ball toward the left-field fence. I turned to face it.

*Season's over,* I thought. *This is a tough way to go home.*

Then I watched left fielder Endy Chávez leap, stretch out his arm, and make one of the most spectacular plays in baseball history, snow-coning the ball to rob Rolen of a go-ahead two-run homer. As Chávez landed, I started jumping up and down, screaming for him to throw the ball to the infield, where Jim Edmonds had ventured way too far off first base. Chávez threw to José Valentín, who fired to Delgado, who caught the ball and slammed his fist down in celebration right in front of Edmonds.

Celebrating that catch, I jumped higher than I think I ever had before in my life. I loved playing basketball as a kid but couldn't ever dunk. I'm pretty sure in that moment I could have spun 360 degrees and posterized Shaquille O'Neal. In those few seconds from Rolen's swing to Delgado's fist pump, my entire mental state had transformed.

*Okay. We're going to win this.*

I think every person in Shea Stadium felt the exact same way. I just wish it could have come true. Despite loading the bases with one out in the bottom of that inning, we couldn't score off Suppan, who did enough in his two starts to win NLCS Most Valuable Player. In the top of the ninth, Molina hit a two-run homer to give the Cardinals their first lead since Game 5. Then in the bottom of the ninth, with the bases loaded and two outs, Beltrán took an Adam Wainwright curveball for a called strike three to end the series.

To this day, Beltrán takes a lot of heat for that strikeout, which I don't think is fair. From my vantage, Wainwright attacked Beltrán with a pitch sequence that was—especially given the context—incredibly nasty. Fastball, inside corner. Curveball, just off the plate, which Beltrán fouled away. Then another curveball that Wainwright dumped from a high release point into the strike zone. At the time, Wainwright was a relatively unknown rookie pitching in relief. Most of our hitters, including Beltrán, had never faced him. Video and scouting reports can only help so much in those situations. It's tough to hit someone the first time you see him. It's tougher still when that someone has elite stuff. Wainwright, who went on to become a three-time All-Star and a two-time World Series champion, had some of the best of his generation.

So, no, I don't blame Beltrán one bit. I don't think anyone should. We never would have gotten to where we did that year without him.

Regardless of how it happened, losing stung. It stayed with me a long while, souring my mood. Watching the Cardinals beat the Tigers in five games in the World Series, I couldn't help but sit on my couch and think, *Man, we could have won it all. If we had just scratched out a couple runs in Game 7, that could have been us up there on-stage, passing the World Series trophy to each other.* I started playing the what-if game in my head, thinking about everything I could have done differently, everything *we all* could have done differently. We had gone into the playoffs missing one of our best relievers and two of our best starting pitchers. If only, if only, if only . . .

For me, failing has always been a big-time motivator, so it's no surprise that the NLCS loss stuck in my mind throughout off-season workouts, throughout spring training, throughout the next couple of years. Just as Willie Randolph had predicted on our walk back from Busch Stadium the previous September, I redoubled my efforts to become the best player I could possibly be—not just for me, but for the team. For the fans. I burned so badly to get back to the playoffs and take that next step.

I knew I never wanted to experience this feeling of losing again.

At least I knew we had a strong roster heading into 2007. With the exception of Floyd, whose ankle injury had limited him to just three plate appearances during the NLCS, every member of our starting lineup was due to return. So were some promising young rotation pieces, as well as Sanchez, Billy Wagner, and other key members of our top-ranked bullpen. So while losing the NLCS was a miserable feeling, we comforted ourselves with visions of better things to come. Talking to both the media and each other in the clubhouse after Game 7, my teammates and I must have repeated some variation of our new rallying cry dozens of times: "This isn't the end. This is the start."

Those weren't just platitudes. Given all the talent in that room, I genuinely felt like we would be back in the playoffs every year. We were not only stacked but young and hungry, clearly on our way up in the baseball world. For those reasons, I probably didn't savor the 2006 playoff experience as much as I should have. Celebrating on the field at Shea Stadium when we clinched the division title, beating the Dodgers in the NLDS, battling with the Cardinals for seven memorable games—those were such wonderful moments that I didn't enjoy as much as I could have at the time.

Looking back, I wish I could have bottled those feelings, bottled those emotions. I just kind of assumed I'd experience them every October.

# TEN

||||||||||

# COLLAPSE

Outside of my daughters, I'm not sure I've ever held a more precious object than the three-and-a-half-by-two-inch business card I received in early November 2006. Printed on it, in characters I couldn't even begin to understand, were the name and address of my Tokyo hotel.

After the 2006 postseason, Major League Baseball invited me to join an All-Star tour of Japan, with three games in Tokyo, three in Osaka, and one in Fukuoka. Having never really traveled outside North America, I was excited to take part. But I'll admit I wasn't the most cultured person in the world. As a kid, I tended to spend my vacation time traveling to baseball tournaments in suburban Virginia, not jet-setting off to Europe or Asia. So this trip opened my eyes to what it's like to travel around the world—including the difficulties of communicating in a country where few people speak fluent English.

After we touched down, I received that business card along with some important instructions. If I ever found myself lost in To-kyo, I was supposed to give it to a taxi driver to communicate where I needed to go. This was before smartphones were prevalent. I hadn't bothered to switch my cell into global mode, anyway. Our traveling party included a couple of interpreters who couldn't be everywhere at once, so that little card was all I had.

I guarded it with my life.

Only a few times did I grow bold enough to venture out for a meal with Mets bullpen catcher Dave Racaniello, my guest for the trip. Once, we tried to ride the subway, but the signs proved too difficult for us so we wound up taking a cab. On multiple occasions, the two of us walked into a restaurant only to discover none of the waiters spoke English, neither of us spoke Japanese, and the menus didn't have pictures. We wound up leaving. Our hotel buffet saved us that week, as did one glorious meal at the Hard Rock Café in Tokyo's Roppongi district. Never in my life had I felt so worldly.

One night, we did manage to enjoy a real, genuine Japanese dinner thanks to one of the Mets' former massage therapists, Yoshi Nishio, who took us out for a memorable evening at a local restau-rant. Learning a few of the local customs and trying to communi-cate despite the language barrier was educational for me. I loved that the trip took me a little outside my comfort zone. It's one I'll always remember . . . and not just because I absolutely raked during the games.

Before the five-game series began, we played an exhibition

against the Yomiuri Giants, who are like the Yankees of Japan. I was pretty upset that manager Bruce Bochy didn't put me in the starting lineup, but I entered late and hit a game-tying home run in the ninth inning. That game finished in a 7–7 tie, and, sure enough, Bochy inserted me into the starting lineup every night from that point forward. Five days later in Osaka, I hit a home run off Kei Igawa, who was about three weeks away from signing a multiyear contract with the Yankees. The following night, in Fukuoka, José Reyes hit a walk-off homer to complete our five-game sweep of the Japanese All-Stars.

Reyes and I were part of a sizeable Mets contingent that also included John Maine and Julio Franco (an active player who served as our hitting coach in Japan), as well as third-base coach Manny Acta. Coming off the disappointment of the 2006 playoffs, the trip was a nice way for all of us to take our minds off the defeat and ease into the off-season while experiencing some culture—and maybe some Hard Rock chicken fingers—at the same time.

For me, the games themselves were the best part. In some ways, baseball is the same in Japan as it is in the States. But culturally and strategically, it can be quite different. Fans all over the country treated us like rock stars, banging inflatable thunder sticks during games and singing songs for the Japanese players. Each time I homered, a kid ran out to meet me at home plate with a gift.

Local media outlets couldn't get enough of the tournament. This was right before Daisuke Matsuzaka, who was an even bigger deal than Igawa, came to the States. Sportswriters kept approaching us with pictures of Matsuzaka, pointing to his face and asking us what we thought. Ryan Howard, who won the National League

MVP that season, was so popular he could barely show his face in public. The entire thing was unlike anything I had previously experienced in my baseball career. I just really, really enjoyed it.

You could call it life-changing in another way, too: Before the series began, while spending a few days training for it in Arizona, I met my future wife. I just didn't know it yet.

||||||||||||||

The Japan Series made for a quick off-season, which was just fine by me. Knowing how much unfinished business the Mets had to tend to, I was eager to get back on the field.

I entered 2007 riding a twelve-game hitting streak, which I only realized because people were constantly bringing it to my attention. Twelve quickly turned to twenty, then twenty-two, then twenty-four. It seemed like every night, reporters wanted to know about the streak, which might have wormed its way into my head a little too much. A couple dozen games in a row honestly didn't seem like a big deal to me—it wasn't like Joe DiMaggio's record of fifty-six was in any danger of falling. Before that year, I didn't even know it was possible to carry a hitting streak from one season to the next.

Regardless, it was still pretty cool—in retrospect, probably a more impressive feat than it seemed to me at the time. On April 18, I singled twice to reach twenty-five straight games, breaking a franchise record that Mike Piazza and Hubie Brooks shared. My streak lasted one more game after that. As much as I didn't enjoy losing it, I was pretty glad to be done talking about the streak so I could focus my mind on other things.

I had big plans for the 2007 season, which was statistically my most productive as a big leaguer. Squarely in my physical prime at age twenty-four, I posted the highest batting average (.325) of my career, as well as my best on-base (.416) and slugging (.546) percentages. I appeared in 160 games for the second time in three years, setting a new career high with 711 plate appearances and proving, just by toeing the line each night, that I knew what it took to endure the rigors of a full season.

I also set a career high with thirty-four stolen bases, which meant a lot to me for two reasons. One, I always had a bit of a chip on my shoulder back from my childhood days as "the pudgy kid at shortstop." I may not have been a burner like Reyes, but I had a quick first step and solid baserunning instincts. I loved using my speed to surprise people, picking the exact right pitch to steal a bag. I was caught only five times that year—all but one of them on pick-off plays—resulting in the best success rate of my career.

The second reason those steals mattered was because they made me the first Met since Howard Johnson—one of my childhood idols and most influential minor league coaches—to hit at least thirty homers and steal at least thirty bases in the same season. A 30-30 season is significantly rarer than a no-hitter or a cycle. Heading into 2007, there had been only forty-eight such seasons in big league history, compared to hundreds of no-hitters and cycles. Willie Mays went 30-30 on two different occasions. Hank Aaron did it only once. HoJo accomplished the feat three times, which said a lot about what kind of player he was.

It was the exact kind of player I wanted to be.

Before the 2007 season, HoJo joined the Mets' big league staff, serving as our first-base coach and baserunning instructor. His being around every day again allowed us to rekindle the lessons we'd begun back in 2003, when I met HoJo at Class A St. Lucie and he began encouraging me to be a better base stealer.

As a prospect, I'd spent hours studying the craft with HoJo—working on pitcher scouting, primary and secondary leads, first-step quickness, and the like. By the time HoJo reached the major league coaching ranks, I had successfully implemented many of his lessons, stealing thirty-seven bases in forty-nine attempts from 2005 to '06. But I knew I had more in me. HoJo thought so, too, urging me to run more often than ever before; he believed I could be one of the most efficient base stealers in the game, which can be even more valuable than being the fastest. All that summer we worked and worked, so it meant a lot to me when, on August 30, I stole my thirtieth against Kyle Lohse and Carlos Ruiz in Philadelphia. Two weeks later, I hit my thirtieth home run, also against the Phillies. Usually, coaches stay near the bench during celebrations, but HoJo was so ecstatic that he bounded out of the dugout to meet me on the field. I was just as thrilled, knowing all the hours and sweat that had gone into the accomplishment.

All told, I finished seventh in the NL with thirty-four stolen bases, which seemed good to me even if it didn't come close to matching Reyes's insane total of seventy-eight. My success rate of 87 percent ranked tenth in the league. I was proud of what I'd accomplished on the base paths and happy to share it with HoJo.

Others weren't quite so impressed. Back home after the season, I probably spent a bit too much time chirping to my brothers at the Thanksgiving dinner table about how fast I had become. Matt, the third oldest of the four of us, challenged me to a sixty-yard dash out in the street in front of our house. Obviously, I wasn't going to back down from that sort of thing, so I dropped my fork and headed to my room to put on tights, a T-shirt, a sweatband, and wristbands. The turkey was still digesting as we ran the race three times on a frigid November night. Ask Matt, and he'll say he won. Ask me and you'll get the truth.

||||||||||||||

I had more reason than usual to be thankful for my brothers' company that holiday. Early in the 2007 season, I woke up to the news that a mass shooting had occurred at Virginia Tech, where Stephen, the second oldest, was a senior engineering major. Flipping on the TV in my Philadelphia hotel room, I learned that one of the shooting sites was Norris Hall, an engineering building where Steve had classes. I began to grow a little frantic, calling my brother without any luck.

I had slept late that morning, so I was rushing around, trying to make the team bus as I worried about Stephen. Each minute that ticked by, my stress level increased. Thankfully, I was able to track down my parents, who relayed the news that Steve was okay. That allowed me to relax a bit, but it was just a scary, scary morning.

Thirty-two people died at the shooting, making it the deadliest in modern United States history up to that time. I learned later that Steve had been on his way to a study group in Norris Hall when the shooting happened. Needless to say, it hit close to home. I had gone to Virginia Tech several times to visit my brother, attending football games and getting a bit of the college experience that I never had myself. Because of Stephen, I was a big Virginia Tech fan, keeping a Hokies helmet in my locker for much of my career.

The shooting shook me. Obviously, all tragedies do, but until a loved one is involved, it's difficult to gain a true sense of how terrifying it is. I can't overstate how important my family is. I was so, so thankful that Steve was okay. My brothers mean everything to me and I never lost sight of that, no matter what else was happening in my life.

llllllllllllll

Steve's experience at Virginia Tech resulted in a rare moment when I found myself focusing on something other than baseball. On the field, things were going largely as planned; by the time I hit my thirtieth homer to join HoJo in the 30-30 club in September, we were right where we needed to be as a team.

We knew we had one of the National League's best clubs, even if some people didn't agree. That spring, Philadelphia shortstop Jimmy Rollins made headlines when he called the Phillies the "team to beat" in the NL East, despite the fact that the Mets had won the division by a dozen games in 2006. We'd brought back much of the same roster, including me and Reyes on the left side of the infield, Carlos Delgado at first base, Carlos Beltrán in center field, and Paul Lo Duca at catcher. A year after shipping six players off to the All-Star Game, we sent a still-pretty-impressive four: me, Reyes, and Beltrán, who were all in the starting lineup, as well as closer Billy Wagner. All three of our position players came away with hits in the game, which was a nice bonus.

Nicer still was the fact that I sat out the Home Run Derby, removing a big stressor from my summer. Having experienced it once, I didn't see a reason to do it again any time soon. I was happy to watch that one as a fan.

After the All-Star Game, things continued to progress. By the end of August, the Mets held a three-game division lead over Rollins's "team to beat," which we extended to seven with seventeen to play. We were right on schedule until things started going haywire. A five-game losing streak put the division back in play for the Phillies, who swept three in a row from us at Shea Stadium.

Just like that, we couldn't win a game. It felt like a bad dream from which we couldn't wake. Our pitching staff's ERA spiked to 5.96 over the final seventeen games of the season, more than two runs higher than it had been the first five and a half months of the season. Our offense couldn't seem to come up with a big hit. We lost five of the six games we played against the fourth-place Nationals, and during that spiral, we began scoreboard-watching on a daily basis.

I can't speak for everyone on that team, but I know I started pressing at the plate.

I always wanted to be the guy people could rely on to get a big hit, which in my opinion is the right mindset for a competitor to have. But that attitude could work against me in the biggest moments, when my adrenaline started pumping and my heartbeat was racing. It could push me farther and farther out of my comfort zone.

This may seem counterintuitive, but as a hitter, I was most effective when my effort level hovered around 75 or 80 percent. When I ramped that up to 100, my whole body tightened to the point where I struggled with pitch recognition and swing mechanics. Everything became rigid because I was trying to hit the ball a mile instead of taking what pitchers gave me. My greatest strength was to right-center field, which meant relaxing, letting the ball travel deep in the strike zone, and then driving it the other way. When I pressed at the plate, I couldn't do that with ease.

Those vulnerabilities had worked against me early in the 2006 NLDS when Derek Lowe coaxed me into chasing pitcher's pitches. They hurt me again in the NLCS against the Cardinals, who took advantage of my eagerness to do damage. I thought I had patched that hole in my game toward the end of the NLCS, but the Phillies, the Nationals, the Marlins, and other teams proved otherwise down the stretch in 2007. Even though I hit .397 in those final seventeen games, which seems excellent at a glance, my slugging percentage dropped almost two hundred points with men in scoring position. In other words, I was playing well and producing to a certain extent, but I wasn't doing the big-time damage that I wanted to.

I wasn't alone. All of us on the team knew what our individual issues were, but that didn't make correcting them any easier. How do you fix a problem when the problem is trying too hard? How do you relax when you're coughing up a seven-game lead with seventeen to play? Even today, I puzzle over what we could have done differently.

At some point, you start to panic a little bit.

It seemed like we were calling team meeting after team meeting, trying to get everybody to calm down and play the type of baseball we had played all season. Those meetings only seemed to make us tenser. Again, what are you going to say? "Play better"? We already knew we needed to do that.

On the final home stand, the Mets installed temporary seating behind home plate at Shea Stadium so they could accommodate more fans for the playoffs. Some people called it tempting fate, considering our suddenly precarious position. All we cared about was winning a game. Four days before the end of the season, we lost for the eleventh time in sixteen games to allow the Phillies to draw even with us. Then we lost again the following night, falling out of first place for the first time since May 15. We no longer controlled our own fate, which was a tough thing for a team with World Series aspirations to accept.

Finally, with almost no time to spare, we caught a break. On the second-to-last day of the regular season, the Phillies snapped their winning streak against the Nationals, boosting us back into a tie for first place. Maine pitched into the eighth inning of our 13–0 rout of the Marlins, allowing one hit and striking out fourteen. It would have been the perfect momentum swing if not for what happened in the fifth inning.

We were already leading by eight runs when Marlins reliever Harvey García threw a pair of pitches near our second baseman Luis Castillo, including a fastball behind him. As tempers flared and the dugouts emptied, umpire C. B. Bucknor warned both benches. I was the on-deck hitter, which put me squarely in the middle of the fray. When our pitching coach Rick Peterson started barking at Marlins catcher Miguel Olivo, I pushed Peterson aside and tried to hold Olivo back from pursuing him. The best I could do was try to play peacemaker—a brawl was the last thing we needed at that point in the season. It seemed to work; after lots of chirping from both sides, everyone filtered back to their respective benches.

Turned out the fracas wasn't over. As a new Marlins pitcher warmed, Reyes and Olivo—two longtime friends, or at least former friends, from the Dominican Republic—began jawing at each other at third base. Reyes later said he thought the whole conversation was a joke, but Olivo clearly didn't see it that way. Minding my own business with my back turned to Reyes, I didn't realize what was happening until everyone in the Mets' dugout began sprinting in my general direction. It was surreal. Players from both teams descended upon Reyes and Olivo, looking for someone to hit.

One of the Marlins' pitchers, Sergio Mitre, seemed particularly fired up, so I wrapped him in a bear hug to immobilize him from behind. That dude was six foot three and weighed quite a bit more than me. I didn't love the idea of getting into a wrestling match with him, but it was better than letting him take free swings at my teammates. Throughout the melee, Mitre kept trying to rip his way out of my grasp. The next day, I woke up with sore muscles from head to toe.

The newspapers described that brawl as the spark our team needed. In reality, it turned out to be better motivation for the Marlins, who had nothing else to play for in a losing season. Their shortstop Hanley Ramírez was particularly vocal after that Saturday game, vowing to play in Sunday's finale despite an injured hand.

"I don't care if it's broke," Ramírez told media members after the game. "I'm gonna play tomorrow. . . . I'm going to kick their asses tomorrow."

Ramírez said some nastier words as well, which weren't taken kindly in our clubhouse. Early the next morning, somebody placed a picture of him and his quote in the tunnel leading to the Mets dugout, along with the inscription "It's never a good idea to wake a sleeping mutt. Somebody pays today."

I don't know who put that photograph there, but I do know how it made me feel. In the years that followed, I always harbored a little extra animosity toward the Marlins, even long after guys like Ramírez and Olivo—whom Major League Baseball suspended for the finale—moved to other teams. I wanted to make them pay for the way they talked coming down the stretch.

And still, despite everything that had happened—the meetings, the brawl, the trash talk—we went into that final game knowing all we needed to do was win one game to keep our season alive. Earlier that month, the Mets had lost a coin flip for home-field advantage in a potential tiebreaking Game 163, so we brought our luggage to Shea Stadium in anticipation of a trip to Philadelphia. We didn't know what the afternoon would bring, but we prepared for the best.

Instead, our nightmare continued. Tom Glavine gave up seven runs in the first inning and our offense couldn't get anything going in an 8–1 loss.

As the innings ticked away and it became increasingly clear that we weren't going back to the playoffs, the whole thing began to feel like an enormous gut punch. Afterward, Glavine took a lot of criticism, but he was a Hall of Famer and one of our leaders, winning thirteen games that season and pitching over two hundred innings. We could have done so much more to support him. Because we didn't, our season was over. Because we didn't, the Marlins

laughed and high-fived and had a grand old time on the Shea Stadium grass, making sure we all noticed. I took the loss personally,
saying afterward that we didn't deserve to make the playoffs. I
meant those words, but that didn't make them hurt any less to say.

People called it a collapse, a choke. All of that was fair.

To me, the whole thing felt even more painful than our NLCS
defeat eleven months earlier. In that one, we'd lost a tough seven-
game battle against a team that went on to win the World Series.
The Cardinals were a championship-caliber group and we were
one clutch hit away from beating them. We played well, fought
hard, and came pretty close to reaching our ceiling.

Despite another stacked roster in 2007, we didn't even scratch
the surface of our potential. Instead, we frittered it away down the
stretch, losing night after night to teams we should have beaten. We
got cold at the wrong time. We pressed. We couldn't do anything
right. For those reasons, the disappointment lingered a long while
after the season. It sticks with me to this day.

That September left a different taste in my mouth than any
other season in my fourteen-year career. In my eyes, it was a complete and utter failure.

# ELEVEN

||||||||||

# DÉJÀ VU

The pain didn't diminish as I returned home to Virginia for another off-season of work, though I was eventually able to reflect on some aspects of the year that made me proud. In November, Rawlings honored me with my first Gold Glove at third base, which meant even more than my 30-30 season. It truly felt like the finest personal accomplishment of my career.

Coming up through Little League, AAU baseball, high school, the minor leagues, and even the majors, hitting came naturally to me. I worked at it tirelessly, sure, but the offensive side of the game was something that never really rattled my confidence, at least not for too long a stretch. Defense was a different story. Defensively, I could struggle, particularly with my footwork and throwing. I knew the Mets had taken notice, considering how much they focused on my issues at the upper levels of the minors. Early in my career, some in the organization feared my defensive limitations might even force me back to Triple-A.

Hearing those whispers as a young, hungry player, I worked my tail off to get to a place where I felt like I was average, then above average, then eventually even better. We're talking hours of fungoes and extra drills in the afternoon sun, hours of work when I could have been doing anything else. To me, putting in the effort was the obvious choice. By 2007, I believed I had developed into one of the better defensive third basemen in the game. Winning my first Gold Glove felt like vindication.

Apparently not everyone saw it that way. No sooner had Rawlings made the announcement than I started receiving text messages from my buddies—things like "Man, what did you do to piss off Chipper Jones?" I had no idea what they were talking about until I fired up my computer and saw Chipper quoted in *The Atlanta Journal-Constitution* saying I shouldn't have won the Gold Glove. He pointed out that I had committed twenty-one errors and had the eighth-best fielding percentage among National League third basemen. (This was before advanced defensive metrics had really become mainstream. Errors were everything.)

"When I found out [Wright won], I was speechless, for quite some time," Jones told the newspaper, calling it "a head-scratcher."

"Certainly the guys with the least amount of errors and best fielding percentage quite obviously didn't win it," he added.

When New York sportswriters called me for my reaction, I told them Chipper's comments didn't bother me. That probably wasn't the whole truth. Not only was I extremely proud of that Gold Glove, but I also thought I had a good relationship with Chipper.

When I was growing up, he was one of the third basemen I admired the most because he could do it all—hit for power, hit for average, steal bases, play good defense. He was the rare number 1 overall draft pick to blossom into a superstar, going on to become a first-ballot Hall of Famer.

Like lots of baseball fans, my brothers and I grew up following the Braves because TBS broadcast their games across the country. I watched Chipper play all the time, taking things I respected from his game and trying to incorporate them into mine. When I made the majors myself and began traveling to Atlanta three times a year, Chipper and I became friendly in the way that opposing players often do. I thought we had a mutual respect. So to read those comments from someone I considered a buddy, yeah, it stung a little bit.

In the seasons that followed, I played with Chipper in two All-Star Games and a World Baseball Classic. I competed against him for years in a fantasy football league. If anything, we grew closer. We've spent a lot of time talking about a lot of different topics, but in all those conversations, I never asked him why he said what he did. I didn't feel like I had to. I knew the work I had put in to win that Gold Glove and I displayed it proudly in my home. A year later, I won another one. As much as Chipper's comments bothered me, I did my best to focus on the accomplishment—not on what people said about it.

||||||||||||||

If nothing else, that award provided another piece of evidence that I was in a good place as a player. I felt it was my responsibility to change the narrative for the Mets following disappointing ends in 2006 and '07.

That winter, everyone on the team—from ownership to the front office to the coaches and players—put their heads together to try to figure out how to improve. I trained as hard as ever with Piney, Cuddyer, and the rest of my usual crew in Virginia. The '07 collapse hurt us all, but we still had the tools in place to be one of the best teams in baseball.

General manager Omar Minaya's response was to be bold, trading four prospects—including Carlos Gómez, who would go on to make two All-Star teams and win a Gold Glove for the Brewers before coming full circle and ending his career with the Mets—for two-time Cy Young Award winner Johan Santana. As a condition of the trade, Santana immediately negotiated a new six-year, $137.5 million contract. He was going to be here for the long haul.

As far as off-season additions go, Santana was as good as it gets. This was a twenty-eight-year-old ace in his prime, fresh off a year in which he'd won fifteen games, posted a 3.33 ERA, and struck out two hundred thirty-five batters—and that was his *worst* season since becoming a full-time starting pitcher five years earlier. On the mound, Santana featured one of the most devilish changeups in the game, a tumbling pitch that could be impossible to touch. (When I faced him in the 2006 All-Star Game, I hit into a double play and was happy just to make contact.) He was an absolute stud. Considering we only missed the playoffs by one game in 2007, the idea was that Santana would put us over the top. His addition did wonders to restore any confidence we'd lost down the stretch.

Twelve months after Jimmy Rollins called the Phillies "the

team to beat in the NL East," Beltrán fired back some similar words
to the reigning champs.

"Without Santana, we felt we had a chance to win our division
last year," Beltrán said. "With him now, I have no doubt we're going
to win our division."

And so we headed into another promising season. Santana did
his part, going 16-7 and leading the NL with 234⅓ innings and a
2.53 ERA, while I chipped in another one of my best years. Although I didn't steal as many bases in 2008, I set career highs with
33 homers, 115 runs scored, and 124 RBI to match Mike Piazza's
franchise record. I made my third All-Star Game, going 1-for-3 as
one of the designated hitters at Yankee Stadium—Chipper played
the first five innings at third base—and I appeared in 160 games for
the third time in four years. Defensively, I committed only 16 errors
in my Gold Glove defense, the lowest full-season total of my career
to that point.

The ingredients were all there, but as a team, we again had
trouble clicking. It wasn't long before rumors about Willie Randolph's job status, which had begun to dog him toward the end of
the 2007 season, grew louder than ever. After we split a double-
header against the Rangers on June 15 to remain stuck in third
place, two games under .500, I admitted to reporters that all the
questions about Willie were getting "tiresome."

"Would I rather talk about baseball? Yes," I told *The New York
Times*. "But I understand that this comes along with it and that we've
underachieved so far this year, and these issues are going to be out
there."

I hated the conversation swirling around Willie, who had

become the mentor I'd envisioned when the Mets hired him shortly after my major league debut. Following Willie's first win as manager in 2005, he shook my hand and told me it was going to be one of many. In the years that followed, Willie and I talked constantly—not just on our walks back from ballparks but pretty much every day in the clubhouse, on the field, in his office, wherever. Over the course of three-plus seasons, we developed as tight a relationship as a player and manager can. Willie showed me a tremendous deal of respect starting when I was still young, treating me like a veteran when other managers wouldn't have. He worked to mold me into a leader. That meant a lot to me—especially from someone who had spent years as a captain in the Yankees clubhouse.

Willie didn't have to treat me the way that he did. To this day, I remain thankful for the type of respect and commitment he showed me when I was a young player.

When the Mets reached the 2006 postseason with Willie managing and me at third base, it felt like his prophecy—"one of many"—was coming true before our eyes. Postseason baseball seemed destined to become an annual tradition in Queens. Willie and I envisioned shaking each other's hands on the field time and time again, piling up win after October win, maybe hoisting the World Series trophy over our heads every now and then. Even our NLCS loss to the Cardinals felt like nothing more than a bump in the road that we would inevitably overcome.

That's what made the rumors so frustrating to hear. Similar to when the Mets had released my friend Joe McEwing two years earlier, I felt personally responsible for Willie's situation. He would never have been in trouble if we had done our jobs as players—and that started with me, a middle-of-the-lineup hitter. If we had played even one game better down the stretch in 2007, the media would probably have spent the winter speculating on a contract extension for Willie rather than a firing.

It was painful to see my shortcomings so directly affect a manager, his family, and everyone else in his orbit. Despite our stacked roster, we lost more games than we won in May 2008, falling to fourth place in the NL East and carrying a sub-.500 record into mid-June. The rumors intensified to the point where even Willie began to joke about them in his daily media sessions. During one nine-game stretch in June, we lost seven times. I was as much to blame as anyone, batting .162 with a .503 OPS. At a time when Willie needed me most, it felt like I was letting him down.

The end came days later, after we flew to California to begin a six-game road trip. We won the first night in Anaheim, only to learn afterward that the Mets had fired our manager. Willie left the hotel early the next morning, before I had a chance to say goodbye or wish him well. I felt sick.

Obviously, by that point, the logical part of my brain had seen Willie's firing coming. The emotional part still struggled to understand the business side of baseball. I knew teams fired managers all the time, but I'd just assumed it would never happen here. Not in Queens, not to the Mets, not to my friend and mentor—not if I could do anything about it. I never overcame the feeling that I could have played better or done something differently to save Willie's job. I felt that way every time someone was cut or fired during my tenure.

The reality is that when a team needs a scapegoat, blame

usually falls on the manager or coaches. It's unfair. It sucks. For me, it resulted in some lost sleep and a lot of guilt.

||||||||||||||||

Willie's firing didn't do much in terms of an immediate spark, considering we played .500 baseball for another three weeks under interim manager Jerry Manuel. Finally, in July, we ripped off a ten-game winning streak to rise from third place in the NL East into a tie for first. Another hot streak in late August put us in an enviable position; by September 10, we were 82-63, sitting three and a half games ahead of the Phillies. It wasn't quite the seven-game lead we'd held with seventeen to play in 2007, but it was still a great place to be.

Then we started losing again, dropping six of our next ten games to fall back to second place. On September 24, we stranded runners on third base in the fifth, sixth, seventh, eighth, and ninth innings in what Manuel called "our toughest defeat," a 9–6 loss to the Cubs. That pushed us into a tie atop the NL wild card race with the Brewers, who were as hot as we were cold. Their ace, CC Sabathia, had produced a 1.65 ERA in seventeen starts after the Brewers acquired him from Cleveland in early July, the last three of those outings on short rest.

Sabathia's performance that September was one of the most impressive things I had seen in baseball, standing in stark contrast to our growing list of problems. Maine was hurt. Wagner was hurt. Castillo was banged up. It seemed like we were running on fumes, losing players to injury as frequently as we were dropping games.

Entering the season's final weekend, we found ourselves a game behind the Phillies in the NL East, tied with the Brewers for the wild card lead, and only barely still in control of our own destiny. That Friday, we lost to—who else?—the Marlins, with Hanley Ramírez going 4-for-5 to stick it to us again. The loss cost us ground in both races, allowing the Phillies to clinch the NL East the next day.

But we weren't dead. Once again, we received a transcendent pitching performance in the second-to-last game of the season to keep our hopes alive, this time from Santana. That pumped me up beyond belief. Pitching on three days' rest and (we found out later) a torn meniscus in his knee, Santana threw a three-hit shutout to draw us even with the Brewers. It was one of the best games of Santana's career—maybe even better than his 2012 no-hitter, given how much it meant. It was exactly why Minaya had paid such a steep price to get him: Thanks to Santana, our playoff dream was still alive. Just like the previous September, all we had to do was beat the Marlins to force at least a one-game tiebreaker.

||||||||||||||

We lost, 4–2. I finished 0-for-4 as we went hitless as a team over the final three innings.

Once again, our season ended in shock and disappointment.

||||||||||||||

People tend to lump together what happened down the stretch in 2007 and 2008, but to me, they were very, very different. Unlike in

2007, when things went our way until the final three weeks, issues surfaced throughout the 2008 season. Our bullpen struggled to stay consistent. Injuries affected our rotation, most notably knocking Maine and Martínez out for significant chunks of the year. Our batting average with runners in scoring position plummeted to twenty-fifth in the majors, and I was a big part of that, hitting .243 in those situations compared to .327 in all others. We just never really gelled as a team.

In 2007, we could beat teams playing our B-plus game or even our C-plus game. In 2008, we didn't have the same thump. It seemed like we had to be firing on all cylinders just to win a game.

In 2007, losing a win-or-go-home game on the final day of the season seemed like a significant failure. I still don't entirely understand how it happened. In 2008, it almost felt like we were lucky to be in that spot. I didn't think we wasted our potential to quite the same extent.

People say the Mets collapsed twice. I say we collapsed once, in 2007. In 2008, we just didn't have the bullets.

The Phillies had their fun, cooling off the Brewers in the first round before going on to beat the Rays in the World Series. At the championship parade in Philadelphia, Rollins went out of his way to take another jab at us, saying, "They brought in that great pitcher, Johan Santana, but they forgot that it takes more than one player to bring home a championship." Cole Hamels called us "choke artists." Obviously, I bristled at those assessments, and at the time we all kind of hated those guys because of their success and their brashness. But it did make for a good baseball rivalry. They had a solid, young nucleus, just like we did, and were able to win with it. We somehow managed to lose twice.

No matter how they happened, those losses stuck with me, especially as the years passed and I gained a greater appreciation for how rare such opportunities can be. I wanted to be the one celebrating on the field, not reading about some other team's party. I saw how fans treated the 1969 and 1986 World Series champions when they returned to Shea Stadium for reunions. Everyone on those rosters, from the biggest superstar to the last guy on the bench, seemed immortal. Decades later, those guys received standing ovations from fans too young to have watched them play.

New York yearns for winning teams, not individual performances. I always loved that about the city because I was wired the same way. I burned so badly to win a World Series. I burned to be a champion. Those three years from 2006 to '08, we had some legitimate chances to do it. We let them slip right through our fingers.

|||||||||

# TWELVE

# RED, WHITE, AND BLUE

Back in 2006, only a season and a half into my major league career, Team USA approached me to gauge my interest in signing up for the inaugural World Baseball Classic.

Just the idea of it bowled me over. As a kid, I never received invitations to play for any of the youth teams that toured the world representing the United States. It seemed like other people were always beating me out, which was totally understandable. (Did I mention I was the pudgy kid at shortstop?) But I burned to play on an international stage all the same, so I was cautiously optimistic when MLB announced the creation of the WBC—a preseason tournament that was essentially baseball's answer to soccer's World Cup. Unlike the Summer Olympics, which always took place during the MLB season and never featured top big leaguers for that reason, the World Baseball Classic promised to be a showcase of the best talent in the world—from the United States to Latin America, Asia, Europe, and beyond.

When it came time to build rosters, third base was a stacked position for Team USA. As a former MVP in his prime, Chipper Jones was a lock. Alex Rodriguez, who had switched from shortstop to third following his trade to the Yankees, was also a strong candidate. The American organizers were honest when they approached me, essentially telling me I'd be an alternate because only two third basemen would make the team. Everything hinged on Rodriguez, a New York native with Dominican parents who was eligible for both Team USA and the Dominican Republic's team. If Alex chose to play for the United States, I wasn't going to get the chance to do so as well. If he chose to play for the Dominican Republic, I'd be in luck.

For weeks, Rodriguez delayed his decision, keeping me in limbo until he finally chose to join the American side about two months before the start of the tournament. I reported to spring training as usual, understanding the situation but certainly disappointed. In that moment, I made it a goal of mine to earn an invitation to the next WBC regardless of Alex, Chipper, or anyone else. I wanted to outplay them. I wanted to force my way onto Team USA by being too good for the organizers to leave me off the roster.

The next three seasons were some of the best of my career, but when the WBC rolled around again in 2009, I found myself stuck in a similar situation. Although Jones was almost thirty-seven at that point, he was coming off a year in which he hit .364 to win the batting title. Insane. And A-Rod was still A-Rod, one of the most successful players in baseball history. Fortunately, Alex announced in December that he would fulfill his mother's dream by playing for the Dominican Republic, which allowed me to check off a bucket-list item of my own.

Considering I had waited a significant chunk of my life to wear a uniform with "Team USA" stitched across the chest, I made it my mission to be as prepared as possible. The most difficult part of the WBC was that it began in early March, at a time when position players are typically just beginning to ramp into game shape. For hitters, the spring schedule goes from cage work and soft-toss flips to batting practice on the field, then eventually to tracking pitches, taking live BP, and facing real pitchers in games. Even at the end of that progression, it can take some time to feel completely up to speed. There's a reason why spring training is six or seven weeks long.

The WBC mandated a different timeline, requiring us to play meaningful games a month earlier than usual. Although I was always one of the first players to get to Florida, right around Super Bowl weekend, I modified my routine even further that winter to prepare for the WBC. I knew I wasn't going to be able to arrive in Port St. Lucie, take a few at-bats, and be ready to go. This might sound dramatic or a little corny, but I had absolutely no intention of disappointing my country, so I used the compressed timeline as motivation. I made it my goal to be in Opening Day shape a month earlier than usual, making March 1 seem like April 1.

I spent a significant chunk of that off-season living in Manhattan with my good friend Dave Racaniello, rather than in Virginia. Together, we commuted to the Mets' brand-new stadium, Citi Field, using a keycard to slip in and use the indoor batting cage. Instead of taking swings off a tee or asking Rac to give me soft-toss flips, I instructed him to throw to me as hard as he could. I wanted curveballs and sliders. I wanted him to try his best to get me out. Rac certainly enjoyed it, talking smack, throwing brushback pitches, and arguing with me over balls and strikes. He could be the fifth Wright brother for how competitive he is.

Because I was away from Piney that off-season, I relied on former Mets physical therapist Jeff Cavaliere to run my strength and conditioning programs. By the time I arrived in Florida for spring training, I felt ready. More than that, I felt eager as I drove three hours across the state to Clearwater, where the Phillies were hosting Team USA at their facility. It was quite the scene. As I put in work at the complex, Philadelphia fans booed me despite the red, white, and blue jersey on my back. Clearly, the Mets' rivalry with the Phillies was alive and well.

I found no refuge inside the clubhouse, where I arrived to find my locker positioned two stalls away from Jimmy Rollins—the man whose "team to beat" proclamation back in 2007 had spawned years' worth of trash talk. I wasn't sure how Rollins would receive me as a teammate, given how many words our teams had exchanged the previous two seasons. *Am I supposed to hate this guy?* In my mind, I was willing to let bygones be bygones, but I didn't know if Jimmy felt the same way.

My plan was to let him make the first move, but it wound up being someone else who broke the ice. The locker between me and Rollins belonged to Yankees shortstop Derek Jeter, whom I admired deeply. I had met Jeter in passing a couple of times, but didn't know him well. When Jimmy and I showed up to the clubhouse that first day, Jeter broke into a grin.

"Jimmy, this is David," he said. "David, this is Jimmy."

We all laughed, taking the edge off any tension that otherwise might have bubbled to the surface. With that behind us, Jimmy proved to be an excellent teammate throughout the WBC, cheering for me as loud as anyone. I had a lot of respect for him as another one of those players who could do it all—hit for power, steal bases, play great defense. I definitely was interested in building a relationship with him.

I wanted to get to know all my new teammates—Rollins included, but Jeter most of all.

||||||||||||||||

Because everyone loves a good comparison, people began stacking me up to Jeter from the moment I arrived in New York. I always considered those conversations unfair to him. Jeter had done so much, accomplished so much, winning four World Series titles by the time he was twenty-six years old. I was just a dude who also happened to play in New York and hit .300 a few times. Of course it was flattering to be mentioned in the same sentence as him, but as far as actual comparisons go, there was no contest. Nobody was ever going to be the next Jeter.

I had met Derek a few times early in my career for some promotional events, but the WBC was my first real chance to see how he operated up close. I was transfixed. Each day, I followed him to the batting cage to try to figure out what made him so great. In the dugout during games, I joined him on the top step to hear everything he had to say. I tried to ask him as many questions as possible without seeming like a superfan. It probably reached the point where I got on his nerves because I wanted to soak up so much information in my quest to figure out what made him tick.

What I came to discover was the importance of his routine. Jeter's was the same every . . . single . . . day. He never strayed from it. He certainly didn't shy away from putting in extra work. During the second of our three Florida exhibition games that month, against the Blue Jays in Dunedin, I was scheduled to receive two or three at-bats as the designated hitter. Derek was off that day, but he didn't feel like his swing was where it needed to be, so he asked our manager, Davey Johnson, for a couple at-bats. Obliging, Johnson subbed Jeter in for me midway through the game.

Those types of substitutions happen all the time in exhibition games, but usually it's the veterans who play the first few innings, followed by the reserves. I got a chuckle out of seeing future first-ballot Hall of Famer Derek Jeter come in to replace me—not the other way around. After the game, I asked Johnson for the lineup card, which had my name scratched out and Derek's written beneath it. Then I asked Jeter to sign it without telling him why. It may be one of the quirkier items in my memorabilia collection, but I've always loved it because of the respect I have for Jeter.

In my mind, that game said a lot about him. The guy owned a handful of World Series rings, but he still wanted to get into a meaningless WBC exhibition game because his swing felt a tick off-kilter. Most guys would have just taken the rest day and been happy with it. Derek was in constant pursuit of perfection.

Later that season, Derek and I did a promotion for Delta that included a competition to benefit our respective foundations:

Whoever posted the highest batting average would win a certain amount of grant money, with the second-place finisher receiving half as much. I got off to a hot start and was batting .356 on June 24—nearly sixty points higher than Jeter. Toward the end of the season I cooled off, but I still finished at a respectable .307. Derek? He hit .363 the rest of the way to crush me with a final average of .334. Because of course he did.

So, yeah, I understood how good Jeter was. I wanted to learn from him in every way possible, and being around him those few weeks in March gave me a firsthand look into how he operated not only as a player, but also as a leader. I noticed that he wasn't the loudest or most boisterous guy, but he didn't have to be because his work ethic was off the charts. His teammates saw the way he prepared and—like me—tried to mimic that routine.

As someone who's not particularly loud or boisterous myself, I could relate to that style. I knew people were counting on me to assume a leadership role on the Mets, particularly as some of the veterans from my early years—Tom Glavine, Pedro Martínez, Carlos Delgado, and others—left our clubhouse. Later in 2009, former Mets captain John Franco publicly criticized me for not doing more as a leader. (He later apologized.) The thing was, I didn't feel like I needed to be that vocal type. I never said anything out loud unless it had to be said, which made my words more impactful when I spoke. I didn't want my team meetings or private conversations to get written up in the newspapers. Most days, I just tried to lead by example, as Derek did throughout his career.

Following those exhibition games in Florida, Team USA flew to Toronto for the opening round of the tournament. One night,

Derek took a group of us out to dinner across the street from our hotel, offering me yet another glimpse into his life. When we walked into the restaurant, the amount of whispering and jaw-dropping that took place was insane. I felt like I was out to dinner with Tom Cruise or Brad Pitt. This guy was on a completely different level, with the paparazzi snapping pictures as often as they could. But the cool part was that at the end of the day, he was still a baseball player just like us. No matter how different our lives might have been, we always had that in common: We could just talk about how it was to play the game that had brought us all here.

||||||||||||||

The WBC gave us plenty to discuss. Even though Team USA failed to reach the semifinals during the inaugural 2006 event, we entered 2009 ranked among the favorites due to our stacked roster. In addition to myself, Jeter, Chipper, and Rollins, our infield included Dustin Pedroia, who became a close friend of mine during that event, and a twenty-three-year-old Evan Longoria. Curtis Granderson and Ryan Braun, both in their primes, highlighted our outfield. Our pitching staff included Roy Oswalt and Jake Peavy, two of the better starters in the game. We were, in a word, stacked.

Our first test was against Team Canada, which hosted opening-round pool play at the Rogers Centre. Featuring a round-robin format with the top two teams advancing, the tournament was designed so that every game mattered—not that we needed a reminder. More than forty-two thousand people crammed into the stadium, most of them rooting for the Canadians. We were the enemy. The place was electric. As Canada took the lead in the top of the first inning, my heart was beating out of my chest.

I finished 0-for-4 with five men left on base that day, which wasn't the best way to introduce myself to Team USA. Still, I'll always remember it because of the atmosphere.

The game was a back-and-forth affair that we led by two runs entering the ninth. To close out the win, Johnson called on J. J. Putz, whom the Mets had acquired from the Mariners a few months prior. During my career, I always tried to reach out to new players by phone, letting them know I'd be there if they had any questions. Between that call and our time together early in spring training, Putz and I had developed a good rapport. We'd driven across Florida together for WBC training camp, bonding a bit as new teammates. I was eager to see him in action.

He was eager just to get three outs. Things grew tense for Putz when Russell Martin and Joey Votto both doubled, plating a run and putting the potential tying run in scoring position with one out. The crowd was going ballistic, screaming and clapping, so I jogged out to the pitcher's mound to give Putz a breather. It felt like Game 7 of the NLCS all over again.

"I don't know if I'm ready for this," Putz said, half joking.

I wasn't sure if I was, either. The atmosphere was everything I wanted it to be, but that didn't make it easy to handle—especially at a time of year when we were typically doing defensive drills in front of a few hundred fans in spring training.

We had to adapt on the fly, which was part of the fun. Putz retired the next two hitters to secure the win, then we crushed an extremely talented Venezuelan team the next night to qualify for the second round. Three days later, when we played Venezuela a second time for seeding purposes, I made a tough play to cut down my old teammate Endy Chávez at home plate. I wasn't hitting as well as I wanted to, but at least some of my off-season work seemed to be paying dividends.

From Canada, we traveled to Miami for another double-elimination bracket, which included two more tournament favorites in Puerto Rico and Venezuela. We lost our first game, 11–1, to a Puerto Rican team featuring my Mets teammates Carlos Beltrán, Alex Cora, Jesús Feliciano, Pedro Feliciano, Nelson Figueroa, and Delgado. It felt like half our clubhouse was in the ballpark that night, and it was tough to let the Puerto Rican guys have all the bragging rights. Worse, the loss slimmed our margin for error to zero. One more defeat would spell the end for Team USA.

Heavily favored the next day against the Netherlands, we won a blowout to set up a rematch against Puerto Rico. The winner of our game would advance to the semifinals. The loser was going home.

After a quiet start to the WBC, this was a chance for me to do something big. Through five games, I was batting .263 with a walk, two runs, and an RBI—fine enough numbers, but far from the type of impact I wanted to make on Team USA. That all changed in our rematch with Puerto Rico. My first trip to the plate, I singled, stole a base, and scored a game-tying run. I later added a walk and a second hit. This was another back-and-forth type of game, which Puerto Rico tied, 3–3, in the fourth inning. By the bottom of the ninth, they were leading, 5–3, with J. C. Romero, a nasty lefty, on the mound to close us out.

What happened next was a little bit of magic. After two singles and a walk loaded the bases, Puerto Rico replaced the lefty with right-hander Fernando Cabrera. Standing on deck as Cabrera warmed, I tried to glean some sort of scouting report against a pitcher I had never faced. It became clear from watching him that I was going to get a steady diet of fastballs and sliders, and probably nothing else.

With the crowd still in a frenzy, Cabrera walked Kevin Youkilis on five pitches to force in a run, drawing us within one and bringing up my spot in the lineup. Yadier Molina trotted out to the mound to try to calm Cabrera, giving me another chance to go over the scouting report in my brain. I knew I couldn't press. I knew I couldn't expand the zone. I needed to stay within myself, play to my strengths, hit the ball the other way if I could.

Those reminders flashed through my head as I stepped into the box for one of the biggest at-bats of my life.

Cabrera wound up throwing me a pretty good pitch—a 2-1 fastball low and inside, probably just a bit off the plate. I swung at it anyway, keeping my hands tight to punch a soft liner into right field. As I ran to first, I contorted my body to will the thing fair. Those seconds seemed to stretch on forever. Finally, the ball bounced just inside the foul line, allowing Rollins to cross home with the winning run.

I'm not sure why, but my first instinct was to start yelling at Delgado, ribbing him for being on the losing end of our little rivalry. The bragging rights belonged to us now. Our tournament status was alive and well. I was so fired up, feeling such immense pride in coming through for my country. Everything just sort of hit me in that moment.

The only remaining question was how my teammates were going to react. As excited as I had been to play in that WBC, I went into the tournament unsure of how much other people would care. This wasn't the World Series. It wasn't the Olympics. I had no idea if anyone was going to take the tournament as seriously as I did.

The answer became obvious when I turned to see everyone streaming out of our dugout with huge grins on their faces.

*Oh,* I thought, *this is going to be good.*

While a few of my countrymen mobbed Rollins at home plate, Jeter led a contingent to meet me out at second. Youkilis joined him, grabbing my jersey as the entire party shifted in my direction. We were jumping and yelling, a giant mob moving as one, and eventually, I collapsed at the bottom of a dog pile on the turf in Miami. I couldn't tell who was on top of me or who was around me as their whoops and hollers mingled with the roar of the crowd.

I couldn't breathe as my teammates crushed me. *I don't even know what's happening,* was all I could think, *but this is awesome.*

|||||||||||||

We played one more game against Venezuela for seeding purposes, losing that one to earn a date with Japan in the semifinals at Dodger Stadium.

It might be easy to say we suffered an emotional letdown after beating Puerto Rico in such dramatic fashion, but the reality is we ran into three of the best pitchers in the world. Japan's starter, Daisuke Matsuzaka, was an international superstar, coming to the majors in 2007 and posting a 2.90 ERA with the Red Sox the following season. The second man out of the bullpen was twenty-year-old Masahiro Tanaka, who would go on to make his own major league debut five years later. (At the time, I had no idea who he was.) I had read a bit about the closer, twenty-two-year-old Yu Darvish, who was on the cusp of a successful big league career himself.

There was no letdown because the atmosphere in Los Angeles, with 43,630 fans at Dodger Stadium, was every bit as raucous as the scenes in Toronto and Miami. We brought our own energy, too. In the third inning, when Rollins stole second base to put a runner in scoring position for me, he kept vigorously clapping his hands in encouragement throughout my at-bat. That struck me as extremely cool. We might have been archrivals throughout our careers, but on this day we were teammates. Friends, even, pursuing a common goal.

With Rollins acting as my personal cheerleader, I came through with a go-ahead RBI double, but Japan scored five times in the fourth to take a decisive lead. I struck out in each of my final three at-bats against Matsuzaka, Tanaka, and Darvish, who was absolutely filthy.

We wound up losing by five runs. Just like that, our tournament was over.

Losing that game stunk, especially considering all the momentum we had captured with our win against Puerto Rico. Due to the WBC's tiebreak rules, we finished fourth, falling short of even a bronze medal. Everyone was down in the dumps, underscoring how much we all cared about the tournament. Nobody wanted to leave. It felt like total culture shock to go from the electric atmosphere of the WBC back to the middle of a routine spring camp in Port St. Lucie.

Still, I wouldn't have traded the experience for anything. To wear "Team USA" across my chest for three weeks in March was a dream come true, a bucket-list item made real. To hit a walk-off against Puerto Rico was a career highlight. The relationships that grew out of that trip were invaluable—soaking up knowledge from Jeter and Chipper, defusing a rivalry with Rollins, making a lifelong friend in Pedroia. This wasn't like an All-Star Game, sharing a locker room with some of baseball's best for a few hours. This was nearly a month of living and breathing alongside perennial All-Stars and future Hall of Famers. I wasn't sure I would ever have that sort of opportunity again.

Losing was tough, absolutely, no doubt about it. The WBC was still one of the most rewarding experiences of my life.

# THIRTEEN

# A STRANGER AT HOME

As I wrapped up 2009 spring training in Port St. Lucie, big things were happening back in Queens, where a steel-and-concrete megastructure was nearly finished rising beyond what used to be Shea Stadium's left-field fence. After more than a decade of planning, the Mets were set to open a new $900 million home across the parking lot from Shea.

It was crucial that I be the first person to hit a homer there. My chance had come the previous September, when the Mets invited me, Daniel Murphy, and Nick Evans to take the first-ever batting practice hacks at Citi Field. It was still an active construction site at that time, with a dirt-and-gravel playing surface and trucks scattered across the outfield. But a ballpark is a ballpark. I grabbed a bat, stepped into my new office for the first time, dug in, and swung.

And swung.

And swung.

Nothing was going over the fence. I'm a competitive person, and for whatever reason, it was extremely important for me to hit the first one out. The simple solution? Refuse to let anyone else try. I just kept hitting and hitting and hitting until I homered.

When I did, a wave of relief washed over me. Finally, it was somebody else's turn.

If that day was a harbinger of things to come, I didn't realize it at the time. A few months later, when a *New York Times* reporter called asking about Citi Field's dimensions, I told him it was impossible to tell how the park might play. The afternoon we took batting practice was cold and blustery. None of us had any idea how balls would travel in the spring breezes and summer heat.

We learned quickly enough. In left field, the fence began at twelve feet high and quickly rose to fifteen, making it difficult even for right-handed hitters like me to pull one out. I was never a typical righty slugger anyway, often sending my homers over the fence in right-center. But that was also a problem at Citi Field, where the deepest point of my power alley was a daunting 415 feet from home. That first season at Citi, I recall watching Chipper and A-Rod hit balls they thought were gone, only to stare in disbelief as they died shy of the wall. Jogging past third base on their way back to the visitors' dugout, Chipper and A-Rod both caught my eye as if to say, *Really?* Those guys combined had nearly a thousand homers at that point in their careers; they knew what it took to hit one out.

I did as well, so it was frustrating to spend the first half of the season spraying balls all over the warning track. In my first seventy-four games that year, I hit four home runs. Four. According to the website Hit Tracker Online, which estimated home run distances before Statcast became the norm, I lost six additional homers to Citi Field's dimensions. In other words, more of my would-be homers turned into outs than actually went over the fence.

When people asked about the dimensions, I told them I was happy hitting doubles, that I didn't need homers to be a productive hitter. That was mostly true. I certainly didn't need big power numbers to be the player I wanted to be, but that didn't stop me from believing I should have been hitting more homers. I always felt I was the type of guy who could hit twenty to twenty-five home runs with one hundred–plus RBI per year, which is exactly what I did my first four full seasons. In my introduction to Citi, I hit ten homers with seventy-two RBI, easily the worst full-season power output of my career.

All told, I still managed a decent year, making my fourth consecutive All-Star team while batting .307 with a .390 on-base percentage. But something was missing. The more I tried to correct what was wrong, the more I struck out, finishing with a career-high 140 whiffs—nearly 19 percent more than the previous season. Typically for power hitters, strikeouts and homers go hand in hand, but not for me in 2009. I became the first player in major league history to hit at least .300, strike out 140 or more times . . . and hit fewer than 20 homers.

As uncharacteristic as that stat line might have been, my mistake was letting it burrow inside my head. My statistics gave me sticker shock. It was a foreign concept to feel like I'd failed in spite of my high average, and while I don't want to say it rattled me, it was more difficult for me to wrap my head around than it probably should have been.

People began questioning the Citi Field blueprints, saying the Mets should have built something a little friendlier to right-handed power hitters. I never felt that way. If I owned a franchise, I would never, ever build a ballpark around a specific player, knowing the park would still be there long after everyone on the current roster retired. So what if I was one of the more prominent players on the team? So what if it cost me a few homers? Over the life of any stadium, thousands of players come and go. It makes no sense to build a park with a single person in mind.

In truth, I could have—should have—used Citi Field to my advantage. My entire life, I'd prided myself on my ability to adapt as a hitter. Need a home run? I can do that. Need a ground ball to the right side? I can do that, too. But I was far from perfect, and that 2009 season exposed some holes in my offensive game. I should have made that park work to my strengths by putting the ball in play as much as possible—taking my doubles, taking my triples, hitting the ball to the opposite field. I could have used it as an opportunity to improve.

Instead, I obsessed over that stupid statistic of ten home runs. It became the most glaring thing I felt I needed to address heading into the off-season, a challenge that I had to overcome. The day after the 2009 season, I began working out in Virginia. Rather than wait a few weeks to give my body rest, I told my trainer Piney that I needed to mix up my routine. And I needed to do it immediately.

"Whatever we were doing before," I said, "I want the varsity program now."

Previously, I'd tended to work out three or four times a week. We increased that to six days per week in 2009. Rather than spend Mondays focused on my chest, Wednesdays on my back, and Fridays on my legs and shoulders, I began cycling through each muscle group twice as often. I wasn't necessarily lifting heavier during those sessions, but I was doubling my amount of time spent in the weight room. I became obsessed with the idea of getting stronger, building muscle mass, bulking up; in my mind, that's what I needed to do to hit more home runs. We took those workouts to a crazy-challenging level. I couldn't get enough of it.

I may not have gained more than five or ten pounds that winter, but I grew stronger than I had ever been in my career, by far. The shape of my body changed. My first day back at spring training, in January, I walked into the weight room and looked around.

*This place can't hold me,* I thought.

Our strength coach, Rick Slate, took one look at me and said I needed to taper things off, because I wouldn't be able to maintain that sort of program once I added the full slate of baseball activities to my routine.

He was right, of course; my off-season program had worked almost too well. I hit 29 homers in 2010, nearly tripling my output from the previous season, but those power gains came at a price. My batting average dropped from .307 to a career-worst .283. My on-base percentage plummeted from .390 to .354, easily the lowest mark of any full season in my career. My strikeout total increased from 140 to a career-high 161.

I had accomplished my goal of hitting more home runs, but at the cost of losing myself as a hitter. I was inflexible, unbalanced. If

I could do it over again, I'd revamp my strategy to reflect more modern sports science models, which say that bigger isn't necessarily better. Proper batting mechanics matter more than brute strength, but I ignored that as I tried to correct my 2009 power drought. All I cared about was heavy lifting, which may be one path to generating power but probably isn't the ideal way to do it.

The funny part is, even back then, I would have happily traded a few home runs for an increased batting average, a higher on-base percentage, better bat-to-ball skills—all that stuff. I wanted to be a complete hitter, not just a power hitter; I never wanted home runs to come at the expense of any other aspect of my offensive game. I just wasn't thinking clearly at the time. I couldn't shake my 2009 home run total from my brain and it affected me for years to come.

Over the seasons that followed, I played a cat-and-mouse game with myself, trying to hit homers without harming the rest of my offensive profile. I treated it like a challenge: Let's see what I can do to try to fit my game into this massive ballpark. I'm not sure I ever met my goals in quite the way I wanted to, but I don't fault Citi Field for that one bit. I blame myself.

||||||||||||||

It didn't help that, for the final month of the 2009 season, I was gun-shy at home plate, stemming from an incident that occurred on August 15. First pitch was scheduled for 4:10 P.M. against the Giants that afternoon, creating shadows that made it tough to see. The sun hadn't quite set when I stepped in for my second at-bat against Matt Cain, a hard-throwing former first-round draft pick with a sub-3.00

ERA and an All-Star Game appearance under his belt. Cain clearly knew how he wanted to attack me, throwing fastball after fastball. Upon jumping ahead in the count, he tried to come up-and-in to mess up my rhythm, but he missed his spot with a 94-mile-per-hour fastball. I had no time to react as the pitch smashed into my helmet.

The next thing I knew, I was lying on the ground, answering questions from our trainer like what the score was, what stadium I was in, which team we were playing. I was concussed.

As I waited to see a doctor in the Citi Field training room, the Mets brought my parents down into the clubhouse from the stands. My mom was extremely emotional, crying despite my assurances that I was fine. Physically, I did feel okay—a bit dazed, a bit shaken up, but not seeing stars or anything. I had managed to answer the trainers' questions correctly on the field, so I figured I had avoided the worst. Looking back, I might not have appreciated the severity of what a concussion entails. I was still just twenty-six years old. Like most athletes that age, I felt invincible. Thankfully, I had plenty of doctors and trainers watching over me, making sure I didn't do something stupid. If nothing else, my mom's emotions kept the sobering thought of how bad it could have been at the forefront of my mind.

As a baseball player, you understand that every time you put on a helmet, there's a chance you could get hit in the head. You just never believe it might happen to you until it actually does.

An ambulance whisked me off to the Hospital for Special Surgery in Manhattan, where doctors ran me through a battery of tests, including a CT scan that confirmed the concussion. My parents followed behind in my own car. I desperately wanted to drive with them because sitting backward in vehicles made me carsick, but the EMTs were having none of it. On this day, no one was going to let me talk my way into anything.

This was two years before MLB instituted a seven-day disabled list for head injuries, along with strict protocols regarding their treatment. As an industry, baseball has learned a lot about concussions over the past decade; even back then, everyone knew this thing was potentially serious. It was obvious I wasn't going to avoid my first career trip to the disabled list, so, for once, I didn't bother trying.

Instead, I opted for damage control. When my agents came to visit me in the hospital, I told them if I had to go on the DL, I had to go on the DL. Fine. But I wanted a plan in place that would put me back on the field after the minimum fifteen days. On day sixteen, I wanted to be back out there playing third base. We worked with the doctors on a blueprint for how to make that happen.

The first requirement was rest, which was no fun at all. I stayed in the hospital for a night, and even after I left, the doctors wouldn't let me do much for several days. They forbade me from leaving my Manhattan apartment and instructed me to keep the lights off as much as possible. That's when the gravity of the concussion really sank in for me. This wasn't just a hamstring tweak—rest, ice, get back out there. This was my brain. This was serious. I did my best to follow the doctors' orders, despite my obvious disappointment over hitting the DL for the first time in my life.

My other overwhelming emotion was boredom, as I lay in bed doing a whole lot of nothing. My parents stuck around town and brought me food, taking care of me like I was a kid again. Each night, I looked forward to watching the Mets, even if that proved more frustrating than uplifting. Beginning with the game in which Cain KO'd me, the team went 5-11 while I was sidelined. I felt personally responsible. Up until that point, I had played in 818 of a possible 833 career games—that's 98 percent, for those doing the math. Playing every day was something I always took a lot of pride in, from childhood on up.

I didn't know it yet, but over the final decade of my career, injuries would prevent me from playing in hundreds of games. Each time, I'd feel like I was letting people down, like I was—and I knew this wasn't true, but it was the way I felt—the sole reason why the Mets were losing.

In reality, our 2009 struggles had all sorts of injury-related roots. José Reyes strained his calf in May and didn't return the rest of the season. Around the same time, Carlos Delgado underwent season-ending hip surgery. A couple weeks later, J.J. Putz had an operation to remove a bone spur from his elbow. He didn't return, either. Our former closer, Billy Wagner, missed almost the entire season recovering from elbow surgery. Our new closer, Francisco Rodríguez, had to go to the hospital due to back spasms. Injuries limited two of the starters in our Opening Day rotation, John Maine and Oliver Pérez, to a combined twenty-nine starts.

With the training room that crowded, I felt even more compelled to return as soon as possible. Lots of well-meaning folks suggested I take the rest of the season off, rest up over the winter, and be ready to go in 2010. I certainly understood that line of thinking, considering we were in fourth place at the time, but I felt it was critical for me to return that year. In my mind, it was important to go through that struggle with the guys. I wanted to be part of the solution, not the problem, which meant being on the field. That's why I insisted to anyone who would listen that I was going to return as soon as I was eligible.

Thankfully, my agents and doctors were willing to indulge me—albeit with some caveats. If I was going to return in 2009, they said, I had to wear a different helmet: a Rawlings S100 prototype constructed to withstand a direct hit from a 100-mile-per-hour fastball. While I was fully on board with that as a means to get back on the field, I didn't realize the stir it would cause. No sooner did I place it on my head than the jokes started flying from all angles, beginning with my teammates during batting practice. Newspaper reporters took to calling it the "Great Gazoo" helmet, in reference to the *Flintstones* character. My first at-bat back from the concussion, I singled against the Rockies, arriving at first base to find Todd Helton guffawing at me. He couldn't even look at me, he was laughing so hard.

"I don't care what I look like as long as I'm getting hits," I told him.

"I wouldn't wear that helmet even if it meant winning a batting title," Helton fired back.

Easy for him to say. He had already won a batting title.

It was all pretty comical. I don't get embarrassed very easily; I've always considered my ability to laugh at myself one of my better qualities, so I was happy to be the butt of some jokes if that helmet kept the Mets' doctors and trainers off my case. Problem was, the helmet was a prototype that had some issues. After reaching base in that first game, I advanced to second on an error, sliding—as was my custom—headfirst into the bag. The helmet banged down into the dirt, temporarily blinding me, then popped back up and hit me in the chin. It completely covered my eyes. I felt like that kid Jake Berman from *Little Giants*—"I can't see with this thing on!"

Right then and there, I knew I had had enough of the S100. I used a slightly modified helmet during a pinch-hit appearance the next day, then convinced the powers that be to let me use a regular helmet with a little extra padding for the rest of the season. This seemed to satisfy everyone.

What I didn't realize was how far I still was from solving my problems. My concussion had healed. My helmet was no longer an issue. But I wasn't myself as a hitter.

Stepping back into the batter's box, I couldn't shake that Little League mentality of bailing out on inside pitches. Getting hit hurts. It goes against human nature to stand, unflinching, as someone hurls a projectile 95 miles per hour in your general direction. Every baseball player has to overcome that mental hurdle early in his life, training his mind to overpower his instincts. But I wasn't some kid facing curveballs for the first time. I was a big leaguer, a multi-time All-Star. I shouldn't have been flinching at pitches that were border-line strikes.

It's not that I was afraid of the ball. I had been plunked countless times before, including shots to my neck and even glancing blows to my helmet. Getting hit is like getting stung by a bee—it hurts for a minute, then you're fine. I knew that as well as anyone, but something inside me seemed to have snapped. That September, I hit .239

and struck out in 29 percent of my plate appearances. I couldn't convince my brain to tell my body to stay in the box and take normal swings. Without the conviction that had come naturally for so long, I stood little chance of success.

Curveballs from right-handed pitchers were particularly tough for me to handle. I found myself turning my shoulder away from routine breaking pitches, despite years of experience telling me they would dive back over the plate. It didn't matter. I fought the temptation to stride at an angle toward left field, bailing out as I unconsciously altered my usual batting mechanics. I struggled to keep my feet planted in their usual position. There are stories throughout history of guys like Tony Conigliaro, a Red Sox star who missed an entire season after getting hit in the face with a pitch in 1967 and was never quite the same. I certainly didn't want to be one of them.

Eventually, I asked my hitting coach, friend, and longtime confidant Howard Johnson for help. I needed to figure out a way to fix this.

We began a batting cage routine that involved HoJo chucking tennis balls as hard as he could, buzzing me inside and sometimes even purposely hitting me with them. I tried to convince my mind that getting hit by a pitch was normal, acceptable. I tried to retrain my body to stay firm in the box, even when pitches looked like they were hurtling toward me.

Late that year, I was in the Citi Field video room working through some mechanical issues when the emotion of the whole ordeal bubbled over. Speaking through tears, I expressed my frustrations to HoJo about not being able to return to form as quickly as

I'd thought I would. This was my future we were talking about, my career, my livelihood, and I was facing adversity I didn't fully understand. A part of me was more scared than I cared to admit.

The issue went unsolved into the off-season, and even as I got off to a decent start in 2010, things still didn't feel quite right. All I could do was what I had always done: work as hard as possible, as much as possible, and hope the answers would eventually come. I took tennis ball after tennis ball off my left shoulder in the batting cage. I watched countless curveballs loop in for strikes before things finally started to change. Finally, on April 21, Cubs pitcher Carlos Silva hit me with a pitch in my first at-bat of the game. It was the first time I had been hit in a game since Cain, and it didn't even really hurt. Something snapped back into place in my brain. *Hey, this is no big deal.*

Sometimes, it's that easy. While I wish I could explain it better, the mental side of baseball can be so complicated and hard to predict. All I know is that I hit .288 with an .851 OPS the rest of the way. The jumpiness was gone. The trepidation was gone. The fear for my career had vanished.

I was ready, in both body and mind, to play some winning baseball again.

# FOURTEEN

# PLAYING THROUGH PAIN

People ask me all the time if I have any regrets from my baseball career. Of course there are small things I would have done differently here or there, outcomes that I would have loved to have changed. But mostly one specific play, on April 19, 2011, stands out in my mind.

This was right at the beginning of the era when teams were shifting their infielders on a regular basis. Our second baseman, Justin Turner, was positioned almost directly behind the bag in defense of Astros infielder Chris Johnson. We were playing the right-handed Johnson to pull, but instead he hit a four-hopper the other way. Turner sprinted back toward his normal position to field it, then spun and fired to shortstop in an attempt to cut down the lead runner, Carlos Lee.

Watching the play develop, I figured I should back up second in case Turner threw wild, which is exactly what happened. As I fielded the carom, I locked eyes with Lee, who was rounding second base and clearly thinking about third. I glanced in that direction to see that our pitcher, Jon Niese, was slow getting off the mound. Lee made a break for it. I sprinted after him. With the bag unoccupied, it became a dead race between us to see who could get there first.

Closing on Lee, I dove to tag him and fell hard on my left side. My shoulder and head both slammed to the dirt, straining my neck and causing all sorts of discomfort in my back.

The good news was that no one seemed to notice. All the attention was on Lee, who had also injured himself on the play, so I managed to hide my slight grimace as I rose to my feet. The bad news was that something clearly wasn't right. I wasn't sure what had happened, but it didn't feel like a garden-variety muscle strain. This was something worse. The only thought going through my mind was that I couldn't let anyone know, because there was no way I was going back on the disabled list.

After recovering from my 2009 concussion, I had managed to construct another All-Star season in 2010, playing in 157 games with 29 homers and an .856 OPS. I had no intention of returning to the DL just a year and a half later, especially knowing how much I'd hated every minute of my first stint—and *especially* with the team off to a poor start in 2011. I didn't want to be the first domino to fall, like in 2009, when every Mets injury seemed to lead to another.

To me, this was a simple logic problem. I needed to play well for us to win. I needed to be on the field to play well. Therefore, I needed to stay as far away from the DL as possible. Spending weeks on the sideline wasn't going to do anyone any good, and telling the trainers about my discomfort meant risking their taking the decision out of my hands. So I kept quiet.

What I didn't understand was the nature and severity of this new injury; I figured I would sleep on it, maybe get a massage or two, and feel fine the next day. Even if it lingered, I thought I could limp to September while still playing at a reasonably high level, then rest over the winter and be back to 100 percent. I had this idea in my mind that the off-season healed everything.

Problem was, I didn't feel fine the next day, or the day after that, or the day after that. My back ached a little more with each flip of the calendar, to the extent that it was obviously affecting my performance. From April 19 through May 15, I hit .205 with a .386 slugging percentage. I stunk. I couldn't drive the ball, which made it harder and harder for me to play this off as a slump.

What finally tipped off the trainers was the fact that I was spending less and less time in the batting cage. From the time I was young, my dad had instilled in me the idea that poor performance should never be due to lack of preparation. As a result, I was always a blue-collar, bring-your-lunch-pail-to-work kind of guy. I loved logging as many hours at the ballpark as possible, clocking in early and taking swing after swing after swing. In the minor leagues, I learned how to work hard without overextending myself, but the batting cage never ceased being my second home. Especially when I was struggling, I wanted to feel like I was doing everything possible to snap out of the funk. My coaches knew that about me, so my absence from the cage raised some alarm bells.

After about a month, the injury began to pain me off the field as well, which caused the rest of those bells to ring. I couldn't hide this any longer. When I finally came clean to the training staff on the final day of a road trip to Houston, they scheduled an MRI for the following morning in New York. I went into the tube with some trepidation, fearing a DL stint. The test revealed something worse: a stress fracture in my lower back that was going to cost me six to eight weeks.

I thought about the play with Lee, how reckless I had been diving after him. Way back in 2005, when I made my diving catch into the stands in Seattle, friends had warned about the risks of playing so aggressively, but I knew no other way. Now their warnings were becoming real. What if I had just let Lee go? What if any number of little things had gone differently? It was all so frustrating to consider.

I spent the rest of that day feeling sorry for myself. The evening at Citi Field was dismal and drizzly, necessitating an eighty-minute rain delay—the perfect capper to a miserable, miserable day. I vividly remember sitting on the end of the dugout bench, bundled against the cold, talking to no one as I blocked out the world. That was so unlike me. I sat there for hours watching Josh Johnson pitch well for the Marlins, powerless to do anything about it.

‖‖‖‖‖‖‖‖‖‖‖

For someone who loved winning as much as I did, those were a tough few years. While the Mets could chalk up their 2009 failures to a constant string of injuries, 2010 was a different story entirely. From the jump, no one outside our clubhouse expected us to compete, even though we all felt like we had the pieces to do so. I never

Here I am as an infant with my dad's parents, Helen (Mema) and Cletis (Pop-Pop). My grandparents on both sides of the family helped nurture my love of baseball. *Photo courtesy of author*

I was the first of four boys to arrive in our Virginia Beach home. It wouldn't be long until our family grew, with a new brother coming every three years. *Photo courtesy of author*

Running with my father, Rhon, circa 1989. Dad used to run charity 5Ks and 10Ks on weekends, and I often tagged along. As I grew older, it taught me the importance of keeping in shape.   *Photo courtesy of author*

My first organized baseball
experience was playing
T-ball for the Dodgers in
Virginia Beach's Green Run
Little League.
*Photo courtesy of author*

**David Wright**

Major Boys     National League

Position: Catcher     Height:   5'
Number: 4     Weight: 123
Date of Birth: 12/20/82     Age:    11
Birthplace: Norfolk, Virginia

| YR. | TEAM | AVG. | GM | AB | R | H | RBI | BB | SO |
|---|---|---|---|---|---|---|---|---|---|
| '92 | Padres | .400 | 16 | 40 | 14 | 16 | 7 | 11 | 6 |
| '93 | Padres | .500 | 19 | 66 | 38 | 33 | 22 | 9 | 6 |
| '94 | Padres | .683 | 18 | 60 | 34 | 41 | 38 | 5 | 2 |

Photo by: Hometown Sports Photography
Virginia Beach, Virginia

© 1994 All American Image, Inc. Glenside, Pa.

Patent No. 5,229,190

I played a little bit of catcher in Little League before becoming "the pudgy kid at shortstop." *Photo courtesy of author*

Hanging with my dad in the early days of the Virginia Blasters AAU team at the Great Neck Recreation Center fields in Virginia Beach. *Photo courtesy of author*

95
12th

NAME: DAVID WRIGHT

I OVERALL GRADES (COMPARED TO THE BEST IN AALL)

A. RUNNING SPEED — B+
B ARM STRENGTH — B+
C. HIT FOR AVERAGE — A
D ON BASE % — A
E HIT FOR POWER — A
F HANDS — A
G AGILITY (FEET) — A
H OVERALL KNOWLEDGE — A
I COMPOSURE UNDER
   PRESSURE — A
J DESIRE — A+
K COACHABILITY — A
   (WILLINGNESS TO CHANGE/ADJUST)

II SUMMARY OF STRENGTHS:

A. AS OUTLINED ABOVE, UNUSUALLY STRONG
   IN ALL AREAS

B.

C.

Blasters coach Allan Erbe wrote out progress reports for every player, grading us on various aspects of our development. Everything he did was professional.
*Allan Erbe*

Playing for the Blasters circa 1996. I wore number 4 throughout my younger years and even early in my minor league career. It wasn't until Triple-A that I switched to number 5. *Photo courtesy of author*

Attempting to turn two at Hickory High School, where I played four years on the varsity team. I spent most of my amateur career as a shortstop until the Mets drafted me. *Photo courtesy of author*

Signing my letter of intent to play baseball at Georgia Tech as my parents and Hickory High coach Steve Gedro look on. I was serious about becoming a Yellow Jacket if I didn't get drafted within the first three rounds.
*Photo courtesy of author*

Here I am with my mother's parents, Bridget (Nena) and Henry (Pops), on the day I committed to Georgia Tech. Even as they grew older, all four of my grandparents rarely missed a game.   *Photo courtesy of author*

My brothers, father, and I posing with Randy "Moose" Milligan, a former Norfolk Tides player who became the Mets area scout who helped sign me. *Photo courtesy of author*

As the senior class vice president of Hickory High School, I delivered a commencement address on graduation day. *Photo courtesy of author*

At my graduation/draft party in 2001 with Blasters coaches Ron Smith (LEFT) and Allan Erbe (RIGHT), who both played significant roles in my development and worked hard to get me noticed by scouts.
*Photo courtesy of author*

I spent barely a month at Triple-A Norfolk on my climb through the minor leagues but the demands of playing at home gave me new perspective on the pressures of a pro-baseball career. *Photo courtesy of author*

Celebrating with José Reyes after clinching the 2006 National League East title at Shea Stadium. Coming up together through the Mets' system, the two of us formed a tight friendship. *Getty Images*

Meeting my wax figure at Madame Tussauds in Manhattan in April 2007. It took me a while to adjust to the idea of being a pseudocelebrity in New York. *Getty Images*

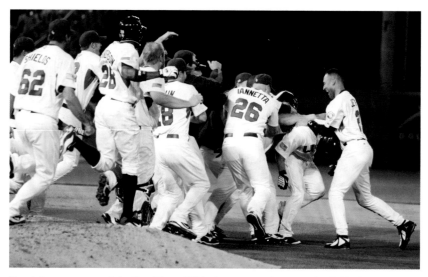

Derek Jeter was one of the first Team USA players to mob me on the field after my walk-off hit against Puerto Rico in the 2009 World Baseball Classic. *Getty Images*

The Wright family on my wedding day (LEFT TO RIGHT): Daniel, Stephen, Rhon, Molly, me, Elisa, and Matthew.    *True Photography*

The first time
I asked Molly on
a date, she said no.
But I convinced her
eventually!
*True Photography*

When I homered in my first at-bat back from the disabled list in 2015, it felt like vindication for months of work and rehab as I battled spinal stenosis.
*Getty Images*

My home run off Yordano Ventura in the 2015 World Series Game 3 was one of the best moments of my fourteen-year career.   *Getty Images*

Playing cards was part of my daily routine. Here I am in my final season playing a game called Pluck with Jacob deGrom, Steven Matz, and Devin Mesoraco.   *Dave Racaniello*

There weren't many people I enjoyed joking around with more than Mets media relations legend Jay Horwitz and my baseball brother José Reyes.
*Dave Racaniello*

Me and my longtime agents, (LEFT TO RIGHT) Keith Miller, Sam Levinson, Peter Pedalino, and Seth Levinson posing before my final game at Citi Field. *Photo courtesy of author*

One of my best friends and the best man at my wedding, Mets bullpen catcher Dave Racaniello, threw my first round of batting practice at Shea Stadium when I was eighteen years old. I asked him to throw with me again before my final game at Citi Field. *Dave Racaniello*

Gathering with my parents, brothers, wife, and daughters before my final game at Citi Field on September 29, 2018.
*Photo courtesy of author*

I thought I was all out of tears coming off the field for the final time, but it turns out I wasn't close. I'll always be thankful for the support of Mets fans.
*Photo courtesy of author*

My family and in-laws joined me for a party that my agency, ACES, hosted after my final game. Left to right: Lisa Beers, Lexy Beers, David Denitz, Mo Denitz, me, Molly, Ralph Beers, Elisa Wright, Rhon Wright, and Brett Beers. (Not pictured is Blake Beers, who was busy pitching for the University of Michigan, and my three brothers, who were obviously "fashionably" late.) *Photo courtesy of author*

Postretirement I've been able to spend so much more time with my wife, Molly, and my daughters, Madison (LEFT) and Olivia (RIGHT).
*Erin Purdy Photography*

A year after retirement, I signed up to coach my daughter (top row, second from RIGHT) Olivia's three- and four-year-old T-ball team in Southern California, just like my dad coached me when I was a kid.   *Kimberli Miller Photography*

Encouraging Olivia at the plate. At this point in my life, there's no greater thrill for me than watching my kids enjoy their childhoods.
*Photo courtesy of author*

It's a boy! Olivia and Madison tee off on the gender reveal for the newest member of the Wright family, Brooks, born in October 2020. *Erin Purdy Photography*

went into a season thinking the Mets couldn't win. I was always the optimist looking around the clubhouse, saying, "If I have my best year, and José Reyes has his best year, and Johan Santana has his best year, and so on and so forth, then we'll be able to do damage."

Looking at things rationally, I understand how rare it is for seven or eight teammates to have career years at the same time, but it did seem realistic to me when I was playing. Maybe I was naïve, lacking enough experience to develop any real cynicism. Maybe it was the competitor in me. Maybe it was simply my personality. Whatever the reason, I never went into a season believing we were going to be a .500 team.

In 2007 and '08, reality didn't strike until the final day of the season. In '09, it bowled us over early as injuries piled up. In 2010, it hit around midseason, when we slid slowly out of the NL East race and began trading away pieces.

I had a regular card game in the clubhouse that year—we liked to play a game called Pluck, which is similar to Spades or Hearts—that usually included me, Jason Bay, Rod Barajas, and Jeff Francoeur. All of us were veterans, good friends, and teammates who spent countless hours together until the game started to fall apart. Bay suffered a concussion in late July and didn't return until the following season. Barajas went to the Dodgers in a mid-August trade. Francoeur went to the Rangers. By September, I found myself surrounded by more and more young players, like Ike Davis, Josh Thole, and Rúben Tejada—guys who were building blocks for the future more than finished products for the present.

And so I tried to be patient as we built. Way back in 2004, I'd received an introduction to the business side of baseball when the

Mets released Joe McEwing. By 2011, I had steeled myself a little better against those kinds of things. I understood that trades were going to take place and I even tried to embrace them, viewing them as vehicles to winning baseball. Nothing against Barajas or Francoeur, who were smart, good players and friends—I was upset when each of them left. It's just that their tenures coincided with a difficult era in Mets history, and when that happens, change is inevitable.

What I didn't realize was the extent of the change heading our way—the departures of not just Barajas and Francoeur, but general manager Omar Minaya and manager Jerry Manuel, too. Omar wasn't technically my first big league GM, but he was there for each of my first six full seasons. He had given me my first contract extension back in 2006, ensuring I could stay with the Mets until at least my thirtieth birthday. Jerry had also been around since 2005, first as a coach and then as a manager. I had spent a lot of time playing for both men and, as usual, felt personally responsible for their departures.

To replace them, the Mets hired two baseball lifers whom I didn't know well: Sandy Alderson as GM and Terry Collins as manager. I had immense respect for Alderson, the mastermind behind the late-eighties Oakland A's teams that won three consecutive American League pennants, and I had met Collins through his work as the Mets' minor league field coordinator. Now that they were coming into bigger roles, I felt it was my job to form the best bond I could with both.

In particular, I wanted to make Alderson understand my devotion to the team. It was widely reported during those days that longtime Mets owner Fred Wilpon had significant money tied up with

Bernard Madoff, who had been arrested in 2008 for running an investment Ponzi scheme. As our team payroll began falling below what the fan base was accustomed to, some media types began suggesting the Mets should trade me and Reyes as part of a full-scale rebuild. Obviously, when I heard that sort of talk, I told anybody who would listen that I had no interest in it. I wanted to be a Met for life, but I knew that decision was out of my hands. Alderson—a man I respected but hardly knew at that point—was the person who controlled my fate.

It would have been devastating if the team had traded me. The orange and blue meant a lot to me. More than a lot to me. The fact that we were struggling only made me want to stick around even more, to shepherd the franchise into a better era.

I knew if I were running a team, I'd want players who passionately wanted to be there. I just hoped Alderson felt the same way.

|||||||||||||||

As all this was happening, Wilpon sat down for a wide-ranging interview with Jeffrey Toobin of *The New Yorker*. Part of the story detailed Toobin's experience watching a game with the Mets' seventy-four-year-old owner, who talked about everything and everyone related to the team. That included some pointed criticisms of Reyes's health and Carlos Beltrán's $119 million contract, which caused the story to blow up. It also included a criticism of me: Wilpon noted that I was pressing at the plate.

"A really good kid," he called me in the article. "A very good player. Not a superstar."

As soon as the *New Yorker* piece ran, all the Mets writers came asking for my reaction. What could I say? Of course the comment hurt my feelings. There was no way around that. But it would have affected me a lot more if not for the relationship I had with the Wilpons.

A few years earlier, during spring training, my grandmother on my father's side of the family had passed away. Mr. Wilpon came up and wrapped me in a big hug, asked me to come to his office, then sat me down and gave a long, grandfatherly talk. He preached that while baseball is fun, family is far more important. His words were deeply impactful.

As it turned out, Wilpon was heading back to New York the next day, so he offered to take me on his private plane and make a special stop in Norfolk so I could be with my family. That always stuck with me, solidifying my relationship with the Wilpons. That conversation, along with some of the family's other gestures to me over the years, far exceeded a little blip quotation in a magazine. Fred Wilpon was frustrated, just like we all were frustrated. His comments didn't sting more than a day or two.

It's possible his words hit closer to home for Reyes, who was due to become a free agent after that season and who, in Wilpon's opinion, wanted "Carl Crawford money"—i.e., the type of seven-year, $142 million contract Crawford signed with the Red Sox in 2010. Although Reyes battled injuries throughout his career, he still averaged 158 games per season from 2005 to '08, playing in 80 percent of our games in 2010 and '11. He was a legitimate superstar capable of doing things I could only dream about, like hitting 16 triples while winning the batting title in 2011, or stealing a Mets-record 78 bases in 2007.

Over the decade I'd known him, José had also developed into one of my better friends in baseball. One of the constants of my career was looking left and seeing him there, and as we grew into adults, our relationship matured as well. I felt like we could talk about anything, at any time.

Years later, when Reyes received a fifty-one-game suspension for violating MLB's domestic violence policy, I criticized him harshly, calling his actions "awful and horrible." I meant that, and he knew it. I had given José a heads-up that if anyone from the media asked me about his situation, as much as I had his back, I was going to be honest. I was going to tell them how I felt—that what he did was unforgivable, but that I still considered him a friend. He understood that completely, accepting it without complaint, and that's part of what made us so close. I could always tell José exactly what I was thinking, and he wouldn't get mad or hold it against me.

With the Mets, it was easy to get lulled into thinking my bond with José could last forever, at least until the possibility of a split started becoming increasingly real in late June 2011. A month after Wilpon's comments appeared in *The New Yorker*, Reyes's agent told Alderson that he didn't want to negotiate a contract extension during the season. In other words, Reyes was heading toward free agency with no guarantee of returning.

The days of Wright and Reyes were coming to an end. Once the off-season arrived and José officially hit the market, the Mets negotiated with him but never made an offer. I found out online when he signed a six-year, $111 million contract with the Marlins that December.

To read those words on my phone felt surreal. Obviously, I had known there was a chance he would leave, especially given the events of the summer. Didn't make it any easier to wrap my mind around the concept. Didn't make it any less painful. Like the departures of McEwing, Willie Randolph, Francoeur, Barajas, and so many others, it was a reminder of how much the business side of baseball can really stink.

Over the years, players create lifelong bonds. From February through September (and sometimes October), we see our teammates more than our families. Tight friendships form quickly but, given the nature of trades and free agency, it's rare for those relationships to last as long as they did with me and José. Seeing him in a different uniform after the two of us had been hyped as prospects together and gone through things like the 2006 playoffs and the '07 collapse together—it was just a strange feeling.

I had known José for a decade. When he left, it was almost like a part of that decade was gone as well.

I sent José a congratulatory message but didn't see him again until the following spring. As he bounced up to me in that flashy Marlins uniform and offered me a hug, I couldn't shake the idea of how bizarre it all felt. José had done what was best for him and his family, and while I never begrudged him for that, I knew I wanted my path to be different. I grew up rooting for the Mets, bleeding orange and blue. It was important for me to stick with the organization if at all possible. To be a Met for life.

Of course, I also understood I had to be smart about the process.

I didn't know Alderson nearly as well as Minaya, and while I trusted the new GM's vision, I couldn't be certain about his long-term plans. Alderson had just let Reyes go to the Marlins without even making an offer. What would he have in store for me?

With free agency still two years away, all I could do was make it as difficult as possible for Alderson to let me leave.

IIIIIIIIIIIIII

The first thing I did to prove my worth was break my finger.

I didn't do it by punching a wall, but I may as well have, considering my frustration when it happened. Throughout my career, I took immense pride in playing every day. I avoided drawing up specific goals, knowing those things could be tough to control—just look at my wonky 2009 stat line as proof. What I could control was how often I played, by preparing and taking care of my body. I wanted to be out there as much as physically possible.

Four games into the 2012 season, that again became an issue. Off to a hot start, I kept it going with a two-out RBI single against the Nationals, then decided to try to move into scoring position. My plan was to run on the first pitch, but Edwin Jackson made a surprise pickoff move to first base. In my haste to dive back, I jammed my right pinky into the bag.

As usual, I did my best to suck it up, striking out and drawing an intentional walk in my final two plate appearances. It hurt like hell but I assumed, as I usually did, that I could sleep away the pain. Better not to let anyone know about it.

That thought lasted only until the next morning, when I awoke to find the finger swollen to three times its normal size. Because I hadn't said anything the night before, my name was penciled into Collins's starting lineup as usual. I intended to do everything in my power to play, reporting to Citi Field and testing it in the batting cage with some swings. Problem was, I couldn't even grip the bat.

For someone like me, who takes so much pride in being out there every day, going into Collins's office and showing him a grotesquely swollen finger was not a fun assignment. Terry took one look at it and called Alderson down from his suite upstairs. Sandy then sent me to the Hospital for Special Surgery, where X-rays confirmed a break. After fitting me for a splint, our medical team scheduled me for a visit with a specialist later in the week.

That all happened on a Tuesday afternoon, which gave me at least some chance of avoiding the DL. Because our Triple-A team was located hours away in Las Vegas, we weren't going to be able to fly in a replacement for that night's game. Wednesday was the series finale and Thursday was an off day, meaning if I could heal up in time for the weekend, the team would have to play shorthanded for only one extra game. In the meantime, our trainers gave me balls of putty that I could squeeze to reestablish some range of motion in my finger. I spent every waking hour of my day working with that putty, determined to avoid the DL.

The hand specialist I saw confirmed the break, which was bad news, but he also noted that this was merely a pain tolerance issue. That was good news. As long as I could grip a bat and deal with the discomfort, there was no reason why I couldn't return to the lineup.

I spent that entire week icing my finger and squeezing the putty, bringing it with me as we traveled to Philadelphia to begin a road trip. I also spent enough time begging Sandy to keep me active that he agreed to grant me another twenty-four hours, which bought me until Saturday morning. If I proved healthy enough to return that day, Sandy was willing to play shorthanded for one additional game. If not, I was going to have no choice but to hit the DL.

I tried to take full advantage by playing all the angles. Later on Friday afternoon, as my teammates took batting practice, I found Terry roaming around the outfield.

"Please, please have my back on this," I said. "I think I'm going to be good to go. And I promise I'll give you a straight answer if I'm not."

I kept using the putty, growing more confident each time I leveled up to a thicker, more resistant gob of it. The problem was that our training staff wouldn't clear me to hit. It was a bit of a catch-22: To stay off the DL, I had to prove I could play. To prove I could play, I had to show I could hit. But the trainers weren't going to let me do that until after Sandy's deadline for me to avoid the DL.

Desperate to find a way to test my pinky, I snuck out of the dugout midway through Friday night's game, made a left turn into the batting cage, and started taking some swings. I actually felt pretty good, until our physical therapist John Zajac walked in and caught me hacking away. As a member of the training staff, Zajac could have blown the whistle and shut down my whole comeback attempt if he wanted to. I stopped swinging for a moment and locked eyes with him.

"You didn't see this," I said.

Zajac just turned and walked away, which I appreciated immensely. In my mind, there was no way I was going on the DL for an injury like this. I burned to compete too much. My strategies may have been a little unorthodox, but they worked. With a splint on my pinky to keep it from bending the wrong way, I graduated all the way to the most resistant putty and convinced Sandy to keep me off the DL. Returning to the lineup that Saturday afternoon, I crushed Phillies starter Vance Worley's first-pitch fastball off the absolute sweet spot of my bat for a homer. All was well again.

Philadelphia was certainly the right place to make my return. I wound up hitting .412 at Citizens Bank Park that season, which wasn't unusual. Over the years, I saw the ball so well there, hitting twenty-two homers and driving in sixty-nine runs in one hundred games—my highest totals at any ballpark outside of Shea Stadium or Citi Field.

Then again, I saw the ball well pretty much everywhere in 2012. In my first six games after breaking my finger, I hit .444 with a .500 on-base percentage. Batting over .400 as late in the season as May 25, I never dipped lower than .304. I wound up finishing a shade higher than that, at .306 with twenty-one homers and ninety-three RBI.

In a lot of ways, I finally felt like I was back to my old self. After a few years of struggling with Citi Field's dimensions, I hit .294 with 12 home runs there, finding that happy medium between selling out for power and hitting for average. I continued to do daily physical therapy exercises for my back, but the stress fracture wasn't a major concern as I appeared in 156 games (missing three for the broken finger and only three more the rest of the season).

My personal highlight occurred at Citi Field on September 26, when I passed Ed Kranepool to become the Mets' all-time hits leader.

So what if the way it happened was a little awkward?

For one, I never loved personal attention. Whenever we stood on the first-base line for introductions during special events, whether it was for Opening Day or the All-Star Game, I always felt a little embarrassed. Curtain calls were flattering, but I could have done without them. Especially when the team was struggling, as the Mets were late in 2012, I didn't need anyone to single me out.

My record-breaker added another level of awkwardness because it was a dribbler down the third-base line, which Pittsburgh's Pedro Álvarez scooped up and threw wildly past first base. In my mind, it could have gone either way as a hit or an error, but somebody from our dugout immediately requested the ball for safekeeping, so the Pirates threw it in. At that point, I figured the official scorer had no choice but to rule it a single.

When he did, the Mets flashed a congratulatory message on the scoreboard, highlighting my 1,419th hit and leading to a nice ovation. The fans were terrific; they couldn't know how uncomfortable I felt. Standing on second base because of the overthrow, I sheepishly waved my hand to thank everybody without really smiling. I just wanted to get the moment over with and move on with the game.

My teammates got a kick out of that. For the rest of the season, whenever anybody did anything good, the clubhouse reaction was to wave it off and try not to act happy. I never heard the end of it.

But of course I appreciated the accomplishment and the ovation. Kranepool was one of the most decorated Mets in history,

joining the team during its inaugural season in 1962, lasting eighteen years in Flushing, and appearing in more games than any other
Met. Even in his seventies, Kranepool spent a lot of time around the
park, which was always nice to see. To be mentioned in the same
breath as him was a pretty cool honor.

I was always only vaguely aware of my place in Mets history.
Any player can do the math and figure if he averages 180 hits per
year, like I did from 2005 to '08, he'll wind up with 3,000 at some
point. Long-term goals like that occasionally crossed my mind, but
I honestly didn't care much about individual achievements. I cared
about winning, knowing how New Yorkers treated guys like Kranepool or Derek Jeter across town. During my lifetime, I saw superstars and role players alike turn into New York legends. The average
Mets fan probably couldn't tell you that Dwight Gooden posted a
2.84 ERA in 1986, but he could tell you all about Gooden's World
Series ring.

To me, personal stats always came second. When my agents at
ACES began negotiating my next contract late in 2012, they created
a file comparing my career through age thirty with some of the
greatest players of all time. At that point, I had amassed 1,426 hits
and 204 home runs. It was more than Carlos Beltrán had at the same
age. It was more than Mike Piazza had at the same age. While I
understood my agents were making a sales pitch, I could read stuff
like that and start drinking the Kool-Aid a little bit, thinking how
neat it was to be listed alongside those Hall of Fame–type players.

Back in 2009, I had spent some time around one of the greatest
third basemen in history, Mike Schmidt, who was a coach for Team
USA at the World Baseball Classic. While there, I bought his

autobiography and asked him to sign it for me. Schmidt did more than that, writing some incredibly flattering words on the inside, and as I read them, I experienced a rare moment when I was able to soak in a bit of what I had accomplished in my career.

*Wow,* I thought, *I must be doing some pretty good things for Mike Schmidt to say these types of things to me.*

But such feelings never lasted long; I truly could dismiss most of those personal accolades with a wave of my hand. It's not that I didn't appreciate them. I did. It's just that I would have cut my numbers in half to win a World Series.

# FIFTEEN

# COMMITMENTS

The only thing more important to me than winning a World Series was winning a World Series with the Mets. Over nine seasons, I'd built a home in New York. I felt secure there, and not just because of my success on the field. I felt comfortable with the entire Mets organization, from ownership on down to the field staff, the clubhouse and training staffs, the cooks, the security guards—everyone. I liked these people.

For me, liking people meant messing with them.

That had been the case ever since I was a kid, warring each day with my brothers. As the four of us grew older, we spent less time pummeling each other and more time cooking up the wildest, stupidest dares we could.

I once challenged my youngest brother, Daniel, to eat an entire gob of wasabi at a sushi restaurant. He managed to do it, but the experience ... let's just say it didn't end well for him. Our bullpen catcher and my longtime roommate, Dave Racaniello, was also a pretty impressive eater, so I set up an Oreo-eating competition between him and Daniel, as well as a pizza-eating contest between Rac and one of my other brothers, Matt. Rac won each of the one-hour, all-you-can-eat duels, taking down more than ninety Oreos and three Patsy's pizzas. Both competitions were as disgusting as they sound.

Of course, eating didn't have to be the main event—I'd put action on anything. In January 2010, Racaniello rode his bike from New Jersey to Port St. Lucie for the start of spring training. I paid to outfit him with a tent and other supplies, then collected bets from my teammates—none of whom thought Rac could complete the journey in three weeks. He faced some challenges along the way, including a pack of dogs chasing him in North Carolina and the sprinkler system "accidentally" going off one night when he camped out in Daniel Murphy's backyard in Jacksonville. But he arrived eight days ahead of schedule, making me a nice profit on my wagers.

As fun as those challenges were, what I really loved was a good old-fashioned prank—after all, I had to pay some of those lessons forward that the Mets' veterans taught me my rookie season, when I found myself singing on team buses and in a Montreal karaoke bar.

In 2014, during Jacob deGrom's rookie year, our hitters adopted a custom of waving towels in the dugout every time someone got a hit. That was not my style at all—I didn't like drawing attention to myself in the first place, so I certainly wasn't going to condone a showy celebration each time I got a hit. But I found myself in the distinct minority on this issue, which everybody in the clubhouse knew. One night in Cincinnati, Curtis Granderson thought it would be funny to take as many towels as he could find and stuff them in my locker. When I came inside and saw the scene, deGrom started laughing out loud at my reaction.

That would not stand. DeGrom returned to his locker after the game to find his pants had been converted into some extremely high-cut jean shorts. I made sure he wore them on his walk back to the hotel.

People knew the risk of sharing a clubhouse with me. One year, I acquired an electric cattle prod, threatening to buzz anyone who was late to stretch or a team meeting. The prod wasn't actually painful, but the sound it made caused even my most hardened teammates to leap in fear.

Setting up pranks meant I was always at risk of becoming a target, like when one of our Citi Field security guards, Dominick Gentile, brought in a novelty pen that shocked me when I clicked it. But I tended to dish out more punishment than I took. I loved putting eye black on the binoculars of our longtime PR man, Jay Horwitz, who was always walking around with rings around his eyes. He never learned.

I once convinced one of my agents, Keith Miller, that I'd lost his dog and was scrambling around the neighborhood searching for it. That one freaked him out. Guys in the clubhouse were constant prank targets for me, but my absolute favorite was Paul Taglieri, who served as the St. Lucie Mets' general manager for many years. Taglieri—"Tags," as we called him—ran things down in Port St. Lucie, which meant he had responsibilities all over the ballpark. His

office was often unoccupied. And he always kept his keys in the top
drawer of his desk.

One day, as Tags was leaving the ballpark after a spring training
game, he noticed a group of fans staring at his car. During the game,
I may or may not have commissioned someone to fill it with Styro-
foam packing peanuts from the floor to the roof. Months later, stray
peanuts were still floating around his backseat.

Another time, I paid our maintenance technician to change the
locks on Taglieri's office overnight. When he finally managed to
open the door the next morning, Tags found that one of my "associ-
ates" had constructed a Sheetrock wall, shrinking the entire office
space to about three by three feet. We arranged it just like his old
office, with furniture in the same positions and pictures in frames.
I wanted to put some farm animals in there, too, but decided that
was probably taking it too far.

My favorite was probably the time Tags entered his office to see
a tire lying on his couch. When he walked outside, he noticed his car
parked in its normal spot . . . resting on cinder blocks. All four tires
were missing thanks to a local tow truck driver who was friends with
our bullpen coach. Understandably a little perturbed, Tags came
rushing into the dugout in the middle of the game to confront me. He
arrived to find everyone pointing to the berm in right field, where a
fan was using another of his tires as a chair. Yet another was in the
batting cage connected to the stadium. The fourth was sitting in the
center field grass on one of our practice fields. We all got a good laugh
out of his exasperation trying to piece his car back together.

A couple times, Tags threatened to retaliate, but he knew better
than to follow through with anything. I may not be the most

talented prankster in the world, but I had plenty of resources and free time at my disposal. Getting into a prank war with me would not have been a smart idea.

Obviously, all that stuff was in good fun, and our laughs spoke volumes about my relationships with those guys. I never messed with people I didn't feel comfortable around or who I didn't think could take it. But when I grew close to teammates or employees, I treated them like brothers—after all, that's the sort of environment my actual brothers and I grew up in, constantly giving one another a hard time at home in Virginia.

In New York, I had grown close enough to pull pranks on more people than I could count. The 2012 season was my twelfth in the Mets organization. Racaniello, Taglieri, Horwitz, so many others—those guys had become my adopted family. Contemplating my future with one year left on my contract, I feared losing the friendships I had built as much as I hated the idea of starting over somewhere else.

I also knew none of this was entirely up to me. Yes, I felt like I had done everything possible both on and off the field, but did that mean I fit into the Mets' long-term plans? Could they make a significant investment in a player about to turn thirty? Would they?

What made me anxious was knowing I would soon find out, one way or the other.

||||||||||||

Financially, late 2012 was one of the best times in MLB history to have an expiring contract. The previous off-season, Albert Pujols had signed a ten-year, $254 million contract with the Angels, the second-largest deal the league had ever seen. Prince Fielder had landed a nine-year, $214 million contract. The off-season before that, Jayson Werth had gotten $126 million from the Nationals, Cliff Lee had landed $120 million from the Phillies, and Adrián Beltré, a third baseman three years older than me, had earned $96 million.

By that point, I knew the Mets were at least somewhat interested in offering me an extension. With one year remaining until free agency, I was happy to negotiate. I just needed some assurance that the team, which had not seriously contended for a playoff spot since 2008, was going to commit itself to building the type of roster needed to win a World Series. We had just wrapped up a fourth consecutive losing season, which wore on me. Fear of continuing to spend Octobers at home gave me pause. Yes, I wanted to stay with the Mets until the end. Yes, I was willing to sacrifice a little money to make that happen. But even I had my breaking point: I had to make sure the organization was going to commit itself to constructing winning rosters over the life of my contract. It was crucial to me to leave the organization in a better place than when I arrived.

Shortly after the World Series ended, Alderson flew from New York to Norfolk to give me those assurances. As I drove to pick him up from the airport, I was incredibly nervous. While I had been around Sandy for two seasons at that point, I couldn't say I knew him all that well.

A marine who fought in Vietnam, Sandy came from a different era. Today, front offices around the league are populated by Ivy League graduates with business and law degrees; back then, that was a novel concept. A lawyer himself, Sandy was the first GM in baseball history to come from outside the industry. But he quickly learned the inner workings of the game and used his unique perspective to outthink everyone, winning three straight American League pennants with the A's from 1988 to '90. Then he went on to work in the commissioner's office and as CEO of the Padres, coming to the Mets right when we needed a guy with his sort of résumé.

Not surprisingly, Sandy was an old-school GM. He didn't make a habit of coming into the clubhouse, plopping down on a chair, and having lunch with the players. Sandy's businesslike demeanor meant he stayed upstairs, in the front office, unless his job requirements sent him elsewhere. As a result, I hadn't gotten to know him much on a personal level. Watching him go about his business gave me a high respect level for him, but knowing he had the power to decide whether I would finish my career as a Met gave me anxiety.

With a list of questions to ask Sandy about his vision for the team, I realized quickly that my worries were unfounded. From the moment I picked him up at Norfolk International Airport, he could not have been more personable. On that car ride from the airport to a local golf course, he put me at ease and made it clear that this was going to be a comfortable, fun day.

Sandy wasted little time, bringing up the topic of baseball as soon as we hit the first tee. Laying out his short- and long-term visions for the Mets, Sandy revealed his plan to trade reigning Cy Young Award winner R. A. Dickey for the types of major league–ready prospects that could help us right away. He told me about the free agents he planned to pursue—guys like Granderson, a consummate veteran who put the team before himself. As we talked, I began to realize Sandy appreciated the same types of players I did—scrappy, hardworking people who valued winning above all else.

What really wowed me was when Sandy brought out some internal scouting reports of the pitchers coming through our system. Midway through 2012, I had had the privilege of seeing the first of them, Matt Harvey, graduate to the majors. A former first-round draft pick with an upper-nineties fastball and a sharp slider, Harvey showed flashes of greatness in ten starts down the stretch.

According to Sandy, we had a lot more coming. Another top prospect, Jeurys Familia, showcased an impressive power sinker during his late-2012 debut. Behind those two in the pipeline were Zack Wheeler, whom Sandy acquired for Carlos Beltrán in 2011, and Steven Matz, the Mets' top draft pick in 2009. Sandy planned on adding at least one more pitcher of that caliber in the impending Dickey trade, and even some of the lesser-known guys coming up through the pipeline, like Rafael Montero and Jacob deGrom, had impressive résumés.

All of them threw in the mid- to upper nineties, making my eyes bug out when I saw the scouting reports. I asked Sandy if what he was showing me was real. In building the team around those pitchers and sprinkling in the types of free agents that we both liked, Sandy intended to construct a winner in just a few short years.

This plan was exactly what I wanted to hear. Throughout my first nine seasons with the Mets, we'd never had a dominant pitching staff. Don't get me wrong—plenty of All-Star and even Hall of Fame pitchers came through Flushing, from Pedro Martínez to Tom Glavine to Santana, Dickey, and more. But even when we were winning from 2006 to '08, we never had the type of lockdown rotation that some other World Series contenders did. The idea of building a team around that kind of staff excited me.

Listening to Sandy speak that afternoon on the golf course, I became pretty convinced I was going to be a Met for life. The next step was to talk things over with my family members, who shared many of my initial concerns. My parents wanted to make sure I saw all the angles, both personally and professionally. My brothers asked if I really wanted to stay with the Mets or if my loyalty to the organization was blinding me from seeing better opportunities elsewhere. They raised valid points, knowing I can be loyal to a fault, knowing I always headed into spring training believing even some of our weaker rosters could win. But after talking to Sandy, I was prepared with detailed answers. Just like Sandy had convinced me about the Mets' future, I convinced my brothers and parents.

I talked things over with my agents as well, telling them I wanted to stay in New York as long as the financial aspect was even close to fair. They did their jobs, running through scenarios of what an extension might look like versus how much money I could make if I waited for free agency. That last part went in one ear and out the other. I probably mentioned to them more than they cared to remember that this was my decision, that this was where I wanted to be. Whatever curiosity I might have had about playing elsewhere was easily outweighed by my desire to win with the Mets. Because of how much I wanted to be a Met for life, maximizing the length of the deal became way more important to me than maximizing the money.

A few weeks later, during a Thanksgiving trip to visit my

girlfriend Molly's family in Los Angeles, my phone buzzed while I was working out at a local gym. It was one of my agents, forwarding along an offer from Alderson and the Mets. And it was a fair one. As soon as I saw those numbers, I knew I was going to re-sign. I wasn't naïve about the way these things worked—I understood my agents still needed to counter, and the two sides had to haggle over details—but I also knew that first offer was good enough that we were going to find a match.

I shot a text back to my agents.

"Just get it done," I wrote. "Let's do this."

IIIIIIIIIIIIII

As I waited for those negotiations to play out, I busied myself ring shopping.

Back in October 2006, in preparation for MLB's All-Star tour of Japan, I had flown to Arizona for a few days of workouts. While I was there, one of my friends tried to set me up on a date with a girl named Molly who was in her senior year at Arizona State. Molly ignored the invitation because she had no interest in dating a baseball player, so I wound up hanging out with our mutual friend instead on Halloween night. Of course, it wouldn't be much of a story if it ended there. When Molly showed up later to give our friend a ride home, she came over to our table and began chatting with me after all. Apparently, my handsomeness swayed her. We hit it off.

Molly and I wound up talking deep into the night, discussing everything from our families and upbringings to our careers, dreams, and more. It's so rare to connect with someone on that level.

When we finally parted ways, I told Molly I wanted to take her on a proper date the following evening, which was my final night in Arizona before the trip to Japan.

We went to Stingray, a sushi restaurant in Old Town Scottsdale, and I was every bit as enamored with her as the night before. I offered to fly her out to see me in New York. She said she'd only accept if I proved I was serious about her, so I spent my entire time in Japan trying to do just that. Because phone calls weren't really an option overseas, I emailed Molly every chance I had. I worked hard to show her how important this new relationship was to me. I guess I did a good job because shortly after I returned, she decided to take a risk on a visit.

That's when I pulled out all the stops. *Jersey Boys* on Broadway. A live taping of *Saturday Night Live* featuring Justin Timberlake. Sushi at Tao. A hotel in Times Square. She didn't even mind when I decided to wear a baggy, two-piece blue velour tracksuit around town, though she did tell me I looked like a Smurf. (I did.) It was just a special, special weekend, and while it went by in a blink, it convinced me that Molly was the right person for me.

Unfortunately, she still had a semester of college left, forcing us back into a long-distance relationship. We made it work. Molly visited me in spring training and on Opening Day. She read *Baseball for Dummies* to learn about the game, because she didn't even know what a third baseman was. After graduation, Molly took an internship in New York, rented a studio apartment, and never left.

By late 2012, I was ready to take the next step. My dad, who was still working at the Norfolk police station at the time, was at a dentist's appointment when he received a call saying an armed courier had come to the precinct with a package for him. Rhon had no idea what it was, but the courier wouldn't let anyone else sign for it. My dad's coworker convinced the guy to stick around until he got back from the dentist, at which point a bizarre conversation ensued.

"Are you Rhon Wright?" the courier asked him.

"I am," Rhon replied.

"I've got a package for you."

"Well, what is it?"

"I can't tell you."

"What do you mean you can't tell me?"

This game of chicken went on a little while longer, until my dad caught a glimpse of the invoice that listed the item's value. At that point, he realized I was the only one who would have shipped something so expensive to his office, so he signed for it. When he called to ask, I fibbed and told him it was a Christmas present for Mom.

Not long after, I flew home and took my parents out to eat at 456 Fish in downtown Norfolk. When I showed them the ring and told them I was going to propose to Molly, we all started hugging and crying. It was one of those real special family moments. And it was about to get more special.

In the middle of all the commotion, my phone began buzzing with messages from the heads of my agency, Sam and Seth Levinson. They were making progress with Alderson on a contract and had gotten close enough that it was time to loop me in. This was real. This was not a drill. I told them to get it done.

How long that would take, I really didn't know. Up in New Jersey, Jeff Wilpon and dozens of other Mets VIPs were attending a benefit auction for Shannon Forde, a longtime Mets public relations official and close friend of mine who was battling breast cancer. With Wilpon and Alderson preoccupied, the updates from my agents came in sporadically for the rest of the night. Eventually, my parents and I parted ways and I headed back home.

"Guys," I texted them around midnight, "I'm tired. Can I go to bed?"

"Absolutely not," came the answer. "Stay up."

By that time, the charity event had long since ended. The messages continued flying back and forth until finally, at around three A.M., we struck a handshake agreement on an eight-year, $138 million deal. We still had to iron out some things, like a full no-trade clause, which was critical to me, and charity commitments on both sides. But with the heavy lifting done, I was able to call my closest family and friends to tell them the news. Problem was, they were all asleep. There I was, bouncing off the walls of my Norfolk condo, unable to tell a soul because it was three A.M.

It didn't matter. I could not have been happier knowing the deal ran through my age-thirty-seven season. We structured it like a bell curve, with smaller salaries at the end, to avoid awkwardness if my production started to fade. The money, honestly, was secondary. Obviously I wanted a fair deal, but this was the largest contract in Mets history (exceeding Johan Santana's by $500,000), so I certainly couldn't complain about the value. My agents made it abundantly clear that I probably could have made more in free agency, particularly given baseball's financial environment at the time. That didn't matter to me. The Mets mattered to me. New York mattered to me. I wanted to be a Met, win as a Met, retire as a Met. This new contract gave me a chance to do it all.

A few days later, Wilpon sent his private plane to Norfolk to fly me to Nashville, where we held a Winter Meetings press conference to announce the new deal. There, I spoke about how critical the no-trade clause was.

"I'm humbled, privileged, emotional," I told the gathered media. "It was very important for me from day one that I finish what I started. Things haven't gone the way we would have liked the last couple of years, but that's going to change.... I've grown up in this organization and made lifelong friendships with teammates, uniformed personnel, and front-office staff. I'm grateful for the opportunity to finish what I've started."

I meant that. I wasn't just talking about the people who made the contract happen, like the Wilpons and Alderson. I was talking about folks like Forde, who helped me in so many ways over the years, and the PR team of Horwitz and Ethan Wilson. Guys like Racaniello, one of my best friends, and the Citi Field security guards, and the clubhouse staffers, and so, so many others. Signing long-term meant committing to all of them as well.

|||||||||||||||

Three weeks later, on the night of my thirtieth birthday, I took Molly on a trip to the Norfolk Botanical Garden's annual Garden of Lights event. I'm a regular Clark Griswold—a big, big Christmas guy—so I always looked forward to driving my car past the different exhibits featuring Santa, his reindeer, you name it. Every year, it was like rolling through a magical forest of lights.

Before going, I arranged for one of the botanical garden

employees to make sure our car would be the last in line that night. As nervous as I was, I tried to play it cool, telling Molly we didn't have to go if she didn't want to. Things started off poorly when I couldn't figure out how to turn on my parking lights. Because I had the engagement ring in my jacket pocket, I refused to take it off even during dinner. The stress was real, but we eventually made it through the exhibit, which was fantastic.

As we approached the end, one of the employees stopped our car and offered to let us walk the rest of the way. Given how cold and drizzly the night was, Molly needed some extra convincing to get out of the car. On cue, the worker produced an umbrella. With that, the two of us strolled along, rain pattering down around us, until we came to a place where one of the displays was unlit.

"We should plug that back in to help them," I told Molly.

"Just leave it," she said. She was afraid I would electrocute myself.

But I had staged the whole thing, so I walked over anyway and plugged it in. The display blazed to life in bright red lights with the message "Will you marry me, Molly?" Dropping to one knee, I proposed. She said yes, we embraced, then we headed over to a tent with red roses and champagne waiting for us on ice.

Twelve months later, with nearly everyone from the Mets' clubhouse, front office, and ownership group in attendance, Molly and I got married in a wonderful ceremony at the Grand Del Mar hotel in San Diego.

She probably disagrees now, but back then, I had a little bit of romance in me.

## SIXTEEN

|||||||||

## CAPTAIN AMERICA

A day after I agreed to terms on my new contract, before I even officially signed the thing, buzz began surfacing that the Mets were thinking of naming me the fourth captain in franchise history. Those whispers only grew louder after media members began their annual migration south for spring training. But no one in the front office mentioned anything to me—at least not right away.

My mind was mostly on a return to the World Baseball Classic, which had evolved into a quadrennial tournament similar in style to soccer's World Cup. Unlike in 2009, there was no drama regarding my inclusion on the roster. I was once again the starting third baseman for Team USA, this time in a lineup that included Giancarlo Stanton, Joe Mauer, Ryan Braun, and other superstars. Derek Jeter wasn't there because he was recovering from a broken ankle, but the new Team USA manager was Joe Torre, which was a thrill for me. In addition to his obvious success as the Yankees' manager, winning four World Series titles in the Bronx, Torre had played three seasons and managed six for the Mets. His career in baseball was one to envy. His role with Team USA made me even more pumped for the tournament.

As in 2009, I began training earlier than usual, taking more serious rounds of batting practice over the winter and asking for extra reps once I arrived in Florida. I really did consider playing for my country a tremendous honor; the last thing I wanted to do was show up unprepared while wearing "USA" across my chest.

When Torre penciled me fifth in his lineup for our opening game against Mexico, it only increased the responsibility I felt to be a run producer. The two-hit game I delivered in response rang a little hollow as our team endured another sluggish start, giving up four runs over the first three innings of another pressure-packed night.

Chase Field in Arizona was full of Mexican fans, which made for a tremendous atmosphere but definitely ratcheted up the level of difficulty. That seemed to be a theme throughout my two World Baseball Classic tournaments—whether it was playing Team Canada in Toronto, Team Mexico in Phoenix, or some of the Latin American countries in Miami, we often felt like the road team in those WBC games. It's part of what made the tournament so memorable: tens of thousands of fans rooting against us in jam-packed stadiums.

Our second game was against Team Italy, which featured lots of American players of Italian heritage, as well as hitting coach

Mike Piazza—my former Mets teammate and a soon-to-be Hall of Famer. We still had the better team on paper, but there was no margin for error. If we wanted to advance to the tournament's second round, we had to win this game.

Long before it started, I knew the atmosphere was going to be as electric as anything I had previously faced in my WBC career. Because Chase Field had only two clubhouses, we shared a room with one of the teams that played before us—on this particular day, Team Canada, which was locked in a critical game of its own with Mexico. As I sat there riding a stationary bike and watching that game on television, several of the Canadian players milled about the clubhouse. All of a sudden, a brawl broke out on the field, stemming from a hit batsman and accusations of Canada's running up the score. It was surreal to watch the Canadian players around me sprint out to the field, where police officers had to help break up the fight.

Hours later, the crowd was still buzzing as we began our own game, falling behind early and carrying a two-run deficit into the middle innings. We slimmed that to a one-run margin by the fifth, when Adam Jones led off with a walk and Jonathan Lucroy singled, prompting Team Italy to turn to a right-handed reliever named Matt Torra.

Like a lot of pitchers we faced during the WBC, Torra was completely unknown to me. We didn't have video on guys like him, a first-round draft pick who'd spent the previous four seasons at Triple-A. But we did have scouting reports and lots of intelligent hitters, so there was always chatter in the dugout when a new pitcher entered the game. I paid close attention as the rally continued against Torra—a fly out by Jimmy Rollins, a game-tying single from Brandon Phillips, then a strikeout and a walk to load the bases with two outs. Over the course of those at-bats, Torra threw everything he had in his arsenal.

Up next was my spot, in a situation that felt enormous. The calendar might have said March, but this was playoff baseball. This was why I prepared the way I did—not just in January and February as I geared up for the WBC, but with all the swings, drills, and ground balls that came before. I worked hard for these moments so that when they finally arrived, they wouldn't overwhelm me.

One of the maxims I've always tried to live by is that good things are rarely due to luck alone. Sure, sometimes a fortunate bounce can decide a game, but far more often, clutch performances are the product of preparation. Through hours, days, months, and years of hard work, players become accustomed to those situations. For the most prepared among us, the game becomes instinctual. It shrinks in those moments—see ball, hit ball. Training takes over and everything else melts away.

That's how I felt stepping to the plate against Torra. I took a couple deep breaths to try to slow my heart rate, stared at my bat for a moment, then thought: *Let's go.*

Early in the at-bat, Torra made it clear that he intended to attack me with soft stuff. I fouled off a breaking pitch and he came back with a fastball, which I also fouled away. On his fifth pitch, Torra tried to bury another slider in the dirt but missed his spot. I saw it well out of his hand and put my best swing on it, crushing it over the left-center-field fence for a go-ahead grand slam.

The feeling was incredible—not just because of what it meant for Team USA, but also because of the legends there to see it. Torre was our manager. Larry Bowa was our bench coach. Greg Maddux was our pitching coach. Impressing those guys even a little bit required doing something pretty significant on the field. As I approached third base, I saw Piazza—a guy who, when I first came into the league, was larger-than-life. He was one of the greatest Mets of all time. To beat his team on that stage, in that moment, meant something significant to me. As I rounded the bag, I locked eyes with him in what seemed like an acknowledgment of mutual respect.

||||||||||||||

Unfortunately, we didn't have much chance for an extended celebration following our 6–2 win over Italy. By virtue of their two victories against other teams, the Italians had already advanced to the tournament's second round. Mexico was out of contention. That left Team USA and Team Canada, both with 1-1 records, set for a winner-take-all showdown the following night.

Given the quality of our roster, we were heavy favorites, which only heaped more pressure on USA Baseball. Back in the inaugural World Baseball Classic, before I became involved with the tournament, the Americans had failed to advance to the medal rounds. Three years later, in 2009, we finished fourth. Japan won both of those and was again a favorite in 2013, but we knew we had the talent necessary to win one ourselves. We also understood the tournament's popularity depended in large part upon how we did. Most of the later-round games were on US soil. Fans wanted to come out to see us play, but they couldn't do that if we lost in the first round.

As if we needed more pressure, our propensity to fall behind early and rely on late comebacks provided it. This game was no different; Canada took multiple leads and carried a one-run advantage into the later innings before we rallied to take back the lead for good. We wound up scoring seven times in the eighth and ninth, which was a relief. Despite slow starts in all three of our pool play games, we managed to survive and advance. I hit .455 with five RBI in those contests, doing nothing to hurt my growing reputation as someone who thrived on the international stage.

Partially because of that reputation, and partially because of whispers back home that the Mets might name me captain, people around the event took to calling me Captain America.

As far as I could tell, it began with MLB Network broadcaster Matt Vasgersian, who coined the nickname during our second-round game against Puerto Rico. It spread rapidly on social media and in newspapers from there; within days, fans were mailing me T-shirts and other paraphernalia related to the superhero. Back in Port St. Lucie, our PR director Jay Horwitz dressed up in a full-body, royal blue spandex suit, taking photos in front of my locker and telling everyone he was Bucky, Captain America's sidekick. Some of my teammates took to wearing screen-printed T-shirts featuring my face and Captain America's body.

As usual, I was a bit uncomfortable being the center of attention off the field. I never felt like I needed a nickname or a superhero persona or anything like that, so I shrugged off the Captain America thing when people asked me about it. But I did appreciate the fans, whose enthusiasm for the concept rubbed off on me. Captain America always looked pretty cool in comic books and movies, carrying around that iconic red, white, and blue shield. Even I could admit the comparison was flattering.

The night Vasgersian coined my nickname coincided with one of the most memorable WBC performances of my career. Having already driven home two runs in the game against Puerto Rico, I stepped into the on-deck circle in the eighth inning with men on first and second, one out, and a 4–1 lead. At that point, pitching coach Ricky Bones came to the mound to make a change.

Ricky had been the Mets' bullpen coach since 2012, which was another fun example of the familiarity between WBC opponents. On nearly every team, I could count teammates and coaches whom I knew well. Those relationships led to a little more trash talking than in regular-season games, like when I yelled at Carlos Delgado following my walk-off against Puerto Rico in 2009. Playing against friends added extra emotion. So when the new pitcher, Xavier Cedeño, walked Mauer, I looked at Ricky and just shook my head. It seemed pretty clear Cedeño was pitching carefully around Mauer to load the bases and get to me. (Ricky later admitted that he liked the matchup better, believing Cedeño could get me out with inside pitches.)

I decided to take it personally.

Cedeño threw me four consecutive curveballs, and on the fourth of them, I hit a towering fly ball to the warning track in right-center to drive home all three runs. Rounding first, I stared into the

Puerto Rican dugout and tossed my bat in the general direction of Ricky. It was all in good fun, but after that walk of Mauer, I wasn't going to let the opportunity to trash-talk pass. For the rest of my career, I brought that game up to him at least once a season, saying decisions like that were why he was a bullpen coach and not a pitching coach.

(Disclaimer: I actually think Ricky is more than qualified to be an excellent pitching coach. But it felt great to make that decision backfire on him, and he will never, ever hear the end of it from me.)

At that point, I was hitting as well as anyone in the tournament, having as much fun as I'd ever had on a baseball field. Most important, we were winning. Thanks to those key victories, the Americans had a real chance to take home the gold.

The only bummer? They were going to have to do it without me.

|||||||||||||

Before the World Baseball Classic began, I started experiencing some left rib soreness. Initially mild enough to ignore, the pain seemed to worsen with each passing day. One off night early in the tournament, my fiancée, Molly, and I went to dinner with Jeff Francoeur and his wife in Arizona. I kept fidgeting in my seat at the restaurant, even standing up during the meal to ease the discomfort I was feeling.

I had ignored plenty of injuries in the past, so this seemed like just another challenge. But as the WBC progressed, the ache grew increasingly worse. At one point, I brought a chiropractor to my hotel room because I thought one of my ribs had popped out of place. I was hoping he could snap the thing back into its proper spot.

Following my five-RBI performance against Puerto Rico, my rib felt sore enough that I had to say something to the Team USA training staff. That set off all sorts of alarms back at Mets camp, where team officials began communicating directly with WBC staffers. As far as injuries go, it didn't seem like a significant issue, but the twists and turns of baseball activities can really wreak havoc on those little core muscles. The Mets were concerned that, with only three weeks until Opening Day, continuing to play would mean risking my health for the regular season. As much as I loved the WBC, it was a bargain we were all unwilling to make.

Minutes before the start of Team USA's next game against the Dominican Republic, all parties agreed it was best for me to shut it down. About an hour later, I stood in a noisy tunnel at Marlins Park to relay the decision to the media: My red-hot tournament was finished.

Mets doctors wanted to examine me personally, so I went up to New York for a cortisone shot and an MRI, which revealed a mild left intercostal strain.

Team USA went on without me. The night I left Miami, my teammates lost to the Dominican Republic. The following evening, they lost a rematch with Puerto Rico as I watched from New York. One of my teammates found a blue-and-red Captain America snap-back cap and placed it on a dugout pillar, where it stayed propped up the entire game. I wish it had bestowed a little more fortune on them. Our bid to become the first Team USA to win the World

Baseball Classic fell a few games short, and while it was frustrating to watch that unfold from afar, I took comfort in knowing I had done the right thing.

||||||||||||||

I knew I might never get another chance to win a gold medal. That sucked. But at least a World Series trophy was still very much in play. And as it turned out, something else was in the works. Shortly after my return to Mets camp, Terry Collins called me into his office for an unscheduled meeting including Jeff Wilpon from the Mets' ownership group, as well as general manager Sandy Alderson and Collins's entire coaching staff. They wanted to name me the fourth captain in franchise history and the first since John Franco retired in 2004—my rookie season.

Although I had heard the whispers earlier in spring training, hearing those words out loud floored me. Captains had become increasingly rare in Major League Baseball; at that time, the only ones were Jeter of the Yankees and Paul Konerko of the White Sox. The Mets had named only three in their history: Keith Hernandez and Gary Carter, who served as co-captains, and Franco, whose leadership helped the Mets and New York City heal after the September 11, 2001, terrorist attacks on the World Trade Center.

To be considered in the same light as those guys took my breath away. I thought back to when I was a kid with the Virginia Blasters, when Coach Allan Erbe conducted annual players-only votes to determine our captains. Everyone would write a name or two on a piece of paper, then Erbe would tally up the results and the top two vote-getters would earn the positions for the upcoming season. The two times I received that honor, I felt so proud knowing my teammates thought of me in that way. To have the same opportunity placed before me as an adult, playing for the team I grew up rooting for, was something I did not take lightly.

Which is why I had to say no.

To be clear, I wanted to be the Mets' captain. Badly. I just didn't want the title to come from ownership, the front office, or the manager. Like when I was with the Blasters, I wanted the decision to come from my peers or not at all.

To me, captain was not just a ceremonial position. It meant being a leader, a confidant, and a trusted authority figure within the clubhouse. It meant setting an example, establishing a culture. Clubhouses are sacred places. I was never going to be some sort of hard-line disciplinarian, but I also wanted the best out of my teammates. If I was going to accept the responsibility of becoming an even more public face of the team, of chastising guys for slacking off or breaking rules—things I tended to do anyway but that were about to become part of my new job description—then I needed to make sure those people accepted me as their leader. If I had the title of captain without the respect of the room, I knew my words wouldn't carry any weight when it came time to fulfill those duties.

Sitting in the manager's office alongside Jeff, Sandy, and Terry, I made it clear the only way I was going to say yes was if my teammates approved the decision.

Locker by locker, I went around the clubhouse and told each of my teammates the story: The Mets wanted to name me captain, but

I wasn't going to accept the role without everyone's blessing. Because I didn't want to put anyone in an awkward position, I told them if they were in favor, they should tell Terry or Sandy. If they didn't want me to be captain, they should voice that opinion, too. If they didn't feel comfortable saying something directly to management, they could tell a coach or a veteran player instead. The whole idea was that, positive or negative, I'd never know who said what.

Going around the clubhouse, giving that spiel to various players, felt a little strange. Some of them, like Daniel Murphy and Dillon Gee, I had known for years. Others, like Juan Lagares and Wilmer Flores, were rookies without much experience. Still others, like John Buck and LaTroy Hawkins, were longtime big leaguers I had only recently met. It was important for me to talk to each one of them personally, regardless of their stature.

I never did find out what anyone said, but the feedback must have been mostly positive. Less than a week after returning from Port St. Lucie, I was in the trainer's room, dripping water onto the carpet from the ice wrapped around my strained intercostal, when Collins called a full-team meeting. The whole room broke into applause as he announced the Mets were going to name me captain. As usual, the attention made my stomach roil, but the feeling of having that support was overwhelming. The entire meeting was kind of a blur, as was the press conference to announce the news in Port St. Lucie.

At that point in my career, I was proud of what I had accomplished, both individually and as a teammate. But it all paled compared to this. Being named captain of the Mets was by far the greatest professional honor I had ever, would ever, or could ever receive. The title meant my teammates respected me as a person, which was a greater accolade than anything that could go on the back of a baseball card.

The only part of the captaincy that didn't appeal to me was the idea of putting a *C* on my jersey. I understood the decades-old tradition, but it just wasn't in my personality to stick out to that extent. My mindset was that a uniform is a uniform for a reason. Even though I might have been a team leader, that was always going to manifest itself behind the scenes. Thankfully, everyone understood, so it was an easy call to leave the *C* off my jersey.

In that and other ways, not much actually changed after the Mets named me captain. I didn't act differently. I might have enjoyed a little confidence boost knowing people were more likely to listen when I talked, but I wasn't much of a rah-rah guy or a team-speech guy to begin with. My goal was always to lead by example. When I did feel the need to speak up, I tried to do so behind the scenes, in private moments, with discretion. If guys took what I had to say more seriously because I was the captain, all the better.

In subtle ways, I do think becoming captain made me a better teammate and person. Had injuries not interfered, it probably would have made me a better player, too. The title held me accountable for a lot of things I did both on and off the field, almost as if I had this new spotlight on myself. I knew my teammates were trying to emulate me, so I redoubled my efforts to do everything the right way, from my interactions with the media to my effort level on the field.

Don't get me wrong, this wasn't a new concept for me. It's just that, as captain, the last thing I wanted to do was have a moment of selfishness or weakness, to give away an at-bat or space out on defense. Rather than spend a single second focusing on, say, how many home runs I had, I focused instead on my preparation and training.

Being captain held me to a higher standard as a player, teammate, and leader. I took that responsibility and honor with grave seriousness for the rest of my career.

# SEVENTEEN

# THE FACE OF MLB

As significant as my role had become within the walls of the Mets' clubhouse, I still had some people to impress outside of it. I had been fortunate to make five All-Star Games in my first six full seasons, starting four of them at third base. The run ended in 2011, when my back injury prevented me from putting up All-Star-caliber numbers, and that lack of support seemed to seep into 2012. Even though I was playing as well as ever, rebounding from my broken finger to hit .355 with nine home runs, 50 RBI, and a 1.013 OPS over the season's first three months, I lagged behind San Francisco's Pablo Sandoval in fan voting.

Give credit to the Giants' fan base: They were aggressive in backing their star, at a time when social media was becoming a factor in All-Star voting. Punching holes in a paper ballot was no longer in vogue; the modern process meant going online and voting up to twenty times in a day. Giants fans were doing a lot of that for Sandoval, who hit .306 with six home runs, twenty-five RBI, and an .848 OPS from April through June.

The Mets lobbied their fans to vote for me as well, but for whatever reason, there was just no stopping Sandoval's momentum. On Sunday morning of our final first-half road trip in Los Angeles, I awoke early, a little jet-lagged, to see about ten missed calls from Sandy Alderson. He kept calling and calling until I finally picked up, still half-asleep as the GM started talking.

"I just want to be the first to apologize that you're not going to be starting the All-Star Game," he told me.

This was news to me. Apparently, Sandy had access to some early voting results, and he sounded legitimately upset—probably even more upset than I was. Later that day, he fired off a series of tweets that received a lot of attention.

"Wright vs. Sandoval: A city of 8 million was outvoted by a city of 800,000," read the first one.

"ASG election of 'Kung Fu Panda' shows the value of a cute nickname. Surprised Giants fans didn't elect a 'ball dude' to start at 3B," went another.

Of course I was also sad to miss out on the All-Star start, but I told Sandy not to worry. I understood how the voting process worked. The Mets were coming off a few lean seasons, and while we were off to a nice start in 2012, we weren't in the same position as the Giants, who were on their way to a second World Series title in three years. Sandoval was a young, exciting star on that team and the Giants did an incredible job incentivizing their fan base to vote for him. I think that's what upset Sandy, who was genuinely apologetic that the Mets couldn't rally their fans in quite the same way. I told him it was totally fine—that I hoped my numbers would be enough to earn me a reserve spot on the team, and the rest was out of our control. When I did wind up making the team as Sandoval's backup, I was happy with that resolution.

The Mets weren't as satisfied. A year later, they redoubled their efforts, making a huge social media and marketing push for me to start the All-Star Game. This one was going to take place at Citi Field, which was a big deal. We hadn't played any postseason games since Citi opened in 2009, so it was our first real opportunity to showcase the ballpark on a national stage. Obviously, I wanted to start the All-Star Game there, and the Mets seemed to want it just as much for me.

I was enjoying another nice year, batting .304 with twelve home runs, forty-one RBI, and a .912 OPS through the end of June. Sandoval was hitting .274 with eight homers, thirty-seven RBI, and a .714 OPS, but he again took an early lead in All-Star voting. In response, the Mets' marketing team put on an absolute full-court press. Between innings, they flashed "Vote for David" messages on the Citi Field scoreboard. They painted the hashtag #VOTEMETS in giant letters behind home plate, urging fans to whip out their smartphones right then and there and punch in my name. The tipping point was when a marketing employee reached out to Cougar Life, a dating site that advertises "women looking to date younger men," and asked if they'd be interested in a marketing partnership. Apparently, Cougar Life had recently named me baseball's "hottest cub." When the potential partnership leaked to the media, it made for an easy punch line and some unwanted attention.

Don't get me wrong—I appreciated everything the Mets were trying to do for me. I badly wanted to start that All-Star Game in front of our home fans at Citi Field. But I didn't want to start because our social media department was better than another team's social media department. I wanted to start because my numbers warranted it. Just as I always aimed to play the game the right way, I wanted to qualify for awards and honors like the All-Star Game the right way, too.

That month, I sent a message up the ladder asking the Mets to cool off their marketing blitz. We were struggling as a team and everything on the scoreboard between innings revolved around me, me, me. Vote Wright, vote David, vote, vote, vote. I asked them to remember that the real goal was not for me to make an All-Star team but for the Mets to make the playoffs.

Understanding my perspective, the marketing and social media departments were sympathetic. They backed off a bit, and I wound up surging in the final few weeks of voting to overtake Sandoval for the start at third base. I do owe the Mets a lot of credit for the work that they did, because I probably wouldn't have started the All-Star Game without them. I'd just like to think my statistics—not any number of likes, hearts, or thumbs-up emojis—were the deciding factor.

|||||||||||||||

Even before I made the All-Star team, MLB approached me about being a captain for the Home Run Derby.

Despite my aversion to derbies, the idea made sense—"Captain

America," captain of the Mets, and now captain of this event in front of my hometown fans at Citi Field. I knew my runner-up performance in 2006 hadn't made me magically good at this sort of thing, so I wasn't expecting much in the way of results. But I liked the format. The league wanted me and Yankees second baseman Robinson Canó to choose the National and American League teams, respectively, with an added sweetener: If an NL player won, MLB would make a generous donation to my foundation, which worked closely with children's hospitals in New York and Virginia.

On paper, my responsibility was simple: choose three NL players to join me on the Home Run Derby roster. In reality, it was stressful. As soon as MLB named me a captain, players started approaching me—sometimes even on the field during games—to campaign for roster spots. A week after the announcement, I stepped to the plate in Atlanta to hear rookie catcher Evan Gattis say hello from his crouch. I turned to my right to return the greeting.

The next words out of Gattis's mouth surprised me: "I will walk to New York if you let me be on this team."

This was a dude who had been to hell and back on his road to the majors, leaving the game for four years and overcoming some serious issues before finally debuting at age twenty-six. If he said he was going to walk from Atlanta to New York, I had no choice but to believe him.

I tried to make the actual process of picking the team as fair as possible, since MLB gave me complete autonomy to choose anyone I wanted. Even though the league allowed us to pick non–All-Stars for the derby, I didn't feel comfortable doing so. That disqualified Giancarlo Stanton, who otherwise would have gotten my vote.

Around this time, MLB ran a poll asking fans which players they most wanted to see in the derby. Bryce Harper won and was having a great year, and the Home Run Derby—to me—should be about putting on a show for the fans. For those reasons, Harper was an easy selection. My second choice, Carlos González, was leading the NL with twenty-five home runs heading into the All-Star break. That seemed as good a reason as any for him to make my team.

For my third and final selection, I chose Michael Cuddyer, based in large part upon my friendship with him. He was certainly deserving, with a .330 average—Cuddyer would go on to win the NL batting title that year—and sixteen home runs before the break. When I picked Cuddyer, he was at the tail end of a twenty-seven-game hitting streak. He never campaigned for a spot and might not have been the household name that some other candidates were, and I knew selecting Cuddyer meant risking a little controversy, given all the other qualified candidates around the league. But I wanted him on my team. Some guys were wishy-washy on the whole idea of participating in a derby. Not Cuddyer. He was beyond pumped to do it, to the extent that his enthusiasm pumped me up as well. Again, this was a show for the fans. I wanted guys who genuinely wanted to be there.

Problem was, there were way more guys who wanted to be there than spots available. That particularly riled up fans and sports talk-radio hosts in Pittsburgh, where Pedro Álvarez—a New York native—went into the All-Star break ranked second in the majors in homers, just one behind González. The Pirates were thriving as

a team, with the second-best record in the NL, making for an electric atmosphere when we traveled to Pittsburgh for three games on
our final first-half road trip.

More than thirty-nine thousand fans packed inside PNC Park
for a sold-out Friday night opener, and it seemed like every one of
them was booing me. The jeers intensified to the point that during one of my at-bats, home-plate umpire Larry Vanover called
time to ask why everyone hated me. Raising my voice above the din,
I tried to explain about the Home Run Derby process. He was completely unaware of it, but the city of Pittsburgh wasn't. For those
three games, every time I stepped near the batter's box or made a
defensive play, some of the loudest boos I had ever heard rained
down on me.

Sorry, Pittsburgh.

As it turned out, González suffered an injury and Álvarez
wound up making my derby squad anyway. If only González had
backed out sooner, perhaps I could have avoided some hostility.

My final pre-derby responsibility was to pick my batting practice pitcher, which gave me a chance to honor a friend. For much of
my career, Mets bullpen catcher Dave Racaniello was my BP pitcher
before games. He was also one of my best buddies. In 2006, I'd
moved from my East Side apartment to a beautiful space in the
Flatiron District that an interior decorator helped design. Rac became my roommate, and for the next eight seasons, we were inseparable. We commuted to the ballpark together, which often meant
my banging on his door early in the morning to make sure he was
awake. For football Sundays, we installed a sixty-inch television
flanked by four other forty-two-inch TVs. The setup included a

very fancy remote control, which of course Rac dropped and broke one day when I was away from the apartment. Other than that, the place was a dream, solidifying my friendship with him.

Heading into the derby, Rac wanted me to choose Mets coach Ricky Bones, a former major league pitcher skilled at throwing BP. Rac thought Bones would give me the best chance to win, but I felt this was a once-in-a-lifetime opportunity for Rac to step onto a national stage and do something incredibly cool, seizing the type of opportunity that most people would never get. I disagreed with Rac's assessment of his own BP-throwing skills. More than that, I told him I didn't necessarily want the best BP pitcher. I wanted the guy who would appreciate the experience the most.

I also wanted someone I could blame forever and ever if I lost. Fortunately, Rac came around on the idea and accepted.

The derby itself went about how I anticipated. I hit five home runs to get eliminated in the first round, taking solace in the fact that the only person I beat was Canó—a crosstown rival and my fellow derby captain. The ovations I received at Citi Field were memorable, both when I initially stepped to the plate and when I hit an early home run into the second deck in left field. Fans stayed on their feet the entire time, cheering and chanting my name. Certainly, I would have loved to have won, or at least made the second round to give fans a show, but I know what I'm good at. Home run derbies aren't it.

The rest of All-Star week was a blur. In an on-air interview during the derby, ESPN announcer Chris Berman called me "the unofficial host of the whole game," given all my responsibilities around Citi Field and New York City. It was always somewhat difficult to enjoy those events, considering how quickly they passed. Players bounced from one interview to the next, from one promotional appearance to the next, from parties to fan events and beyond. The game was actually just a small part of it.

The game was also always my favorite part. That night, I hit cleanup, finishing 1-for-3 with a single. I didn't know it at the time, but it was my final All-Star appearance. Playing in seven of them over the years, I hit .389. I like to consider it more evidence that I could compete on baseball's biggest stages.

IIIIIIIIIIIIII

In terms of wins above replacement, 2012 and 2013 were the third- and fourth-best seasons of my career. Despite being on the wrong side of my thirtieth birthday, I felt like I was at the top of my game. I had conquered Citi Field to a certain extent, hitting thirty-nine homers those two years while batting above .300 in each of them. I had silenced any lingering doubts about my defense, following up two Gold Glove seasons with more solid work at third base. I had overcome my troubles after being hit in the head with a pitch in 2009 and my physical issues after breaking my back in 2011. I was in possession of a long-term contract with a full no-trade clause, which I hoped would allow me to retire as a Met. I was the captain, well established both on the field and off it, with two World Baseball Classic appearances and seven All-Star Games on my résumé. I had become, in some small ways, an ambassador of the game.

During spring training 2014, Major League Baseball ran a bracket-style contest called the Face of MLB to determine, via fan voting, which player most deserved that title. There was no avoiding it in Port St. Lucie, where the clubhouse televisions were constantly tuned to baseball channels.

My daily routine was to drive to the ballpark, eat breakfast, lift weights, and then head back to my locker. That walk through the main clubhouse room always seemed to coincide with MLB Network's daily update on the contest, and each time I advanced, my teammates rose to give me a standing ovation. Knowing how uncomfortable I was with the attention, they had a grand old time with it.

The finals came down to me and A's infielder Eric Sogard, a relatively unknown player with six home runs at that point in his career. He stood five foot ten and wore glasses on the diamond. Sogard went on to have a long, successful career, but at the time, he was not a household name; my teammates certainly got a kick out of the fact that he had turned into a social media sensation. "Captain America" or not, there was a real chance this dude was going to beat me.

I'll admit I felt some relief when I outlasted Sogard in the competition. Thanks in large part to the Mets' social media efforts, MLB awarded me a nice plaque, which I added to my memorabilia collection. But similar to how I felt during my recent All-Star ballot experiences, what I really wanted was something no social media department could provide. As fun as off-field things like the Face of MLB were, my priorities were on the diamond. To me, "Captain America" meant little if it didn't come with a World Series title.

At age thirty-two, it was time to tackle some unfinished business.

## EIGHTEEN

||||||||||

## SPINAL STENOSIS

Early in March 2015, I walked into the Port St. Lucie clubhouse to find rookie pitcher Noah Syndergaard sitting at a table, eating his lunch during a game. This was something players knew not to do; that spring, manager Terry Collins and pitching coach Dan Warthen had made it abundantly clear that they wanted everybody on the dugout bench, even if they weren't scheduled to play. So when I saw Noah sitting there, my instinct as captain was to teach him a lesson.

In doing so, I made what I consider one of my biggest mistakes as a leader.

Let me preface this by noting that, throughout my career, I never tried to embarrass anyone. I only ragged on players, especially younger ones, if I knew they could take it. Noah was that type of player, so my idea that afternoon was to get on him in a big-brother-type way, making my point and ending the conversation with a hug or a fist pound. What I didn't notice were two things: a group of beat reporters busy conducting an interview on one end of the clubhouse, and another veteran teammate, Bobby Parnell, by his locker across the room.

Oblivious to all that, I walked over to Noah and told him to get back to the dugout. When Noah didn't move right away, Parnell came up behind me, grabbed his lunch, and threw it in the trash. One of the reporters, *Newsday*'s Marc Carig, had his head turned in our direction and began tweeting play-by-play of the incident, which prompted several other writers to ask me about it after the game. I didn't realize anyone had seen what had happened. Catching me completely off guard, the questions twisted me in knots as I tried to answer them. I usually prided myself on being well prepared for my interactions with the media, but this was one instance in which I found myself tongue-tied. What was meant to be a lesson for Noah turned into a lesson for me.

After the game, I apologized to Noah for the way I went about teaching him that lesson, telling him I never would have said anything in that moment if I had known the media was within earshot. I assured him the last thing I wanted to do was embarrass him. Noah was only twenty-two years old. Certainly, I could look back on my own experiences as a young player—showing up late on my first day of pro ball or wearing flip-flops on my first big league road trip, for example—and understand that mistakes happen. My only goal was to make sure with Noah that this particular mistake didn't happen twice.

The whole episode became an unwanted distraction, but it was important for me to establish that type of winning culture in our clubhouse. Thankfully, Noah understood, which gave us a solid foundation for our relationship going forward.

I knew that Noah, a former first-round draft pick acquired in the R. A. Dickey trade, was a critical part of the vision Sandy Alderson had laid out in Virginia three years earlier. Capable of throwing 101 miles per hour with a breaking ball that Collins dubbed "the hook from hell," Syndergaard was one of the top prospects in camp, dripping with potential.

Our pitching staff also featured Matt Harvey, who was still rounding back into form after undergoing Tommy John surgery in 2013; Jacob deGrom, the reigning NL Rookie of the Year; Zack Wheeler, who was coming off his first full, successful big league season; Steven Matz, another top prospect on the cusp of the majors; and several others.

My job was to get those guys to commit to the sort of culture that championship teams require. I had long been fascinated by the "Cardinal Way" in St. Louis. Over the years, I became friendly with some of the players who implemented it, including World Series champions Adam Wainwright, Yadier Molina, and Matt Holliday. Those three were part of something called a "veterans' council," which solved problems in the St. Louis clubhouse. That seemed like a smart idea to me. As the Mets' captain, I wanted to create the same culture of accountability, especially with our roster looking as strong as it had in a long time.

The 2015 Mets appeared to have playoff potential, and I wasn't going to let anything off the field interfere with that. If we went about our business the right way, I knew, six straight losing seasons could quickly turn into something much, much better.

IIIIIIIIIIIII

For the team, the regular season began almost perfectly. After opening the year with a series victory over the Nationals, who figured to be our chief NL East rivals, we reeled off eleven straight wins against the Braves, Phillies, and Marlins to build an early division lead. Or at least, my teammates did. I only stuck around until April 14, when a stolen-base attempt resulted in a pulled right hamstring. Hitting the dirt awkwardly, I tried to tell myself it was just a cramp, but I realized pretty quickly it wasn't going to disappear on its own. When an MRI revealed a Grade 2 hamstring strain, I mentally prepared for what I figured would be a one-month absence.

In a weird way, the injury almost felt like a blessing in disguise. For much of April, my back had been feeling a little achy. At first, I considered it normal soreness—annoying, sure, but nothing really troublesome—and I managed to play through it, batting .333 with a home run over eight games that month. Taking some time off to rehab a hamstring tear, I realized, could give my back a chance to calm down, too.

Problem was, as I began to ramp up my rehab down in Florida, my back was absolutely killing me. Just trying to run at a 50 percent effort level sent pain ripping through my core and legs. As the days went by, standing for more than ten or fifteen minutes at a time began to cause significant discomfort. Driving forty minutes to the restaurants I liked to frequent in Jupiter or West Palm Beach was agony. As usual, I began running all the worst-case scenarios through my mind. I feared I had fractured another vertebra.

One morning, as I drove from a physical therapy session to the field in Port St. Lucie, I did what I often did when facing difficult decisions: Call Dad.

"I don't know what to do," I told him. "The Mets expect me to come back from this hamstring injury, but they don't know my back is in pain."

Rhon's advice was simple: "You've got to be smart."

He said everything a dad is supposed to say, and I probably should have listened to him. Instead, I kept trying to push through it, push through it, push through it, hoping I'd wake up one morning and everything would just feel good again. I prided myself on being available to play every night, even when I was a little hurt. I had hated going on the disabled list for my 2009 concussion, then in 2011 for the stress fracture in my back, then again in 2013 and '15 for hamstring injuries. After avoiding the DL for more than half a decade, I seemed to be establishing residency on it. But what could I do? My back became so debilitating that I sat awkwardly in the car on my short drive to the stadium each day, squirming in search of a position that wouldn't shoot knives of pain up my spine.

Eventually, it reached the point where I knew I had to say something. I was nearing the start of a rehab assignment, but there was just no way I could play through this.

In the staff office in Port St. Lucie, I found Dave Pearson and Jon Debus, two longtime Mets employees who ran our rehab program. Those guys worked hard to get players back on the field as quickly as possible, so it sucked to walk into that room and say that, yeah, my hamstring was fine but my back was hurting. I knew they weren't going to tell me I'd be normal again after a couple days of rest. I figured this would spark a chain reaction of events: a trip to New York, an MRI, a new diagnosis, a new rehab plan, an expectation of significant lost time.

The bottom line was I was nervous, maybe even a little scared of what this new injury might be. Breaking the news to Pearson and Debus, I found myself close to tears.

As expected, they relayed the message to our staff in New York, including team physician Dr. David Altchek. The next thing I knew, I was on a flight from West Palm Beach to LaGuardia, fretting about what I'd learn on the other side. Testing at the Hospital for Special Surgery resulted in a diagnosis of spinal stenosis and a conversation I'll never forget. Dr. Altchek sat me down, delivered the news, and gave me one piece of advice: "Don't Google it."

Of course, the first thing I did was tap the words into my phone. Spinal stenosis? That had never come up in all the time I'd spent sifting through possible diagnoses on the Internet.

I realized instantly why Dr. Altchek had wanted me to keep my phone in my pocket. Every website ran through the same buzzwords: *Numbness. Weakness. Tingling. Pain. Cramping. A debilitating and irreversible narrowing of the spinal column that worsens with time.* A jumble of thoughts began racing through my mind. *Oh my God, my career is over. Nobody comes back from this sort of condition. This is the type of thing elderly people get. Why me? Why now?* I started feeling sorry for myself.

Mentally, the diagnosis was crushing. I kept thinking back to my collision with Carlos Lee four years earlier, how I had tried to play through the stress fracture in my lower back. What I learned later is that, after fracturing a bone, calcium deposits cause it to regrow a little thicker so it can repair itself. In my case, I was already genetically predisposed to having a narrower spinal canal than most people. My thickened bone mass was likely clogging up the area even more, leaving less room for nerves to function. The general wear and tear I had placed on my lumbar discs over the years only made matters worse.

All that doctor-speak was scary. Terrifying, even. I'm a fairly optimistic person, but the news hit me really, really hard. This was something I not only couldn't understand but couldn't easily fix.

Back in 2011, when I'd collided with Lee, I'd received a checkup in Los Angeles with spinal expert Dr. Robert Watkins, whom I liked and trusted enough to head back to for a second opinion four years later. From New York, I flew to LAX, hopped in a car, then drove up to nearby Marina del Rey to visit Watkins's home office. As far as doctors go, this guy was legit; he grew up in Tennessee and trained in England and Switzerland before moving to Southern California to focus on athletes under the direction of legendary surgeons Dr. Robert Kerlan and Dr. Frank Jobe—the guy who completed the first successful elbow-ligament-replacement surgery on pitcher Tommy John.

Watkins was the surgeon who repaired Dwight Howard's back and Peyton Manning's neck. He worked closely with the Los Angeles Dodgers, the Los Angeles Kings, the Anaheim Ducks, the University of Southern California football team, the PGA Tour, the acrobats of Cirque du Soleil—you name it. Walking into his sixth-floor office overlooking Marina del Rey Harbor, I saw dozens of signed sports jerseys lining the walls. Watkins understood the human spine as well as anyone on earth. If anyone could fix my back, it was him.

As I suspected, Watkins confirmed Altchek's diagnosis, administered a series of six epidural injections, and set me up with a team of physical therapists in Los Angeles. Surgery wasn't an option for my condition, but we had a rehab plan in place, which would theoretically have me back on the field at some point in 2015.

What the exact timing might be, no one could say, which frustrated me to no end. Up to that point, most of my injuries had come with clear timelines: three or four weeks for a muscle pull, six weeks for a broken bone, and so on and so forth. This was not a muscle pull or a broken bone. This was entirely new, uncharted territory.

That first week, I checked into a hotel, not knowing when I might be able to check out. It wound up being the first of many temporary homes. One hotel booted me for a weekend to accommodate a wedding block. A nearby rental home was available only for a week or two. I moved up and down the California coast, from Marina del Rey to Manhattan, Hermosa, and Redondo Beaches and back again, staying as long as the places would let me. Over the course of three months, I cycled through five or six different spots.

The baristas at hotel coffee shops all over Los Angeles began to learn my name, probably thinking I was some high-powered businessman, given how much time I spent in those places. Each morning I went downstairs, grabbed a cup, then drove to my daily session with a physical therapist named Michael Schlink. Working closely with Dr. Watkins, Schlink ran me through a system designed to help athletes with back trouble return to the field. The program may have been well tailored for people like me, but that didn't make it exciting; it involved lying on my back for about an hour and a half each day, staring at the ceiling, doing exercises that required minimal movement yet left me soaking in sweat.

The foundation of my physical therapy was an exercise called the dead bug, which involved lying with my knees bent and my arms pointed upward. Keeping the small of my back pinned to the floor, I raised one leg while lowering the opposite arm. Then I did it again. And again. And again and again and again, eventually introducing light weights into the motion as I grew comfortable with it. Other exercises followed—partial sit-ups, hip bridges, bird-dogs, and more. The idea was to work my core in a way I never had before. Those six-pack abs people like to show off at the beach? That's not what I needed. What I needed was to strengthen the less glamorous muscles all around my spine so that they could protect it.

As the weeks passed, Schlink added modifications to make the program increasingly difficult (but just as boring as ever). It's not like I was lying back for ninety minutes each day, getting a massage. This was an absolute grind, with no end in sight.

Each Monday, I met with Dr. Watkins in his Marina del Rey office, hoping he might clear me for more intensive activities. Each Monday, he said no. Next came a weekly conference call to update Mets trainers, who wanted to stay in the loop. Watkins was adamant that I needed to complete every level of physical therapy without pain before I could advance to more functional exercises for baseball players. It was frustrating because it felt like I was doing so little, unable to jog, run, or lift weights. Even standing in one position for too long caused discomfort. In those early days of rehab, we judged my progress on how far I could walk without keeling over.

Dr. Watkins gave out homework assignments, telling me to walk for five or six minutes without stopping. Simple things became big things. Actions that had been easy my entire life were suddenly difficult. It was also tough on a mental level, because in my mind I was a professional athlete. I was a multi-time All-Star. I wanted to be sprinting, hitting, fielding ground balls, slinging around heavy weights to mold my body back into peak condition. Instead, I was walking a quarter mile and hoping it wouldn't bring me pain.

What Dr. Watkins knew was that spinal stenosis would eventually end my career, due to the weakness it would cause in both my core muscles and my throwing shoulder. He had a plan to delay and alleviate those symptoms, giving me a chance to play for years to come—potentially even at a high level. I just had to trust in the system and put in the work.

When the Mets came to play a three-game series in San Diego in early June, I drove down the 405 to check in with the team and update reporters on my situation. Over and over, they asked about my timeline. I didn't have any good answers because I genuinely didn't know when I might be able to pack my suitcase for good, leave the coffee shops behind, and head to Florida to ramp up baseball activities.

It wasn't just the media. Teammates and friends were constantly reaching out to ask how I was doing, how I was feeling, when I might return. Athletes are taught not to be overly forthcoming with injury updates due to the uncertainty that surrounds them. In this case, I truly had no idea. The situation was so fluid. One day, I'd experience little to no pain during a morning of rehab. The next, walking ten minutes would feel like a Herculean task. One day, I'd wake up feeling like my old self. The next, driving five minutes in my rental car would make me want to scream. Given the lack of any pattern, it was difficult to predict how I might be feeling in a week, or two, or six. If my doctors couldn't provide concrete time lines, how could I?

Inwardly, I still had more questions than answers. Outwardly, I tried to project confidence.

"You've got two options," I told the Mets writers that day at Petco Park. "Either you allow this to get to you and you just kind of check out and moan and groan, or you keep your head up and you push, and every day in the rehab you challenge yourself to do the best you can, and understand how good it's going to feel when you get back and get a chance to put the uniform on for real, and go out there and play.

"This is probably overused, but you don't understand how much you miss something until you're away from it for so long. From the moment I was diagnosed with this, from the information-gathering stage, there has never been a question in my mind. Not only am I going to come back, but I'm going to come back sooner rather than later."

||||||||||||||||

Each night in Manhattan Beach or Marina del Rey or wherever I happened to be staying, I found a comfortable position that wouldn't hurt my back, settled in, and flipped on the Mets game. From afar, I watched the team's early eleven-game winning streak give way to a sluggish May and June. Perched four and a half games ahead of the Nationals on May 1, the Mets went 24-32 over their next fifty-six games to fall back to .500 and second place. I watched my team-mates score one run in the Cubs' three-game sweep from June 30 to July 1, then—as newspaper writers and radio hosts completely wrote them off back home—fly to Los Angeles for a six-game road trip against the two best teams in the NL West, the Dodgers and the Giants.

Thanks in part to Syndergaard and Matz, who'd both earned first-half call-ups, we were pitching well. What we weren't doing was hitting; our offense ranked twenty-eighth in baseball heading into that road trip against the Dodgers. It hurt to watch from my couch; I wanted to help but was unable to do so. Then a funny thing happened out in Los Angeles: The Mets held their ground. Syndergaard pitched well in the opener at Dodger Stadium and our offense cracked closer Kenley Jansen for a go-ahead run in the ninth. Two days later, Matz and Logan Verrett combined on a shutout. My teammates won that series and the next one in San Francisco, and suddenly were no longer dead.

I made the drive downtown to Dodger Stadium each day, fighting traffic to watch the games in person, check up with the Mets' training staff, and spend some quality time around the guys. I missed being in the clubhouse. I hated feeling disconnected from my teammates. Most nights, I texted a few of them after games, congratulating guys for big hits or pitching performances. It may not have been much, but it was a small way to stay involved.

One day that week, hitting coach Kevin Long asked if I would be interested in talking with Dodgers manager Don Mattingly, who'd worked with him for four years in the Yankees organization.

I was plenty familiar with Mattingly's story: He was a former Yankees captain who'd made six All-Star teams, won a batting title, and been the 1985 American League MVP, but whose back trouble had forced him into early retirement at age thirty-five. Knowing Mattingly never overcame his physical issues, I wasn't necessarily eager to hear his take. I had spoken to a few athletes with conditions similar to mine, including Giants running back David Wilson, who retired at twenty-four due to stenosis. The bottom line is back pain sucks. No one seemed to have an uplifting story.

Because back injuries tend to affect people in different ways, those sorts of conversations also tended not to be that useful. But I grew up a huge fan of Mattingly's, so, if nothing else, this was a chance to get to know a New York baseball legend. I wasn't going to say no to a chat.

At Long's instruction, Mattingly met me behind the plate during batting practice. He couldn't have been nicer, laughing about all the dead-bug exercises he had done in his life—something I could very much relate to. Mattingly's primary issue wasn't stenosis but a degenerative disc in his back. His rehab was nonetheless similar, involving countless hours lying faceup on a medical bench. Recalling his experiences, Mattingly talked about the frustration of having days when he felt good, days when he needed to test his back with batting practice or other activities, and days when he couldn't even think about playing baseball. I could hardly believe the words coming out of his mouth.

*Oh my God,* I thought. *This is me.*

Hearing something so relatable from a former All-Star player comforted me. Up until that point, I had received far more sympathy than empathy. I could always talk about my condition to my doctors, trainers, or physical therapists—smart, educated people who were some of the top experts in their fields. They all helped in significant ways, but everything they knew about stenosis they had either read in books or learned by treating other patients. They couldn't know what it felt like to wake up with severe lower back pain, to lie on a bench and do dead-bug exercises for hours, to feel helpless watching on TV as somebody else took your place on the infield dirt.

Mattingly understood all that and more. He'd continued his back rehab into retirement and, just like me, expected to do it for the rest of his life. Meeting someone else in that situation gave me perspective on not merely the short-term challenge that awaited me but also the implications for my life after baseball—something that, to this point, I had given relatively little thought to at all.

Those types of things could be scary to think about. It was comforting to know others had traveled this path as well.

||||||||||||||

By the time I met Mattingly, I had graduated to more intensive physical therapy, increasing my optimism that I might soon be cleared for baseball activities. Those around the team noted I was in far better spirits than when I had visited them in San Diego one month earlier, and for good reason. My doctors still weren't giving me a clear picture of my timeline, but, given how I was feeling, I figured I could return at some point in August. That would give me plenty of time to round into form before the postseason. It was slow progress, but progress indeed.

Although I still spent my mornings doing Schlink's exercises, I had been cleared to complete them without supervision. To add to my workload, I began to train at a new center run by John and Lisa Meyer, a husband-and-wife team who operated a physical therapy center for athletes throughout Los Angeles. As a sports fan, I found it was neat going there every day, not knowing who else might walk through the doors. Blake Griffin was among those who showed up that summer. Anthony Davis. Matt Cassell. Maria Sharapova. Once, I shared a soccer field with Tobin Heath of the women's US National Team, who demonstrated pretty quickly how much better an athlete she was than me. I often worked out alongside members of the Los Angeles Kings.

At that facility, my rehab exercises were specialized for baseball. Using movements designed to prepare my body for the rigors of throwing a ball or swinging a bat, the Meyers created a program specifically tailored to me. I spent hours doing exercises with resistance bands and TRX straps, relying on my own body weight rather than dumbbells or iron plates. I had to protect my spine. If I were to put a big bar across my back, load it down with weight, and do a set of squats like I was twenty-five years old again, it would send lightning bolts of pain through my back. I had to take everything slowly, progressing to the point where I could accomplish even simple tasks like jogging or running.

Eventually, I advanced to light baseball activity under the Meyers' supervision. Near their office was a pair of public turf fields where Heath and others performed their drills. I began throwing baseballs to John Meyer from forty feet away, doubling and tripling that distance as I grew stronger. We went from there to a dirt-and-grass baseball field, which made me feel like I was back with Coach Erbe and the Blasters. Meyer stood at first base, rolling ground ball after ground ball across the infield. All the while, he focused on my throwing form, imploring me to incorporate my legs and core muscles into throws as much as possible. When it was time to start hitting, Meyer worked with me at a batting cage that Giancarlo Stanton was known to frequent about fifteen minutes from Manhattan Beach.

Each day, I inched forward. Each day, I did a little bit more. Each day, I felt a little more optimism that the end of this rehab slog was near.

Finally, on July 24, Watkins cleared me to return to New York, where I could ramp up baseball activities under the Mets' care. To the surprise of the front desk, I checked out of my hotel, flew across the country, and returned to Citi Field, where I resumed throwing, taking ground balls, and hitting with even more intensity. I couldn't have been happier. Not only was I doing what I loved and making tangible progress toward a return, but I was back around my teammates on a daily basis.

All told, I had been away three months. It had felt more like three years.

The day the Mets cleared me to restart baseball activities, July 24, was significant for another reason. Around the same time Dr. Watkins was giving me the okay, the team was making arrangements to call up Michael Conforto, a 2014 first-round draft pick barely a year removed from college. Arriving in New York straight from Double-A, Conforto provided an immediate spark, collecting four hits in his second career game and batting .270 with nine home runs over the balance of the season.

Truth is, we had been searching for something to spark us. Despite holding ground on their West Coast trip in early July, the Mets had played sub-.500 ball over the ensuing two weeks. Fortunately, the Nationals were also struggling, allowing us to hang within a few games of them in the NL East race. No matter what the standings said, it was clear to everyone that something needed to change.

Conforto offered the first piece of evidence that something would. The second came that night, when Sandy Alderson traded for veterans Kelly Johnson and Juan Uribe to plug infield holes. (In Uribe's case, that meant largely playing third base in my absence.) I thought back to my time on the golf course with Alderson in 2012, when he'd shown me a list of the types of free agents he valued. It was largely made up of grinders like Johnson and Uribe, who had been battle-tested in October and knew exactly what it took to win. I felt strongly that we needed as many of those players as possible— guys who were going to put in the work, play hard, get dirty, and put winning before everything else.

Another such grinder was Wilmer Flores. A onetime top prospect who struggled to hit consistently and find a defensive home early in his career, Wilmer wasn't always a household name in Flushing. But his desire was unassailable, which the world came to realize on the night of July 29. Done with my rehab for the day, I was sitting on the bench in the middle of a game against the Padres when reports began leaking that the Mets had traded Flores and Zack Wheeler to the Brewers for Carlos Gómez. A fan near the dugout rail actually shouted out the news to Wilmer, and the next thing we all knew, he was standing on the infield dirt crying. Collins asked me to go into the clubhouse to see what the TV announcers were saying. I went in, listened for a bit, and told Terry that Wilmer had been traded.

"There's no way he's been traded," Terry responded, incredulous. "The front office hasn't told me to take him out of the game."

I wasn't sure how to reply. By the end of that half inning, we still hadn't received any word from the front office. When I saw Wilmer jog off the field and go straight into the clubhouse, I followed close behind.

Understand that Wilmer signed with the Mets out of Venezuela when he was sixteen years old. He grew up in the system, learning the English language and American culture and making many of his closest friends. As much as baseball is a business, I couldn't blame Wilmer for losing his composure because I couldn't even begin to understand what he had gone through on his baseball journey. What I could understand was his heart. I had been in the majors for more than a decade, spending all that time with one team. For me, as for Wilmer, the Mets were family.

In the clubhouse, I found Wilmer by his locker, his eyes red. Taking a seat beside him, I tried different tactics to calm him down.

"If they had traded you," I said, echoing Terry's words, "they would have taken you out of the game. So if you're not out of the game, you're not traded. You've got to focus up here because you're going to get another at-bat in a close game."

That didn't work, so I tried the speech I've used on about a dozen other players over the years.

"I know you're going to miss a lot of this," I told him, "but it will create an opportunity where you have a better chance of getting more playing time, and more important playing time than you'd have over here."

Although Wilmer completely understood, I could tell he was flashing back through his baseball journey, from Venezuela to the present day. In a way, his reaction was refreshing, because very few guys would respond in such a genuine fashion. It showed how much he cared.

He wound up becoming a cult hero for it. As it turned out, the trade fell through due to issues with Gómez's medical report. Wilmer stayed with the Mets and, two days later, hit a walk-off home run to spark a three-game sweep of the Nationals, which vaulted us into first place for the first time since June.

That same day, thirteen minutes before the trade deadline, Alderson acquired superstar outfielder Yoenis Céspedes from the Tigers for two minor league pitchers. The mood around the team was unlike anything I had seen. It was an incredibly emotional day for everyone, capping a week that included near-constant drama both on and off the field. That month had it all, from trades (and a nontrade) to crushing losses and uplifting wins. Even though I was sidelined, I was elated to be in New York to help, in my own small way, guide some of the younger players like Wilmer through it.

IIIIIIIIIIIII

About a week after Wilmer's walk-off, I flew to Port St. Lucie to begin a minor league rehab assignment. My back was feeling better, or at least good enough to play. With two months left in the regular season, I felt like I had one shot to get this right.

It didn't go well.

A quick glance at the statistics might tell a different story, considering I hit .321 with five walks in eight games for Class A St. Lucie. The truth is, I was flat-out garbage. I was fielding like garbage. I was hitting like garbage. I felt like garbage. I committed three errors in those eight games, and of my nine hits, none went for extra bases. I had just one RBI.

During those games, I thought back to my only other career rehab stint, as I recovered from the 2011 stress fracture in my back. I hit .476 with three doubles in that one, tearing the cover off the ball and playing good defense, too. The Florida State League prospects facing me that week must have felt like the big leagues were far away.

Flash forward four years, and the prospects facing me must have thought that if David Wright could make seven All-Star teams, it must not take much to play in the big leagues. It honestly felt like they were laughing at me. I doubted my health during that rehab stint, doubted my ability to make an impact. The back of my baseball card might have looked nice at that point in my career, but it didn't mean much considering the big-time physical limitations I was battling. I wondered if I would ever be the same. I knew what people were saying back in New York, in the newspapers, and on the radio. I couldn't argue with it. My confidence hadn't been this low in a long, long time.

Regardless of how I felt, though, I was edging close to a return. All I could do was challenge myself to make the most of the situation, which meant putting in as much hard work as possible.

The final test was playing in consecutive nine-inning games, which I accomplished twice on rehab without a major issue. It was enough to convince the Mets' doctors and trainers that I was ready to rejoin the team. They conferred with the front office, which scheduled my reunion for the start of a three-game series in Philadelphia in August. As the Mets wrapped up their final game in Denver, I arrived in Philly a few hours ahead of them.

To say I was fired up would be an understatement, but that didn't erase the discomfort I felt waiting for my teammates to arrive. Given the moves we'd made for Céspedes, Uribe, and others, it felt like I was captaining a roster full of strangers. The time I spent with them in July was nice for introductions, but it wasn't the same as going through the grind with them night in, night out. Give my teammates credit: At times during the summer, when they were out to dinner on the road or hanging around the clubhouse, they Face-Timed me into conversations just to keep me involved, which helped me continue to feel like one of the guys. But I was eager to be back among them for real.

To break the ice, I thought it would be cool to be down in the hotel lobby when they arrived that evening. The check-in area of the Westin Philadelphia was on the second floor, so I knew everyone would come piling out of the elevator at the same time and see me.

As I waited, I couldn't shake one other thought from my mind. *Man, I'm hungry.*

I hadn't really eaten dinner that night, and while I knew it wasn't the best thing for my diet, I couldn't stop thinking about the Insomnia Cookies bakery across the street from the hotel. I loved that place and knew my teammates did, too, given how many late-night orders we'd placed there over the years. I also figured a little comfort food would help ease my mind.

Walking in, more brilliance struck me. *Better idea: Let me get cookies for the whole team. Then I'll have something to give them when they get here.*

As I returned to the Westin with a whole tray of cookies, one last idea worked its way into my brain. I had my baseball bag with me in my hotel room, so I changed into full uniform in hopes of giving everyone a chuckle when they arrived. Random hotel guests shot me curious looks as I sat there waiting in the lobby, cookies in hand, before my teammates finally came crashing through the elevator doors. Their smiles and laughs proved well worth the effort.

I think the only person who actually ate the cookies was longtime public relations director Jay Horwitz, who loves his desserts. It wound up being a great icebreaker regardless, giving me a chance to talk to some of the new guys and feel a lot more comfortable going into a game the next day—especially knowing some of their playing time was going to suffer because of me.

Given my performance on rehab, I wasn't sure I deserved to take away anybody's at-bats. In my absence, Uribe had been starting most days at third base and thriving. The team had performed consistently well after the final week of July, expanding its NL East lead. I didn't want to be a distraction. I just wanted to contribute in any way I could, which I made clear to Collins.

"Terry," I told him, "I don't know what I'm capable of doing. I'm sure you saw the reports from those minor league games. Don't feel like you have to utilize me in a certain role. You're not going to hurt my feelings. My ego is checked at the door. Use me where you see fit to help this team."

Collins said he understood. Then, that first day back, he wrote my name fourth on the lineup card. Cleanup.

*Oh, dear God.*

I had always hit well at Citizens Bank Park, but that didn't ease my mind during batting practice. Historically, when I was in a good hitting zone, my BP sessions featured lots of line drives to right and center field, very few fly balls, and even fewer home runs. I was at my best when my effort level felt closer to that 80 percent, when my bat almost felt a little slow at the plate. It's a big reason why my swing wasn't conducive to home run derbies.

That BP session in Philadelphia was different. I found myself hitting lots of homers and duck-hook, topspin liners to left. Due to my pure excitement to be back, I was swinging harder than usual, which historically meant I was going to have a bad game. I was early, jumpy. I couldn't do anything but pull the ball. It was one of the worst BPs I could remember.

With that experience fresh in my mind, I tried to settle my nerves in the visiting clubhouse as I changed into my game uniform. It didn't do much good. When I ran out to the field for the first time, Mets fans were all over the place, making my heart beat through my chest.

The Mets went down in order in the top of the first, giving me a little extra time to compose myself, but those butterflies came roaring back when I approached the on-deck circle to lead off the second. I vowed not to swing at the first pitch, figuring it would bounce ten feet in front of home plate and I'd come away looking like an idiot. Of course, left-hander Adam Morgan's offering was a fastball on the corner. Strike one.

Seeing that pitch at least made me feel a little more comfortable, a little less jumpy. Morgan backed it up with a low curveball, then another fastball through the fat part of the strike zone. I saw it well out of his hand and, for one of the first times in my career, just completely let it rip. As amped as I was, I knew there was no chance of dialing anything back, so I swung as hard as I possibly could.

When bat hit ball, the sound was so pure. Striking a baseball perfectly like that almost feels effortless, like the ball makes no vibration coming off the bat. As it rose, I did a little skip step coming out of the batter's box and looked up in disbelief. *This thing is going to leave Citizens Bank Park.*

Maybe not quite, but I did absolutely crush it, and took my time going around first. As much as it wasn't in my nature to revel in a home run like that, when I saw it arc toward the second deck in left, I reflected on what this small personal triumph meant to me.

A few months earlier, I had Googled my diagnosis and considered it catastrophic. Spinal stenosis had ended plenty of athletic careers in the past. A lot of people were questioning if I would ever play again. I worked my tail off to overcome that and get back on the field, doing two-a-day rehab sessions, trying to get my body right to go out there and play baseball, all the while feeling heartbroken that I couldn't be with my teammates as they went on an amazing run up the standings. After hitting my home run and high-fiving everyone in sight, I made a beeline to the clubhouse to thank John Zajac, a Mets physical therapist who had sacrificed countless hours to help me that summer.

On the bus back to the hotel that night, the Mets' radio broadcaster Howie Rose—a Mets fan since childhood who had witnessed most of the greatest moments in franchise history, often up close—told me that home run was one of the few times in his career he'd gotten chills calling a game.

I felt similarly. That entire year was just such an emotional roller coaster. I didn't know what the future held, but I did know that for this one pitch, this one at-bat, I'd beaten the odds. I'd made it back. It looked like the Mets were heading to the playoffs, and I was at least going to be a small part of that. It was just a huge personal win for me, one of the biggest individual accomplishments of my career.

||||||||||||||

At that point, five weeks remained in the regular season. More importantly from a personal standpoint, only one week remained until September 1, when rosters expanded from twenty-five players to a maximum of forty. While that Philadelphia home run was sweet for me, preceding a couple other multi-hit games later in the week, my back still didn't feel even close to 100 percent. I knew I was going to need regular off days down the stretch, which became easier to achieve thanks to the expanded roster.

On one hand, hitting a homer in my first game back allowed me to take a deep breath and focus my mind on playing baseball, as opposed to worrying about what people might think of me in my diminished state. On the other, I was still very much doubting my health and future. Of the Mets' thirty-nine games after my return that season, I appeared in thirty of them. Essentially, I was playing in three out of every four, scheduling regular maintenance days for my back. On days I didn't start, I never came off the bench. My routine was too long and intricate for the unpredictability of pinch-hit appearances. As much as I relished batting with a game on the line, it just wasn't realistic to think I'd be useful in those spots down the stretch in 2015.

I wound up hitting .277 with four home runs, thirteen RBI, and an .818 OPS in those thirty games, which seemed like another significant win considering the state of my back. Unlike during my rehab stint, when I couldn't seem to hit anything beyond shallow left field, eleven of my thirty-three hits went for extra bases.

My final regular-season home run came on September 26, in the Saturday game of a weekend series in Cincinnati. Entering that day, we had built an eight-and-a-half-game lead over the Nationals, sweeping them again in early September to build what seemed like an insurmountable lead. Still, after going through what we did in 2007 and, to a lesser extent, 2008, I knew better than to start preparing for the playoffs. We had to finish this thing.

Needing only one more win to clinch the NL East, we turned to Harvey, who pitched effectively into the seventh inning. By that point, we had taken a nice lead thanks to a Lucas Duda grand slam, a Curtis Granderson solo shot, and a two-run double from my friend Cuddyer, who had joined the Mets as a free agent the previous winter. We were on the precipice of a division title when I came to the plate in the ninth inning with two men on base.

As far as at-bats go, this one didn't have a ton of juice; we were already leading by five runs with our closer, Jeurys Familia, warming up in the bullpen. But when I squared up a Burke Badenhop sinker for a three-run homer to ice it, the dugout absolutely exploded. The reception I received after that relatively meaningless homer is something I'll remember forever. Everyone realized the game was pretty much over at that point, that we were about to clinch the NL East and rush the field. More than that, as guys hugged me and shouted congratulations to me in the dugout, I realized that they were, in a way, acknowledging what I had done to make it back to the field. It was an exclamation point to a tremendous season for us as a team and an absolute grind of a year for me personally. Much like my first home run back in Philadelphia, this one was hugely satisfying.

When Familia locked down the final three outs a short while later, I jumped higher than I had on a baseball field in a long time. I know I enjoyed the celebration more than in 2006, when the Mets clinched a postseason berth for the first time in my career. Back then, looking at our core as a young, optimistic player, I figured I'd receive a playoff invitation pretty much every October. Over the nine years that passed between appearances, I gained a new appreciation for how difficult it is to win. I was also thirty-two years old, playing through a major back condition that I knew was going to affect me for the rest of my life. I had no idea if this playoff berth would be my last, so I resolved to enjoy the run as much as humanly possible.

After celebrating in the clubhouse, I ran with my teammates back onto the field, where hundreds of Mets fans had stuck around to wish us well. It was humbling to see how many of them had made the trip from New York, holding signs and chanting the names of me and my teammates.

"We deserve this," I said to a group of reporters in the middle of that celebration. "The fans deserve this. The city of New York deserves it. I'm glad we could deliver for them."

In a selfish way, I also felt like I personally deserved it. I had faced my diagnosis the only way I knew how, with hours upon hours of hard work. I had done what I could to stay mentally and physically strong, knowing I might only have one shot to get this thing right.

# TWENTY

# OCTOBER, AGAIN

In the months following my return from injury, the book on me was obvious. Whether as a direct result of my back issues or a product of my months away from the field, my bat speed had slowed. Opponents tend to pick up on that sort of stuff quickly. As a result, I found pitchers challenging me with fastballs much more often than earlier in my career.

To combat all the heat, I did my best to get into favorable counts and gear up for something straight, which is how I found myself hunting fastballs from one of the National League's most electric relievers in a playoff game at Dodger Stadium.

The Mets' roll through August and September was strong enough for us to clinch our first NL East title since 2006, but not strong enough for us to secure a postseason home-field advantage. We actually finished with the fewest wins of any NL playoff team, which meant we'd have to go on the road to face the Dodgers—the same club we'd beaten in my 2006 playoff debut—in a best-of-five series. Worse, the Dodgers were one of the few teams with a pitching staff that could rival ours. Their rotation may not have been quite as deep, but they planned to take advantage of the best-of-five format by using only three starters: reigning Cy Young Award winner Clayton Kershaw, former Cy Young Award winner Zack Greinke, and lefty Brett Anderson. To advance, we would need to beat Kershaw and/or Greinke at least twice.

Fortunately, Jacob deGrom was ready for the challenge, striking out thirteen batters over seven electric innings in NL Division Series Game 1. He was incredible. We entered the later innings of that game leading, 1–0, thanks to Daniel Murphy's home run off Kershaw.

Otherwise, Kershaw was cruising, retiring nine of ten after Murphy's homer and needing just five pitches to carve us up in the sixth. But when Kershaw walked the leadoff man and two other batters in the seventh, Dodgers manager Don Mattingly came to remove him with the bases loaded and two outs.

Normally, I'd have been thrilled to see a three-time Cy Young Award winner leave a playoff game, but the Dodgers' stacked bullpen made me rethink that. Out went the left-handed Kershaw. In came right-handed Pedro Báez, who threw in the upper nineties and hadn't pitched since the regular season ended five days earlier.

Báez was part of a new wave of relievers who threw harder than ever. Back in the day, the reward for knocking out a starter was facing a lesser pitcher in the later innings. By 2015, the reward was facing someone who threw BBs. It seemed like every reliever in baseball was throwing in the upper nineties, at a time when I was struggling to hit those sorts of pitches. In a small sample, I batted .231 down the stretch against fastballs of at least 95 miles per hour. I fouled off more than half of those I swung at, compensating for my lost bat speed by spoiling as many top-flight pitches as possible.

For those reasons, Báez was a bad matchup for me on paper, but he did me a favor by missing inside with each of his first two fastballs. His next two pitches both came sizzling in at 99 miles per hour; I fouled off one, then took the other for a ball. Yet another foul ball ran the count full.

As Báez prepared to throw his sixth pitch of the at-bat, I mentally committed to hunting another fastball. The heater was, without question, Báez's best offering, and the one he turned to almost exclusively when the count ran full. If he decided to stray from that pattern and throw his second-best pitch in this spot, with a playoff game on the line, with the scouting report on me what it was, so be it. I would have tipped my cap and said, "You got me."

He didn't. Báez's pitch wasn't a bad one, whistling in at 99 miles per hour, but it caught enough plate for me to line it back up the middle for a two-run single.

It's difficult to describe the intensity of my emotions after that hit. When I reached first base, I unleashed a huge fist pump with my right hand, screaming with passion. Everything just poured out of me in that moment. This was more than just a two-run single. This was more than even my August home run in Philadelphia, which had provided proof that I could overcome my physical limitations. This was better. This was evidence that I could still contribute to something meaningful not just for me, but for the Mets.

I was right back where I wanted to be—playoffs, big situation, under fire in a difficult spot. And I had come through. To do something like that after months of uncertainty made it so much sweeter.

||||||||||||||

We won that game but lost the next one on a play that turned the series on its head. After the Dodgers put runners on the corners with one out in the seventh, Terry Collins replaced Noah Syndergaard with Bartolo Colón, a veteran starting pitcher working in relief during the postseason. Enrique Hernández was on third. Chase Utley was on first. Colón's job was to induce a double-play ball, which he did with a fastball that Howie Kendrick one-hopped toward second base.

That's where the chaos unfolded. Murphy fielded the ball and flipped to shortstop Rúben Tejada, who had to reach high above his left shoulder to grab the feed. As Tejada spun to try to unleash a throw, Utley slid late into second base, toppling him to the dirt.

Standing at third base, my eyes were focused on Kendrick to see if we had a chance to turn two; by the time I realized what was happening, Tejada was already crumpled on the ground. Trainers carted him off the field, taking X-rays that revealed a broken right leg. His postseason was finished. To make things worse, the Dodgers successfully challenged that Tejada's foot ever touched second base. We didn't record a single out on the play, leading to the four-run rally, a 5–2 loss, and a 1-1 series split.

Like most of my teammates, I realized the aggressiveness of Utley's takeout slide only later, after I watched video of it in the clubhouse. There was no daylight between Utley and second base when he dropped to the dirt. Guys were angry. Our shortstop had broken his leg on a slide that even Utley had to admit was late. Emotions were running high in our locker room.

"*Slide* would be generous," Murphy said when asked about it after the game. As a middle infielder, Murphy would know; he had twice torn knee ligaments attempting to turn double plays. Other veteran infielders, like Kelly Johnson, were livid. Outfielder Michael Cuddyer told reporters it was up to them "to decide if tackling is legal in baseball."

As for me, I wasn't any happier, though I was willing to give Utley the benefit of the doubt. "You are going to have to ask Chase what the intent was," I told the media, which is about as short as I ever got with reporters. "Rúben had his back turned to him; obviously he can't protect himself. Only Chase knows what his intent was."

What I didn't tell the media was that I also wanted an explanation. I knew Utley reasonably well from playing against him in the NL East for more than a decade and alongside him on four NL All-Star teams. He debuted a year before me, in 2003, serving as the Phillies' everyday second baseman until a trade to the Dodgers midway through 2015. I had a lot of respect for Utley's hard-nosed style, which I considered similar to mine. Like me, Utley was a loyal player who really cared about winning. When the Phillies traded him, I took his spot as the longest-tenured major leaguer to play for only one team. It meant quite a bit to hold that title until I retired.

So, yeah, I wanted an explanation. Shortly after the game, Utley texted me asking for Tejada's phone number to apologize. Before I gave it to him, I took the opportunity to tell Utley that I didn't think he intended to break Tejada's leg but that I also didn't consider the play clean. He responded that, as a second baseman, he understood the risk of takeout slides. He essentially said the same thing to me that he had said publicly in his postgame press conference: that he saw an opportunity to take out Tejada and prevent us from turning two, but that he never wanted to hurt him.

"Obviously I feel terrible that he was injured," Utley had told reporters. "I had no intent to hurt him whatsoever, but I did have an intent to try to break up the double play."

Texting with me later that night, Utley said he was eager to get in touch with Tejada and apologize, so I facilitated the exchange of numbers. I could tell Utley was sincere, which took some of the edge off the whole situation for me.

I may have been more forgiving than most. The next morning, the *New York Post* headline blared one word: "SCREWED!" The *Daily News* went with "UT-TER DISGRACE!" Guys in our clubhouse were still angry. So were our fans, many of whom called for Major League Baseball to suspend Utley. He received some violent threats over the incident, which I hated to see. Again, I believed Utley when he said he had no intention of hurting Tejada. He just wanted to break up a double play. Did he go about it the right way? Not in my opinion, and not in the opinion of MLB, which rewrote its slide rule after the season. But the public reaction, especially the threats to Utley and his family, went well beyond what I considered proper.

If a silver lining existed, it was that the episode proved galvanizing as we returned to Citi Field to play in front of a fired-up crowd. Not only was Game 3 our first home playoff game since 2006, it was our first at Citi Field, ever. Everyone was motivated and the Tejada episode charged our emotions even more, turning Citi Field into an extremely hostile environment for the Dodgers. During pregame introductions, Utley stood stone-faced as boos rained down on him. A few minutes later, when Tejada came limping out with a cane, the place went berserk.

Inside our clubhouse, guys really rallied behind Tejada. As cheesy as this might sound, we started getting an idea in our heads that we were going to win it for Rúben. While it may not have been a direct cause and effect, we scored ten runs in the first four innings of Game 3 and went on to win 13–7. A Game 4 loss sent the series back to Los Angeles, where we needed to beat Greinke to advance.

I had spent nearly a decade craving playoff baseball; this was exactly what I had signed up for. I was enjoying every bit of the drama.

||||||||||||||

Because Los Angeles is such a sprawl, walking to the ballpark wasn't an option for the road games that series. For me, neither was taking the team bus. We stayed in Pasadena, about a twenty-minute drive from Dodger Stadium. As much as baseball players love to get to the park early, especially in the playoffs, the first bus generally didn't leave until early afternoon. Given my rehab regimen, I needed to be there around eleven A.M. to ready myself for a major league game.

The solution was to ride in with head trainer Ray Ramirez and his assistant Brian Chicklo. Each morning during the NLDS, I texted to ask what time they were leaving. Then I grabbed a ride with them, hours before my teammates and coaches arrived at the park. Once there, I immediately began my preparation with our physical therapist, John Zajac.

Back when I was rehabbing in California that summer, Zajac had frequently flown out on team off days to oversee my progress. Since this wasn't all stuff I could do on my own, I monopolized a ton of his time in Los Angeles and elsewhere, getting daily personal attention from a guy responsible for twenty-four other players. The least I could do was be out of his way by the time my teammates began arriving in the early afternoon.

With Zajac, I generally began with stretches and physical therapy exercises—dead bugs, bird-dogs, all that stuff. A big part of his job was helping me with active release techniques that promoted blood flow and recovery. I also received massage therapy, followed by time on the stationary bike to warm my entire body. From there, I cycled through various skipping and plyometric exercises, which readied me to swing a bat. Everything had a purpose. Once I completed those exercises, I began to swing lightly off a tee, intensifying the movements until I felt loose enough for batting practice.

The entire process took about three hours, and, really, it was just the warmup to the warmup. When it was finished, I stretched again with my teammates and went through the Mets' regular pregame routine. If that sounds tedious, it's because it was. I didn't want to do this. I *had* to do this. Without that routine, my back never would have cooperated.

The sequence was easier when we were on the road, like in Los

Angeles, because visiting teams took batting practice last. That allowed me to go straight from my warmup into BP, then into the game about an hour later. At home, an awkward break of about ninety minutes forced me to perform a second, modified version of my warmup closer to first pitch.

Home or away, it was a major investment of time, but it was so, so much better than missing a once-in-a-lifetime playoff run. I also had a significant factor working in my favor. Baseball's playoff system included regular off days, including two in the middle of the best-of-five NLDS. This afforded me even more rest than I received during the regular season without any loss of time on the field.

My body needed those breaks. Yes, I was playing and, yes, I felt like I was doing so at a reasonably high level. I hit second in the lineup during the NLDS and felt like a threat, even though my two-run single against Báez was my only hit of the series. But I knew that, to stay capable, I needed to put in more hours than ever before. This wasn't about getting better. This was about maintaining a reasonable level of production, because if I couldn't, I would have taken myself out of the lineup. It was incredibly time-consuming and, up to that point, the most difficult physical fight of my life.

It was also well, well worth it. Rolling into Dodger Stadium the morning of October 15 gave me emotions that I hadn't felt in nine years. I felt fortunate to experience them again.

|||||||||||||

Early in my career, I had the privilege of playing behind Hall of Fame pitchers Pedro Martínez and Tom Glavine. Later, I was lucky to watch Cy Young winners Johan Santana and R. A. Dickey take the mound every fifth day. I was Matt Harvey's teammate during his best years, Noah Syndergaard's when he was at his most electric, and so on and so on.

I mean no disrespect to any of them when I say there's no one—no one—I'd rather give the ball to in a big game than Jacob deGrom.

The night that cemented that legacy in my eyes was Game 5 of the NLDS. DeGrom had come a long way already, from being a relatively anonymous prospect—I certainly didn't know much about him when Sandy Alderson was talking up our farm system on the golf course—to being the 2014 NL Rookie of the Year. He debuted early that season, starting against the Yankees only because multiple other pitchers were injured. He would have found a path to the big leagues regardless. DeGrom had this mental toughness, this bulldog mentality, this competitive streak, that I had never seen from anyone else. It didn't matter if we were playing basketball on a little Nerf hoop in the clubhouse or pursuing an NL pennant. He always had this intenseness about him, which manifested itself in an ability to compete at an elite level—even when he wasn't feeling his best.

On the evening of Game 5, deGrom was decidedly not feeling his best. As the sun set over the San Gabriel Mountains behind Dodger Stadium's outfield fence, he allowed a pair of quick runs in the bottom of the first to flip a one-run lead into a one-run deficit. When a walk and an error put two more men on base in the second inning, Collins asked Syndergaard to begin warming in the bullpen.

That's when deGrom's legendary competitive streak kicked in. With the game on the line, he retired the next two batters, then stranded runners in the third, fourth, and fifth innings as well. In the top of the sixth, Murphy homered off Greinke to put us back on top, where we stayed as deGrom, Syndergaard, and Familia combined on the final twelve outs.

At that point, we erupted, mobbing our closer on the field and partying together for the second time in three weeks. The carpet in the visiting clubhouse became so soaked with champagne and beer that a pool formed in the center of it. Some of the younger guys ditched their spikes and even kicked off their shower sandals, using the carpet as a makeshift Slip 'N Slide. It was a happy, disgusting mess.

"This champagne tastes even sweeter having gone through what we've been through as an organization these last nine years," I told reporters in a quieter corner of the clubhouse, steering clear of the mosh pit on account of my back. "This city, this fan base, the guys that put this uniform on, it's very rewarding to be here now, having experienced everything we've experienced."

I was talking about the team, but those words applied to me as well. Throughout that postseason run, I never lost sight of everything I went through just to get back on the field. Doing so would have been difficult, considering all the daily work required just to keep my back in playing shape. That, combined with a nine-year wait between playoff appearances, made the whole thing sweeter. I understood as well as anyone what sort of achievement this was.

I intended to enjoy it for a night—really, really enjoy it—and start thinking about our next-round opponent, the Chicago Cubs, in the morning.

|||||||||||||||||

Like us, the Cubs were an up-and-coming team with a young nucleus. In other ways, they were our opposites. Unlike Alderson, who built the 2015 Mets around a core of starting pitching, Cubs general manager Theo Epstein constructed his roster around promising young hitters. Most of them, including Kris Bryant, Anthony Rizzo, and Addison Russell, were entrenched as big league regulars by 2015.

The Cubs presented a different sort of challenge than the Dodgers, who could match our pitching strength in a way few teams could. As a hitter, I understood as well as anyone that good pitching tends to beat good hitting. But the Cubs, who ranked second in the NL in runs after the All-Star break, could overpower our pitchers if they made enough mistakes. The only NL team with more second-half runs was the Mets, thanks in large part to a guy named Daniel Murphy.

A thirteenth-round draft pick, Murphy was even less hyped than deGrom coming through the farm system, but he raked at every minor league level before debuting in 2008. Murphy spent the next six years serving as a good contact hitter with marginal power, averaging eight home runs per season.

That changed in 2015, when Murphy, under the tutelage of Mets hitting coaches Kevin Long and Pat Roessler, became a poster child for the "launch angle revolution" sweeping across baseball. By urging Murphy to pull the ball and hit it into the air more often, Long and Roessler worked to tap more fully into his natural power. That's the simple explanation, anyway. Murphy was like a mad scientist in the batting cage, always tinkering with his swing. He could talk about hitting in ways that even I barely understood.

Whatever he changed that year worked for him. After hitting a typical five home runs before the All-Star break, Murphy nearly doubled that to nine after the break, with no loss in contact skills. Then he became a one-man wrecking crew in the NLDS, hitting three of the Mets' seven homers against the Dodgers. In that fashion, Murphy became just the second player in 2015 to homer off both Kershaw and Greinke, doing a ton of damage at a time when I personally wasn't hitting very well.

As much as Murphy was a close friend of mine, I'd be lying if I said I saw that type of breakout coming. Looking back on it, I think the mechanical changes he made led to something just as important: a monster leap in confidence. Murphy was always a self-assured hitter, but in the 2015 postseason, he became borderline arrogant—in a good way. He started believing pitchers could no longer get him out. He started thinking he was better than them. I think every All-Star–caliber hitter finds that zone at some point in his career, but for Murphy, it was so stark and so sudden, right there for everyone to see on a national stage. He wasn't just hitting home runs off middle relievers. He was going deep against guys like Kershaw, Greinke, and—in Games 1 and 2 of the NL Championship Series— Jon Lester and Jake Arrieta of the Cubs.

Arrieta was the NL Cy Young Award winner that year. Lester was a World Series hero who finished in the top five in the Cy

Young voting three times. In homering off both, Murphy guided the Mets to victories in NLCS Games 1 and 2 at Citi Field, bringing us halfway to the World Series. Murphy hit another in Game 3, because of course he did, putting us on the precipice of a pennant.

The next day was unseasonably warm at Wrigley Field. We felt a little bit like a team of destiny at that point, like we couldn't be stopped, so we showed up to the field with more than our share of swagger. As usual, I arrived in the late morning, running through my stretching and physical therapy routine to prime my back for the grind of nine innings. My Game 3 contribution had included three hits, a walk, and two runs scored. I was feeling good. The Mets were feeling good. A Game 4 win would not only send us to the World Series but also afford my back some extra days of rest.

Any nerves we might have felt disappeared when Lucas Duda and Travis d'Arnaud homered in the first inning off Jason Hammel, giving us a four-run lead. Duda homered again later in the game, putting it well in hand by the time Murphy took his final at-bat in the eighth inning.

At that point, Murphy had homered in five consecutive postseason games. "Legendary" doesn't even begin to describe how hot he was as he stepped in against Fernando Rodney, a successful veteran who threw in the mid-nineties with a "Bugs Bunny" changeup that seemed to take forever to get to the plate. That didn't deter Murphy, who told me he planned to hunt a changeup from Rodney. Hitters do that sort of thing all the time, looking for a certain type of pitch in a specific area of the strike zone. A correct guess makes the pitch a lot easier to hit, but a wrong guess makes it extremely difficult to adjust.

None of that applied to Murphy, given the rare sort of zone he was in. Waiting on a changeup, Murphy saw nothing but fastballs, crushing the third of them for another home run. Curious, I approached him when he finished rounding the bases.

"I thought you were looking for a changeup," I said.

"I was," Murphy replied.

I just shook my head. The only thing I could compare it to was when Michael Jordan made six straight three-pointers in Game 1 of the 1992 NBA Finals, shrugging his shoulders like he felt sheepish about the performance. This was the Murphy Shrug. It was one of the most ridiculous offensive performances I had ever seen, and it could not have come at a better time for the Mets. That home run gave us an 8–1 lead with six outs standing between us and a pennant.

When Familia locked down the last of them with a called third strike on Dexter Fowler, the feeling was unlike anything I had experienced on a baseball field. It wasn't just the fun of another champagne celebration, this time in a cramped Wrigley Field clubhouse. It was the perspective of knowing my entire baseball life had led to this point.

Every kid who grows up playing baseball dreams of making the World Series. It's the pinnacle of the sport. Early in my career, I assumed I would get there eventually. As the years passed, I held out hope but started to wonder. When my back trouble grew serious early in 2015, I lost confidence that it would happen for me. Lots of good players go their entire careers without making the World Series. What made me special? What made me any different?

The difference was the team. I don't know what the Vegas odds were for the Mets to win the NL pennant back in July, but they couldn't have been good. For months, we struggled to keep afloat, while I fought to get back on the field. Then we caught fire and accomplished the stuff of dreams.

It's not that I didn't think we could make it. I did, every year, year in and year out. It's just that, after going through so much both on and off the field, I couldn't believe it was really happening to me. During the celebration I turned to Cuddyer and blurted out: "We're going to the World Series. Who goes to the World Series?!"

The Mets were. I was.

Somehow, some way, we had made it.

## TWENTY-ONE

||||||||||

# FALL CLASSIC

The downside of our sweep over the Cubs was that we had to wait almost a full week for Game 1 of the World Series. Reporters kept asking if that was a help or a hindrance. I didn't really know how to answer. Certainly, the rest helped, especially for my back. But going five days without facing live pitching threatened to make staying sharp difficult.

Our coaches debated the best way to go about things, whether that meant setting up intrasquad scrimmages or simulated games at Citi Field, or having our hitters face our pitchers in live batting practice. One day, I stepped into the box against Noah Syndergaard, who was throwing upper-nineties fastballs as the outside temperature dipped into the forties. That wasn't fun. Another afternoon, sixty-six-year-old Terry Collins threw BP, chucking the ball as hard as he could from about twenty feet in front of home plate. We did all sorts of atypical drills as we tried to fill the time between NLCS Game 4 and World Series Game 1. All told, it was our longest break of the season, longer even than All-Star week, and I think it really affected us. I don't want this to sound like an excuse—it definitely was not the reason why we came out sluggish in the days that followed. It was just a different experience preparing with such a long layoff.

Over on the American League side of the bracket, the Royals dispatched the Blue Jays in six games. Kansas City was about the worst opponent we could have drawn. Not only were the Royals battle-tested, having lost the World Series just one year before, but they also featured a lineup full of contact hitters capable of neutralizing our hard-throwing starting pitchers. Their own starters threw nearly as hard. In their bullpen were three of the best relievers in baseball: Greg Holland, Wade Davis, and Kelvin Herrera. The Royals were damn good.

They had also gone decades without a title, making their fan base every bit as hungry as ours. Two days before Game 1, we flew to Kansas City for a workout at Kauffman Stadium, which shares its parking lots with the football stadium, Arrowhead. Our timing couldn't have been worse; the Chiefs had scored a big conference win over the Steelers that day, and the game was letting out right as we were arriving. The place was packed with tailgating fans. Kauffman Stadium didn't have a dedicated players' entrance, either—the Royals were kind enough to set up a few flimsy ropes to separate us from the fans. As we walked from our bus into the ballpark, people were yelling and screaming and berating us, making us feel about as unwelcome as possible. It was a hell of an introduction to what the World Series was going to be.

||||||||||||||

One upside of our NLCS sweep was that it allowed Collins to line up the rotation how he wanted. That meant giving the Game 1 ball to Matt Harvey, a first-round draft pick who had burst into New York City's consciousness with a dynamic All-Star season in 2013. Matt blew out his elbow toward the end of that campaign and didn't return until 2015. When he did, he resumed his place as one of the best pitchers in baseball, going 13-8 with a 2.71 ERA during the regular season.

He was confident and brash, having spent most of his life dominating on the mound.

The problem that month was Matt's innings total. In an era when pitchers were throwing harder than ever, resulting in escalating injury rates, baseball was struggling to keep some of its best players healthy. Theories abounded, but one thing most doctors and executives agreed on was the need to limit pitcher workloads after Tommy John surgery.

Early in September, as it became increasingly clear that we were heading to the playoffs, Matt—sitting on 166⅓ innings and counting in his first year back from Tommy John—told reporters he considered 180 his limit. He refused to answer questions about his postseason availability, leading to a days-long story in which everyone tried to figure out if he was going to pitch in October. We were in Miami at the time, playing a three-game series that Matt wasn't scheduled to appear in. I also sat out the Sunday afternoon finale to rest my back, so I used the opportunity to sidle up next to Matt on the dugout bench.

Some people didn't think I had the greatest relationship with Matt, probably because we were opposites in a lot of ways. I was married, getting ready to start a family. Matt was single, looking to enjoy different aspects of what New York had to offer. Whereas I tended to shy away from the celebrity element of playing professional baseball, Matt took to fame in a way I never did. He also earned a superhero nickname, in his case "the Dark Knight," which seemed to increase his status as a budding superstar. He tended to put himself in tough situations, like when he missed our team workout at Citi Field before NLDS Game 1. The New York tabloids and talk-radio hosts jumped on that sort of stuff, turning him into a pseudo-villain.

The reality is I had a great relationship with Matt. During spring training, he rented the house next door to mine. I regularly hosted cookouts and Matt was always among those who came to grill out, to relax, to talk about baseball and life. I felt comfortable discussing anything with him. On those occasions when Matt got in trouble, I explained to him how important he was to our success and how critical he was as a role model to younger guys like Syndergaard and Steven Matz. He had the ability to shape those players into the next Matt Harveys, but to do it, he needed to lead by example.

Matt was always quick to apologize when he messed up. At times, I criticized him publicly to get across a message, but I think he respected that I never went behind his back. I never said things to the media that I wasn't willing to say to his face. The only reason I said those things at all was because I wanted him to be a leader, which is a big part of why I felt I needed to bring up the topic of his innings limit. It seemed like he was really wrestling with the issue.

"I get it," I told him that afternoon in Miami. "I truly do. You're coming off Tommy John surgery and you have a bright future ahead of you. Obviously, I want you to pitch because we've got a good opportunity here, but I'm going to give you the pros and cons of both sides."

We spent several innings ticking through them. I understood the checkered prognosis for guys eclipsing two hundred innings in their first seasons back from Tommy John surgery, which Matt risked doing if he pitched in the postseason. I also understood we had a real chance to accomplish something special as a team, and we needed Harvey there to do it. For about half the game on the dugout bench, we talked through various scenarios. I urged Matt to do as much research as he could about the two-hundred-inning mark. I told him I understood his need to look out for his financial future. And yet, as he bounced ideas off me, I challenged him to think about his legacy, the team's legacy, the idea of winning in New York and becoming a legend.

While I'm not sure how much difference the conversation made, Matt ultimately decided to keep pitching, going 2-0 over the first two rounds of the postseason. He was dynamic, throwing in the upper 90s, burning passionately to win—the Matt of old. For that, I'll always be thankful. We wouldn't have reached the place we did that year without Harvey on the mound every fifth game. No chance. In my eyes, what Matt accomplished coming off Tommy John surgery was the second-most impressive pitching season I ever witnessed in my career, right behind deGrom's 2018 Cy Young campaign.

That's not something I say lightly, given the caliber of pitchers I played behind. What Matt did in carrying me and a lot of other guys to the World Series was so impactful on a personal level. Even if his road was turbulent, we owed him a debt of gratitude for traveling it.

|||||||||||||

It wasn't Harvey's fault that we lost World Series Game 1; I pinned that one squarely on myself and the offense. Harvey delivered a quality start, putting us in position to take a 4–3 lead on an eighth-inning error. But Alex Gordon hit a game-tying home run off Jeurys Familia in the ninth, and our offense couldn't touch the Royals' potent bullpen in extra innings. We simply gave them too many chances. Our own bullpen also pitched well, but an error, a hit, and an Eric Hosmer sacrifice fly finally sank us in the fourteenth inning.

Even if it didn't end the way I wanted, that night was the culmination of a dream for me. I was proud to be playing in a World Series, proud to stand on the third-base line as the Kauffman Stadium PA announcer introduced the New York Mets. Losing Game 1 only intensified my resolve to win the whole thing.

The next night, we mustered two hits in nine innings against Johnny Cueto to fall behind the Royals two games to none. As a team, our fears of coming out rusty seemed warranted. Personally,

I was struggling to gain any momentum at the plate in October, which I chalked up more to Kershaw, Greinke, and Arrieta bottling me up than to anything involving my back. After my two-run single off Báez in NLDS Game 1, I hit .158 with two extra-base hits in my next forty-six plate appearances. The hits I did get at least tended to be big ones.

Given all that, I didn't take it personally when some of the talk between games revolved around the Mets' potentially benching me. I knew I was in a place where I could do damage, and I knew Collins had faith in me. So I just went through my usual physical therapy and prepared as best I could for Yordano Ventura, the hardest-throwing starting pitcher in Kansas City's playoff rotation.

As a team, we understood that no matter how badly we were struggling, Citi Field was going to be humming for the first World Series game in ballpark history. The Mets hadn't been to the Fall Classic since 2000, the year before I was drafted, and hadn't won it since 1986. I knew the '86 Mets had also fallen behind in the World Series, 2-0, before roaring back to win in seven games. We did our best to feed off that history, telling ourselves: "We've still got this."

It wasn't just talk. Especially after grinding out a series win versus Kershaw, Greinke, and the Dodgers, we felt like we had a real chance against the Royals. The first task was to take care of business at home. That meant taking care of leadoff man Alcides Escobar, who was on fire swinging at first pitches that postseason. Feeling Escobar had grown a bit too comfortable in the box, Syndergaard opened Game 3 by knocking him to the dirt with a 98-mile-per-hour first-pitch fastball. The crowd went nuts.

People were still buzzing when I came to the plate with a man on base in the bottom of the first. As expected, Ventura opened me with a fastball, which I swung on top of and pulled foul. On paper, Ventura wasn't an ideal matchup for me, averaging 97 miles per hour with his fastball that postseason. But when he threw a 96-mile-per-hour heater in almost exactly the same spot as the first one, I jumped on it, meeting the ball with the sweet spot of my bat. Like my welcome-back homer in Philadelphia two months earlier, it was one of those rare shots that I knew was gone as soon as I hit it.

For a moment, I did something I never did, allowing myself to look up into the stands and soak in the moment as much as possible. Even before the ball landed over the left-field fence, people were screaming, high-fiving, holding up signs, going crazy. I felt weightless rounding the bases. Glancing behind home plate, I saw my wife, parents, and brothers sitting in the Wright family seats, as thrilled as anyone in the park. In the midst of all that Citi Field bedlam, time slowed. I became hyperaware of everything going on around me.

*Remember this,* I thought.

Just like that, the stress of trailing in the World Series melted away. The stress of my interminable rehab program vanished. Any pain I might have been feeling no longer seemed to bother me. I had just hit a home run in the freaking World Series. I was locked into that moment.

Crossing home plate, I almost bowled over Murphy and Yoenis Céspedes with high fives. I felt like I floated from one end of the dugout to the other, slapping every hand that popped up in front of me. Above, I could hear the thunder of the crowd.

Over the first decade of my career, I probably spent a little too much time looking toward the next big thing, the next big challenge, always worrying about tomorrow. Never being satisfied was part of what allowed me to become the player I did, but for those few minutes of Game 3, I let myself forget about the next inning, the next at-bat. I will never ever forget that home run. I will never ever forget how I felt in that moment. It's something I will hold close to me for the rest of my life.

On one of my early days as a minor leaguer, I scribbled down a famous quotation painted on a wall in the Mets' spring clubhouse: "If what you did yesterday still looks big today, you haven't done much today." Each time I advanced to a new level, I hung those fourteen words in my locker, always trying to abide by them. That's why I almost never reveled in accomplishments as they were taking place. My mind was always looking forward to what more I could do.

But as I rounded the bases in World Series Game 3, having been through so much, having wanted this for so long, I allowed myself to get caught up in the moment and just really, really enjoy it as it was happening.

||||||||||||||

Later that game, I punched a two-run single into center field to seal our victory. It wound up being our only win of the series. We dropped another tough one in Game 4, giving up three runs in the eighth, before Harvey's eight dominant innings in Game 5 seemed to save the Mets' season. With the Citi Field crowd chanting Matt's name, I watched him walk off the field after the eighth with this intense determination in his eyes, and I knew right then that

Collins would let him go back out for the ninth. Collins absolutely made the right decision in relenting, but the Royals managed to tie the game off Matt and Jeurys Familia. They won it in twelve innings, celebrating on our field as our fans went home unhappy.

If the greatest thing to happen to me on a baseball field was to play in a World Series, then the worst thing was to lose it. I found myself reflecting once again upon how rarely those opportunities occur. Throughout 2015, I had faced my own baseball mortality. My back injury forced me, whether I was ready to or not, to acknowledge that my years as a big leaguer might be numbered. And I hadn't accomplished what I'd set out to.

The only solace was that my injury also gave me perspective. As much as the loss hurt, I felt so proud and thankful to be a small part of that October. In mid-July, the Mets had no business even sniffing the playoffs, but they played hard and stayed focused, reaching a better place because of it. I burned to win—make no mistake about it. Given what I had gone through physically, I worried that this might have been my last real chance to win a World Series. But in a way, given both my injury situation and the way in which the Mets rose from the dead, everything that happened from August through September felt like playing with house money. We took those chips and came within a few tough breaks of being the best team in baseball.

So, after Game 5, I didn't pout. Instead, I went around the room and shook everyone's hand. I thanked Céspedes for the historic way he led our offense, especially at a time when I wasn't much help. I thanked Kelly Johnson and Juan Uribe for not complaining when I cut into their playing time. I thanked Michael Cuddyer, one of my best friends, not only for gracefully ceding some of his own playing time to Michael Conforto but for doing everything in his power to help the younger player succeed. I thanked Harvey for putting aside his personal concerns to lead our pitching staff in October. People love to throw blame around when things don't go their way, but I had only warm feelings for my teammates and coaches. Those guys allowed me to fulfill a lifetime dream, playing in my first World Series. It was their dream, too. Without pulling together as a team, we never would have made it.

For a long time that night, I stayed in uniform, standing in front of my locker to answer question after question before the media finally ran out of things to ask. Leaving would have meant acknowledging the start of the off-season, so I wasn't eager to drive away from Citi Field anyway. No one was in a hurry to go home that night. After the initial commotion of the loss died down, Collins gathered everyone together and addressed the team, thanking us for everything we'd accomplished. I asked to speak next.

"Let's treat our off-season like we don't want this to be the pinnacle of our careers," I told the guys. "Let's not let going to the World Series and losing it be the best thing to happen to us. Let's use this as motivation."

My speech ended with another heartfelt thank-you. I meant it. To this day, thinking about 2015 brings a smile to my face. I can't put into words how much it means to me that in my personal collection is a National League championship ring.

# BACK, NECK, SHOULDER

ive short months after our World Series loss to the Royals, we opened the 2016 season with a two-game rematch in Kansas City. It was my twelfth consecutive Opening Day start for the Mets, setting a franchise record for the longest streak in history. At least some of my pride in that record stemmed not from the streak itself but from the fact that I was starting Opening Day less than a year after my back diagnosis. Every opportunity to step on the field became more of a blessing.

Each step literally was also more challenging than ever. In the sixth inning of a two-run game, Eric Hosmer—the Royals' cleanup hitter, of all people—dropped a bunt down the third-base line to catch me off guard. Playing deep to respect Hosmer's opposite-field ability, I rushed in, grabbed the ball, and fired sidearm to first base. Due to the element of surprise, Hosmer stood a decent chance of being safe no matter what. But the throw didn't have much oomph on it, exposing me to questions after an 0-for-4, two-strikeout game. Was my arm okay? Could I be the same type of defensive player despite spending months on the sideline, unable to lift weights or do baseball activities? Could I be the same type of player in general?

Personally, I believed I could do all of it despite my physical issues. That didn't mean it would be easy. My 2015 return was unique because it occurred on a first-place team using an expanded roster. I could take as many days off as I needed without hurting the club. Postseason play was similar thanks to all the built-in off days. I knew the training wheels would come off in April, when we returned to the grind of a 162-game National League season. If I planned to be a regular player again—i.e., not on the disabled list— I was going to need to take the field often.

Talking things over with my doctors, my trainers, Terry Collins, and Sandy Alderson, we settled on 120 games as a reasonable expectation. That meant playing, essentially, in three games out of every four.

We also agreed to take things easy during spring training, considering I spent most of the winter doing physical therapy instead of baseball activities. Rather than make my Grapefruit League debut five weeks before Opening Day like most of my teammates, I remained sidelined until sixteen days before the opener. All told, I logged only fifty-five defensive innings at third base that spring, spending as much time off my feet as possible. No doubt, the rest helped my back. But all that time off also affected me as a player.

My frustration stemmed not necessarily from my back pain, which I had learned how to semi-manage, but from the limitations it forced me to accept. Because of my stenosis, I couldn't do cardio or lift weights the way I wanted. I couldn't take as many swings or ground balls as I preferred. Following the World Series, I didn't take any time off, maintaining an in-season rehab schedule as I tried to reduce my pain levels. None of it helped me get bigger, faster, stronger. Long gone were those sweat-soaked off-seasons with Piney, bulking up and trying to become the most dominant player I could be. Long gone were the sprints up and down Mount Trashmore with my brothers. All physical therapy was doing was giving me the best chance to manage my pain.

For years I had grown accustomed to waking up, rolling out of bed, and heading to the cage, the field, or the gym to work. I prided myself on putting in as many hours as I could. That off-season, I couldn't do it. My body badly needed rest and, for the first time in my career, I had no choice but to comply.

Understanding I was a diminished version of my old self, I found it frustrating to see teams notice and try to take advantage of that. It began with the steady diet of fastballs pitchers fed me down the stretch in 2015. It continued with plays like Hosmer's bunt in Kansas City, designed to test my arm strength and defensive range. I'd like to think that if a cleanup hitter had tried to bunt on me earlier in my career, I'd have grabbed the ball, dusted it off, and thrown behind my back to first base. Bare-handed bunt plays were supposed to be my specialty. Suddenly, simple stuff like that wasn't so simple.

My mind hadn't entirely caught on to what was happening. *You're still the player you've always been,* it kept telling me. My body disagreed. *Take a few steps back. This is the player you are now.*

After the 2016 opener in Kansas City, I at least began to see some results, batting .271 with four home runs and a .909 OPS over my next twenty-three games. It probably seemed like I had settled into a routine, playing roughly four out of every five games while hitting for some power, drawing some walks, occasionally even stealing a base. But body parts ached on a constant basis. In addition to my back, my shoulder felt weak, as Dr. Watkins had anticipated. I was also feeling some unexpected neck pain; most mornings that spring, I woke up feeling like I had slept the wrong way.

On days I played, I continued to show up to the park three hours before the rest of my teammates. On days I didn't, I was a cheerleader, resting my body as much as possible.

During one of those rest days, May 23, I sat in the dugout as the Mets fell behind by a run in Colorado. Even though Rockies closer Jake McGee was a hard-throwing lefty, the exact type of pitcher I had historically hit well against, Terry Collins was preparing someone else to pinch-hit for the pitcher in the ninth. To me, that seemed ridiculous. If I couldn't help the team in a situation tailor-made for my skill set, then I probably shouldn't be on the roster at all. Finding Collins in the dugout, I urged him to let me hit. We both knew I wouldn't be able to complete anything close to my full warmup routine, but the Mets were in a tight game and my competitive juices were flowing. I told Collins I could take a couple quick swings off a tee and figure out the rest on the fly.

As committed as Collins was to giving me my scheduled day off, I kept pressuring him until he relented. When he did, I scrambled into action, doing some quick back stretches and taking swings in the cage. A few minutes later, I grounded into a game-ending force out.

The result was disappointing, but that sort of thing happens. What I didn't anticipate was waking up the next morning in so much pain that I needed two more rest days just to return to the field.

I never really got healthy. About a week later, despite homering against the Nationals, my back and neck continued to ache. I took another day off and homered again on May 25, which only disguised the fact that my neck was increasingly becoming a problem. Following a team off day, I played on May 27 and homered yet again. Things deteriorated from there. By my final at-bat that game, I couldn't even turn to look at the pitcher. I struck out looking, swinging at none of the six pitches I saw.

At that point, I had no choice but to say something, setting a familiar sequence of events into action: another trip to the Hospital for Special Surgery, another MRI, another anti-inflammatory injection, another murky prognosis. Tests revealed a herniated disc in my neck, which was difficult to hear. For over a year, I had focused most of my mental and physical energy on my back. Slowly, my shoulder was becoming a problem. Now my neck was an issue, too?

Dr. Altchek initially hoped I might be able to rehab it, recommending rest and anti-inflammatory injections, all while knowing surgery loomed as a threat. We sent the results to Dr. Watkins in

California, but Memorial Day weekend caused a delay in process-
ing them. A day or two later, I returned to the clubhouse after a
game to find a voice mail from Dr. Watkins, who was concerned
enough that he wanted to see me in person.

My wife, Molly, was seven months pregnant with our first child,
so it pained me to leave her alone in New York even for a few days.
I told myself I'd head out to Los Angeles for a night or two, Dr.
Watkins would fix my neck, and I'd fly back home, good as new. Of
course, a part of me braced myself for something worse.

It arrived in the form of Watkins's telling me I needed surgery.
Immediately. Playing baseball with my specific type of herniation,
Dr. Watkins said, put me at risk of doing further damage to my
spine. I was crushed. Stunned. Considering the goal I had of appearing in 120 games, this seemed like a worst-case scenario.

When I called Molly to relay the news, she broke down in tears,
more nervous for me than for herself. I was nervous, too. Never in
my life had I undergone surgery. I wasn't sure what the recovery
would be like, how long it would take, how much I would be able to
help Molly once the baby arrived. Dr. Watkins said I wouldn't be
able to lift anything heavier than ten pounds for two weeks after the
operation. There were so many unknowns, so many stressors, without even considering what it might mean for the rest of my baseball
career.

As Dr. Watkins and I planned the operation, trying our best to
work around Molly's due date, he laid out two options. One was a
newer procedure similar to a knee or hip replacement, in which he
would insert an artificial disc into my neck. It sounded promising,
but the research associated with it was limited—I would have been

the first high-performance athlete in a contact sport to undergo the surgery. The other was an old-school fusion, requiring Watkins to go in through the front of my neck and push aside my throat to access my spine.

Sounds fun, right? These were major, major operations. Neither choice promised to be simple. There I was, alone in Los Angeles, scared to death, feeling completely on an island as I made a major decision about my career and long-term health.

Because Watkins saw benefits to both operations, we spent several days debating. That week, one of the pioneering doctors for the disc replacement method happened to be giving a talk at a nearby university. Not only did Dr. Watkins attend the conference on my behalf, he stuck around afterward to grill the guy about the long-term prognosis for a baseball player.

Dr. Watkins knew that, even in nonathletes, the newer surgery had a history of failure. He worried that the artificial disc might wear out over time, or possibly even snap under the wrong conditions. Finally, he understood we had little margin for error; if my operation failed, my career would end. From his colleague, Dr. Watkins gleaned enough information to recommend the fusion, which gave me a 90 percent chance to return with only a 5 percent loss of range of motion in my neck.

I consulted with the Mets and others on what to expect, even reaching out to Braves outfielder Nick Markakis, who had come back strong after a similar surgery in 2014. Everyone was optimistic. That was the hope—that I, too, could return to the field in months, not years. Molly was too far along in her pregnancy to fly, so my parents came out to Los Angeles to help me through the recovery.

The operation required Dr. Watkins's team to insert all sorts of metal into my neck, including a cage containing bone marrow from my hip and screws to hold it all together. Surgeons removed bone fragments and the herniated disc, relocating a nerve in the process.

One of them had told me I might wake up with a bit of a sore throat. Big understatement. For about ten days after the operation, I had trouble swallowing, forcing me to subsist on smoothies and soup. I couldn't really move my neck muscles, to the extent that I had to call my parents each morning for help getting out of bed. Affixed to my neck was a brace plus a large bandage just beneath my Adam's apple—nice fashion statement, I know. Unable to shave due to all the sensitivity, I grew a beard instead. This was serious stuff: Doctors told me if I sneezed the wrong way, I could do damage.

The one benefit was that my rehab didn't require the same type of constant supervision as my back rehab, which allowed me to fly home to a very pregnant wife about a week after the operation. The first day Dr. Watkins cleared me to return to Citi Field, I asked Jacob deGrom for a ride to the stadium because we lived in the same building. Wearing my brace, I instructed deGrom to take it slow, drilling home the point that any unexpected movement could hurt my still-tender neck.

"Dude, I'm serious," I told deGrom, fearing he might take my insistence as a joke. "Drive carefully."

He may have taken my orders a little *too* seriously, crawling up FDR Drive at 20 miles per hour with his hazard lights blinking. Cars were zooming by, honking at us, and I'm sure a few of them recognized deGrom with his distinctive shoulder-length hair. That didn't stop them from cursing out the former National League Rookie of the Year. DeGrom was doing it to make fun of me, but I'm pretty sure that's actually how he learned to drive where he's from in Central Florida.

By some miracle, we did make it to Citi Field before game time, which was an experience in itself. Even though I was back around the team, it didn't feel normal. Out of concern that a foul ball might slice into the dugout, forcing me to dive out of the way and jerk my neck, my doctors mandated that I watch games from the bullpen. So I sat out there with a different perspective both literally and figuratively, feeling detached.

The good news was that the Mets were a handful of games above .500, very much back in playoff contention. The bad news was that I had no idea if I'd return to be a part of it. Fans and media wondered as well, but there wasn't much I could tell them. I didn't have a great answer as far as my timetable. The problem was not just my neck, which I knew would heal, but the spinal stenosis that lurked below it. Each day that passed was another day I was unable to do my regular back rehab exercises, let alone the types of baseball activities I'd eventually need to conquer to return to the field. I didn't know how my body might respond once I ramped up again.

It wasn't the most comfortable thing in the world to consider, knowing the road ahead was sure to be painful. Shortly after I returned to Citi Field, a reporter asked me if it was all worth it.

That one, at least, was easy to answer.

"You know the risk of doing anything physically for a living, but it's something that I love to do," I said. "If you told me you'd have to have a neck surgery, you'd have some back issues, hell, I'd do it all

over again because I enjoy what I do. And I plan on continuing to
enjoy what I do."

IIIIIIIIIIIII

The toughest days, at least mentally, were when the Mets were on
the road. Thankfully, my wife helped with that. Each morning, I
checked in at the Hospital for Special Surgery around nine A.M.,
completed my regimen with a physical therapist named Terrance
Sgroi, came home, then had the rest of the afternoon completely
free with Molly.

To fill the time, we walked.

Walking was the only cardiovascular exercise my doctors allowed, as well as something Molly's obstetrician encouraged her to
do during her pregnancy. So the two of us—me in my neck brace,
Molly in her third trimester—frequently wandered for miles
around the city. Depending on the day, we would walk up through
Central Park, or around the reservoir, or across the Upper West
Side, or down to Battery Park and the Financial District. We would
go wherever the mood happened to take us. For years, I had spent
summers (and sometimes winters) in New York, but always with so
many responsibilities cutting into my time. Walking around while
recovering from neck surgery allowed me to see my adopted city
with new eyes. Molly and I went to museums, tried new restaurants,
explored neighborhoods that we didn't know well, and so much else.
It provided a sense of peace during what was otherwise a trying
time for me.

As the weeks and months passed in that fashion, it became clear that I wasn't going to get back on the field in 2016—the physical obstacles stacked against me were simply too great to overcome. As much as that sucked, I tried to stay confident, never allowing myself to consider failure as an option. I thought about how I'd played after returning in 2015, batting .277, then coming up with some big postseason hits despite not being at my best. If I could return from four months of rehab to accomplish all that, surely I could achieve even more with neck surgery behind me and a full, healthy off-season under my belt.

Looking back, my mindset was probably foolish (or foolishly optimistic), but that's the way it had to be in the face of tough odds. I had this idea in my head that if I kept working hard and sticking to my routine, I would wake up one day and everything would feel good again. Like magic, I would be fixed. I would be normal. I tricked myself into believing it.

The only thing I could control was how hard I worked, so I buried myself in that pursuit. All the hours I had put into becoming a big leaguer? All the sacrifices I had made to stay in the league, then to become an All-Star and captain? I was going to have to do it all over again, staying as disciplined as ever during every rehab exercise, just to give myself a chance to return to the field. Shuttling back and forth from my Manhattan apartment to the Hospital for Special Surgery during that time, I wasn't even considering being an All-Star–caliber player. I was thinking about survival.

By the end of 2016, my career seemed so delicate. As confident as I was that I could return, I could see the window closing.

||||||||||

# TWENTY-THREE

# LAST CHANCE

The most difficult part about my 2016 neck surgery was that when the doctors cut into me, they had no choice but to literally touch a nerve.

The human body features a nerve running from the neck to the shoulder that, if poked by an outside force, can essentially shut down. Due to the nature of my surgery, the doctors needed to move it to access my spine. They hoped it wouldn't react poorly, but that's exactly what happened as I ramped up baseball activities the following spring. Despite a full winter of physical therapy and rehab, I entered 2017 unable to throw with any real strength.

This situation was far worse than the previous April, when Eric Hosmer had tested me with a bunt in Kansas City. In addition to the nerve issue, I was still battling stenosis, which weakened my core and, in turn, my shoulder. Each new issue affected the ones already in place. It felt like I was pushing hard uphill, unable to make any real progress.

The Mets kept me out of regular team workouts, setting up a program that involved physical therapy for my neck and back, plus lots of strengthening exercises for my shoulder. I spent most of my days indoors, away from teammates, who were busy taking batting practice and doing defensive drills. At one point, I tried a throwing program, which yielded embarrassing results. In addition to the knifing pain in my shoulder, everything felt so mechanical, almost like I was throwing left-handed. I had to relearn how to do everything, giving myself the same kind of advice I would eventually give my children when they first learned to throw. One of the simplest actions for a baseball player had become physically too much for me to handle.

At the end of March, the team broke camp without me for the first time in thirteen years. Officially, the Mets placed me on the disabled list with a right shoulder impingement, but so many things pained me at that point—my back, my neck, my shoulder—that they could have said anything. I stayed behind in Port St. Lucie to continue my program indefinitely, spending a summer there for the first time since I was in Class A ball.

St. Lucie is a great place, but as any rehabbing Met can tell you, it's not where you want to be from April through September. Once the spring training carnival ships out of town, it can be lonely. It can be frustrating. The days that summer were hot and humid, filled with sweaty, monotonous rehab work. More dead bugs than I could count. More resistance-band reps than I could possibly remember. Hours upon hours upon hours spent at the field. As much as I had grown accustomed to that program, it never became fun. Most evenings, I met up with my longtime friends, St. Lucie Mets executives Paul Taglieri and Traer Van Allen, to eat and watch the big-league game on TV. Throughout the long summer, those nights became important for my sanity.

My doctors told me I would eventually need surgeries on both my shoulder and back, but I put them off as long as possible, knowing the operations would destroy any chance I had to play that year. Instead, I strengthened my core and shoulder until I couldn't really do anything more. I didn't feel good at that point—far from it. I just felt like I had reached the end of the road for all that rehab stuff. By late August, it was time to test out my body in games. I needed to know if it could still take the abuse of nine innings, and the only way to answer that question was to play.

It didn't go well; in three games for St. Lucie, I went 1-for-10 with five strikeouts. My shoulder felt so small and weak.

My agent Keith Miller had driven up to watch the last of those games. I was scheduled to play only five innings at third base, so when I returned to the clubhouse midway through the game, Millsy met me inside. He pulled up a stool next to my locker.

"What did you think?" I asked him.

"What did *you* think?" he replied.

"I think I looked like someone who needs shoulder and back surgery," I said.

There was no use sugarcoating anything for Millsy, who could always see through my overly positive airs and bring me back down to reality. Watching me play that week, Millsy saw a guy who could barely lift his shoulder. He saw a guy who just couldn't do the things he used to do. Millsy wasn't ever going to say that to me outright, but he had a way of helping me see it myself. As the game played out a few dozen feet away from us, Millsy and I sat on those clubhouse stools for about half an hour, just talking things out. By the end of the conversation, I knew continuing to rehab was pointless. The next morning, I called Sandy Alderson to shut things down for the season.

Without a realistic path back to the field in 2017, my next move was to fly to Cincinnati to talk with shoulder specialist Dr. Timothy Kremchek, who recommended surgery to repair my rotator cuff. At that point, there was no reason to avoid it, so I doubled back to New York to have Dr. Altchek perform the operation. I felt like a nomad. From the time Dr. Altchek diagnosed me with spinal stenosis in 2015 through the end of my playing career, I crisscrossed the country on a regular basis, flying from New York to Los Angeles to Florida to Cincinnati to New York, and so on and so forth. I spent more time in hotels than I'd care to admit. I spent depressingly little time around the Mets. I'd be lying if I said doubts didn't creep in about my career, doubts that felt more real to me than any I'd had before.

What helped me through that time was family. In July, my daughter Olivia Shea celebrated her first birthday. (Yes, we gave her the middle name as a tribute to Shea Stadium. I'll always have a place in my heart for the ballpark I once called home.) A little less than two years later, Molly gave birth to another girl, Madison. My growing family provided not only a much-needed distraction from the grind of rehab but also some perspective. At a point when the end of my career was staring me in the face, I didn't have to fear life after baseball. I knew with my wife and two daughters there to support me, along with my parents, brothers, in-laws, and friends, I had wonderful things waiting for me.

I just wasn't ready to begin that chapter quite yet.

|||||||||||||||

Staring at another winter of rest and rehab following a 2017 season that never got going, I elected to undergo a third surgery in seventeen months: a laminotomy, a procedure designed to relieve pressure in my spinal canal. Dr. Watkins carved me open again to remove bone spurs, a ligament, and a herniated disc from my back, which did make me feel better. But that surgery was designed more for my future quality of life than anything; while it would help with the pain, I knew it wasn't going to have a significant effect on my ability to return to the field.

More and more, I was questioning whether I could do so. Early in the summer of 2018, the Mets cleared me to restart baseball activities. I felt like I was picking up a ball for the first time in my life. Three of the five throws I made that day sailed well wide of the target. I had this idea that throwing a baseball should be like riding a bike, which was so obviously wrong. Not a second of my experience felt natural.

Each morning, I woke up and tested my neck, my back, my shoulder, to see which of them would be the issue. Some days were good—just a dull ache somewhere. Others, I literally had to roll out of bed because I couldn't sit up straight. The pain started to affect my everyday life, knifing through me when I tried to pick Olivia up out of her crib. One morning, I asked Molly to tie my shoes because I couldn't bend over to do it myself. I learned later that I had torn the lining of a disc in my back. Nothing major, just another few days of crushing pain to endure.

I tried everything. Pilates. Massages. Chiropractors. Jacuzzis. At one point, my wife bought a back stretcher off an infomercial, just to see if it would bring some relief. Most of that stuff helped a little, but nothing was permanent. People close to me began questioning my sanity, urging me to reevaluate my situation, hinting that maybe I should call it a career. They all meant well, worrying about my long-term health and life after baseball, but I found it so difficult to silence the little voice inside my head saying, *Maybe I can still play. Maybe if I can get back to the big leagues, adrenaline will take over and I'll feel better. This doesn't have to be the end.*

It was all wishful thinking; eventually, I realized I was going to have to either play through severe discomfort or retire. I couldn't wait for the pain to diminish because it wasn't going to. Ever. I was thirty-five, more than two years removed from my last big league game. I had gone as far as my body would let me. Of course I hated that the end had come so quickly, robbing me of what should have been the later stages of my prime, but sitting there whining about it wasn't going to do me any good. So I did what any normal person would do: I began ramping up baseball activities in the hopes of taking one last crack at a return. I couldn't entertain the thought of retiring unless I knew, without a doubt, that I had followed every possible path to the end.

I don't love to admit this, but I wasn't always completely honest with the Mets during that 2018 season. I told them what I needed them to know so that I could receive the proper treatment for my back, neck, and shoulder. Had I said more—had they known the type of pain I was really going through—they would have shut me down in an instant. I couldn't let that happen. As far as the Mets knew, I was feeling okay, doing my best to check off the benchmarks they had established for me. For the team to let me go on another rehab assignment, I needed to do things like face live pitching and perform advanced defensive work. I sacrificed my body, gritting my teeth through pain as I ticked off each item.

My idea was to spend around three weeks in the minors and, if my back responded well enough, return to the Mets once rosters expanded in September. But I was a mess. My first five games for Class A St. Lucie, I went 0-for-14 with six strikeouts. My strength had evaporated. My bat speed was gone. I couldn't play back-to-back games at third base without succumbing to pain. Simply put, I just wasn't a major league player.

During that assignment, the Mets gave me another checklist of accomplishments to complete. I quickly became more concerned with hitting those benchmarks than with playing good baseball. My goal at third base was to avoid diving, because one sharp movement could put me out of commission for days. I silently begged batters not to hit the ball to me. At the plate, I prayed for contact, knowing swinging and missing could send me through the roof with pain.

One day, Keith Miller drove from West Palm Beach to Port St. Lucie to watch me take another lackluster round of batting practice. Millsy had been by my side from the beginning, meeting me as a teenager and advising me at every step along the way. Outside of my coaches, he knew my swing better than anyone. Outside of my family, he knew my heart best. So Millsy certainly understood the train wreck he was seeing that day in Port St. Lucie. Afterward, he approached me.

"Dude," he said. "Are you okay?"

I assured him I was fine, even though it was clear to both of us that I wasn't. I just wasn't ready to give up. I couldn't give up. My only path to the majors was forward, so I continued to grind, dragging myself to the field, managing to go 6-for-18 over my next five games. The numbers looked so, so much better than how I felt. They allowed me to fool everyone a little bit longer, but I knew I couldn't keep playing that game.

I talked things over with Molly, who was my rock throughout the whole ordeal, and my parents, who had been a steady source of advice during my career. We all agreed that I had to come clean. When I called Millsy to admit that, no, I was not fine, it was an emotional release for me. We had the first of several heart-to-hearts about my situation, as I began to wrap my mind around the idea of retirement.

I still waited to tell the Mets, knowing they were on the verge of activating me. I had put in so much work and, despite the pain, was so close to my goal of returning to the majors. I felt like I owed it to myself to make one last attempt, so I stuck to the rehab plan, flying out to Triple-A Las Vegas with less than a week left in August. I needed to play back-to-back nine-inning games for the Mets to consider activating me, and my first night there, Drew Gagnon threw a shutout in two hours, six minutes. That was a freaking blessing. Standing at third base, I was in agony. How I managed to make it through that night and the next, I'm really not sure. I just knew this couldn't continue. Had Gagnon not thrown the gem he did, I might have had no choice but to take myself out of the game.

That Las Vegas experience forced me to accept reality. For the first time in my life, I wasn't enjoying baseball games. I was surviving them, which wasn't how I ever wanted to play. As I came to that realization, I finally became willing to admit that the pain was overwhelming me. I finally became willing to accept that I couldn't continue. A strange sort of peace settled over me once I knew I had done everything possible to extend my career. My mind, heart, and body were all on the same page.

Preparing to give up the game I had loved since childhood was still a massive decision. Baseball had dominated my existence from the moment I was old enough to know what it was. I had spent almost half my life playing professionally. It was heartbreaking to put that aside. I badly wanted a sense of closure.

Before leaving Vegas, I shared a meal at the Wynn with Millsy, who had flown out for the games. He also seemed relieved to hear my decision, knowing I was no longer doing anyone any good. We agreed that I had to be honest with the Mets about how I felt, because it was unfair to keep them in the dark as they tried to plan their short- and long-term future. During that conversation, I told Millsy I wanted to find a way, if at all possible, to get back into uniform one last time. I had worked too hard, for too long, to fall just short of my goal. I knew my body couldn't handle a full major league workload. I knew I couldn't really contribute. Selfishly, though, I still wanted one last chance to step in front of the fans in Queens.

I had played for thirteen seasons, giving so much of myself to

the team and the game. It felt right to go out with one last moment
under the lights.

||||||||||||||

The next morning, I flew to San Francisco to join the Mets as scheduled. When I arrived, I asked to meet privately with Omar Minaya
and J. P. Ricciardi, the ranking front-office executives on the trip.
There, in the visiting manager's office at AT&T Park, I unspooled
emotionally. I felt an enormous weight lift off me as I described how
I was feeling, for the first time, to people outside my innermost
circle. People with the power to take action regarding my career. As
expected, Omar and J.P. alerted Mets owner Jeff Wilpon and GM
Sandy Alderson, who flew out to meet the team in Los Angeles. I
took the team charter down to meet them.

Sitting in the visiting manager's office with Jeff at Dodger Stadium, I had to hold my legs to stop them from shaking. I had known
Jeff for the better part of two decades. He was like family to me. The
entire Wilpon family was, from Fred, who had let me tag along on
his private jet after my grandmother's passing; to his wife, Judy, who
gave me advice when I was looking into adopting a golden retriever
after my retirement; to Jeff and his kids, who had grown up alongside me in the Mets organization. I often get asked about my experience with the Wilpons, who owned the Mets throughout my entire
tenure as a player. I can only speak to the way they treated me. That
was with class, every step of the way.

I wanted Jeff to hear the truth from me, resulting in another
emotional breakdown as I described the pain I was feeling. With

tears staining my face, I relayed my request to play again before retiring, understanding what a big ask it was. I still had two years and $37 million left on my contract, much of which the Mets were recouping via insurance. Nonetheless, Jeff assured me he would do everything possible to get me back on the field. I never got involved in the financial details, because they didn't personally affect me much. My contract was guaranteed. But I knew it was something the Mets would have to square with their insurance company, and I was thankful they were willing to do so just to indulge my personal dream.

More than anything, I wanted to play baseball in front of my daughters, who had both been born after my last big league game in 2016. I wanted to thank the Mets fans who had rallied behind me from the day I was drafted in 2001. I wanted to acknowledge all the support I'd received over seventeen years in professional baseball.

As a group, we figured out the logistics. It made more sense for my final game to occur at night, given the hours of rehab and stretching I would need to prepare for it. The Mets had a ten-game road trip scheduled in the middle of September, followed by a three-game home series against the contending Braves. Knowing how far I was from approaching a major league skill level, I didn't want to do anything to undermine the integrity of Atlanta's playoff chase, even though we were out of contention. I also didn't want to play behind Jacob deGrom, who was closing in on his first National League Cy Young Award. If I committed some sort of defensive misplay to affect his stat line, I would never forgive myself.

Given all those stipulations, we penciled in my return for September 29 against the Marlins, on the second-to-last day of the season. When the Mets returned home in early September, we scheduled a press conference to reveal the plan to media members, who still thought I intended to make a fuller comeback.

As I prepared for that press conference, the finality of my career really started to set in for me. I had no idea what to say. Despite having weeks to write my address to the media, I came to the ball-park empty-handed. That was so unlike me. At my locker, I scribbled out the names of people to thank, sticking the paper into my back pocket. Then I holed up in the equipment room with bullpen catcher Dave Racaniello, whose career with the Mets had begun a few years before mine. The two of us sat there laughing and reminiscing, talking about everything we had been through together.

Because none of my teammates knew this was the end, I wanted to make sure a few of them heard it from me directly. I first approached José Reyes, who had rejoined the team as a free agent in 2016. My nerves were relatively unfrazzled at that point, but when I opened my mouth to tell him this was the end, I completely lost it. I was a blubbering mess as José wrapped me in a hug.

Still a bit shaken, I went over to deGrom, who had become one of my closest friends since he'd joined the team in 2014. That conversation went about the same way.

Finally, I called a meeting with the rest of the guys, many of whom I didn't know well because of how little time I had spent around the team in recent years. It didn't matter. My face was swollen. I literally couldn't talk. Between tears and sniffles, I think I managed to get out about a dozen words, none of which made all that much sense. Mostly, I tried to relay the news that this was it, that this was the end, that I physically couldn't play anymore. I suspect it was one of the worst speeches anyone in that room had ever heard.

I remember watching Mike Piazza grow emotional during his final appearance as a Met in 2005 and wondering why a future Hall of Famer like that, who had accomplished more than I could dream of, would be so sad at the end of his tenure. Fast-forward a decade and I finally understood. I had spent my entire life doing one thing, pouring so much time and effort into it and loving every piece of it—the good, the bad, the ugly, the wins, the losses, the laughs, the tears. To have that taken away was difficult to accept. The emotion of it hit me all at once.

I knew my press conference wasn't going to be pretty. So did Rac, who slipped a Gatorade towel into my back pocket as I headed out of the clubhouse. Most of my teammates beat me into the conference room, lining the walls to listen to my speech. I got through about a minute of it before my eyes grew wet again, especially as I thanked my teammates, friends, and family. I could barely choke out the names of my two daughters, Olivia and Madison, before moving on to a more general thank-you.

"I said it when I was a younger player and I'll say it again: I truly bleed orange and blue," I said. "And throughout this process, the love and the support and the respect from inside and outside the organization has meant the world to me. Thank you to everybody involved, and you'll never have any idea how much it means to me."

# TWENTY-FOUR

# A NIGHT TO REMEMBER

I awoke the morning of September 29, 2018, having barely slept. My anxiety was real, which surprised me. I hadn't been this nervous for my first professional game, my big league debut, or even the World Series. This was a new level I had never previously reached.

When I arrived at Citi Field for the final game of my career, dozens of fans were waiting outside the players' parking lot. What struck me more than anything was the graciousness of that group and others throughout the weekend. In the days leading up to it, fans stopped me on the sidewalk just to say they had tickets to my final game. Citi Field had sold out within hours of my tearful press conference. Realizing my career was this important for a generation of Mets fans was a difficult thing to wrap my head around.

All told, I spent about two weeks preparing, doing my usual hours of rehab exercises, stretching, and baseball activities. But everything had changed. No longer did those steps feel tedious. I almost relished the dead bugs and resistance-band work, knowing I had a finite amount of time left as a professional athlete. I went through every rep with renewed purpose. As much as the exercises were still physically painful, I was so grateful that the Mets were, in a small way, giving me a chance to go out on my own terms.

I was under no misconception that I would do anything special in my final game; I just wanted to make sure I didn't embarrass myself. During batting practice sessions, I felt like I had a hole in my bat, except for one afternoon when the Mets set me up with some live BP reps. Facing Tim Peterson, a rookie reliever trying to stay sharp because he wasn't getting much game action, I squared up a pitch and sent it probably a dozen rows up the right-center field seats. I couldn't believe it.

*Oh my God. I hit that good.*

It had been a long, long time since I had squared one up against a real pitcher like that. As a baseball player, I lived for the feeling of hitting a ball, hearing a satisfying crack, and knowing immediately that it was gone. Rediscovering that feeling after so long sparked something dormant within me.

It wound up being my last home run as a big leaguer.

Each time I did something at the ballpark, I made a little mental note of the fact that I might not do it again. Most of it was just the daily clubhouse nonsense I had taken for granted for so long—private jokes, Ping-Pong games, things like that. I developed a routine with Jacob deGrom, Steven Matz, Jay Bruce, Michael Conforto, and some other guys, showing up early to eat lunch together and play a few rounds of Pluck, the card game I had never seen anyone play outside a baseball clubhouse. We laughed, joked, talked. After the season, Dave Racaniello presented me with a book of pictures he took during those weeks, snapping away with his cell phone camera as the rest of us bonded. Those little moments were what I knew I'd miss most.

Thinking about the end, I tried not to get too emotional, but it was difficult to avoid. Guys I'd played with at various times throughout my life were reaching out, from Virginia Blasters buddies to minor league teammates to former members of that clubhouse card game. When I tagged along with the Mets on a trip to Boston in mid-September, one of my old World Baseball Classic teammates, Dustin Pedroia, presented me with a number 5 panel from the Fenway Park scoreboard. I couldn't believe how heavy it was. Later that week, ex–Phillies manager Charlie Manuel gave me a similar "NYM" panel from Citizens Bank Park, where I had enjoyed so much success over the years. Finally, my old Tidewater friend Ryan Zimmerman gifted me a Mets flag from the out-of-town collection at Nationals Park.

This may sound corny, but during those weeks, I spent so much time reminiscing. I felt like Kevin Costner in *For the Love of the Game*, mentally reconstructing my career as I prepared for that last at-bat, that last game, that last appearance on a major league field. Each day, the finality of it pressed against me a little more.

‖‖‖‖‖‖‖‖‖‖‖

I knew the night of my final game would affect me deeply, but at least I had plenty of time to prepare for it. Technically, I came off the DL earlier that week, joining the active roster for the first time since the May 2016 game when I couldn't turn my neck to face the pitcher. It had been twenty-eight months, more than two full years since my last big league appearance.

Leading up to the weekend, I talked through various scenarios with Mets officials. Understanding how physically and emotionally exhausting Saturday was going to be, I knew we couldn't plan anything more for Sunday. Someone suggested I pinch-hit Friday instead, as a way to squeeze a little extra out of the weekend. That seemed perfect. With limited time left as a big leaguer, I wanted to maximize the experience.

Our first-year manager, Mickey Callaway, told me I would be the first man off the bench that night, so I began stretching early to prepare my body for an appearance. All the while, I kept one eye on the scoreboard, knowing rookie starter Corey Oswalt was on a strict pitch count. He wasn't likely to bat more than once.

As much as the Mets tried to script things for my benefit, baseball is rarely neat and easy. A few minutes before the pitcher's spot came up in the fourth inning, I emerged from the dugout to a paralyzing ovation. Standing on the dugout step, then the on-deck circle, I felt physically nauseous, my mind spinning as the weight of the situation bore down on me. Before the game, deGrom had presented me with an engraved bottle of wine on behalf of the starting rotation. He'd tried to make a little speech but didn't do so well, stopping midsentence and shoving the gift into my hand.

"Here, just take this box," he'd said. Maybe it was the emotion getting to everyone, or maybe it was deGrom's 2.0 GPA at Stetson that wasn't letting him find the right words.

Whatever the case, luck was on my side. Kevin Plawecki grounded out to end the fourth inning, allowing me to regroup from the comfort of the dugout. By the time I reemerged in the on-deck circle, I had regained some composure. The competitor in me began to stir, worrying more about making contact than what was happening in the stands.

Blocking out the noise, I cycled through the warmup routine that had grown so familiar over fifteen seasons, then stepped to the plate. Given my physical limitations, I wasn't about to let a good pitch go by me, so I pounced when José Ureña threw a first-pitch fastball. The resulting groundout seemed like a significant victory. I'm not trying to be modest here: I was so far removed from major league shape that I was happy just to hit a pitch relatively hard.

With a sheepish look on my face, I jogged back to the dugout, waving an arm to the crowd. I was satisfied with the night.

|||||||||||||||

The crowd reaction to that pinch-hit appearance jacked me up so much that I barely slept. When I finally dragged myself out of bed early Saturday, I spent some time playing with my daughters, said goodbye to them and Molly, then left our apartment on Sixty-First and York for a David Wright greatest hits tour. First up was my usual coffee shop, the Coffee Inn, where I grabbed a toasted almond drip with a splash of almond milk. Next, I visited my favorite deli, Space Market, for a honey turkey sandwich with Swiss cheese, lettuce, tomato, onion, avocado, and honey mustard. Then I met up with Racaniello, who lived nearby and had been my carpool buddy for years. Because Rac is a terrible driver, I insisted on being the one behind the wheel. I was hyperaware of everything I did that morning, knowing each little action would be my last as a major league player.

My childhood idol turned big league teammate, Michael Cuddyer, mused that it would be like my wedding day all over again. I'd be the center of attention, the star of the show, and everything would be over in the blink of an eye. Friday's pinch-hit appearance had at least given me a frame of reference for what to expect, but Citi Field had only been about two-thirds full that night because the Mets hadn't publicly confirmed that I would appear in the game. Lots of people kept telling me how jam-packed the stadium would be on Saturday, but I honestly didn't believe it until Rac and I pulled up to the main security gate. Waiting there, hours before game time, were dozens of well-wishers. The support was breathtaking.

After signing autographs for that first wave of fans, I went through my usual routine of lunch and cards with the guys, then launched into my rehab exercises one last time. I paid special attention to how I felt putting on my uniform, knowing I would never do it again as a player. When the Mets lit up the scoreboard with a pregame montage of my career highlights, the crowd reaction was incredible. I couldn't stop grinning and bouncing up and down in the dugout as I waited to take the field. When I did, the Mets asked me to jog out alone, creating another incredibly emotional experience. I made a beeline for third base, gave the bag a respectful kick with my cleat, then raised a hand to salute everyone in the crowd. Next out of the dugout was José Reyes, who wrapped me in a big hug before taking his position beside me at shortstop.

Only one last thing remained before we could play. When the Mets had begun drawing up plans for my final game earlier that month, Jeff Wilpon had suggested my dad throw out the ceremonial first pitch. As touched as I was by the offer, I wanted my older daughter, Olivia, involved in some way, and I knew Rhon would want that, too. So I asked if Olivia could throw out the first pitch instead; if she needed some prodding, my dad could be there beside her to help. Jeff loved the idea.

Molly and I spent some time practicing in our apartment with Olivia, who had a pretty good arm for a two-year-old, but we didn't have any idea how she would react with 43,000-plus people screaming around her. I figured there was a 50 percent chance she would throw the ball to me and a 50 percent chance she would just run around wildly, trying to play keep-away.

I shouldn't have worried. Before the PA announcer could finish introducing her, Olivia grabbed the ball and, grinning, fired it right at me. I picked it up, lifted Olivia, and kissed her on the neck. Then I turned to my five-month-old daughter, Madison, who was also on the field with Molly and my parents, and kissed her on the forehead. In that moment, I couldn't have been happier. Sharing those few seconds on the field with my family was one of the most special moments of not just my career but my life.

||||||||||||||||

Retaking my place at third base, I ceased trying to steady my nerves because I knew that wasn't possible. Instead, I just attempted to settle into the rhythm of the game, hoping no one on the Marlins would hit a ball in my direction. Thankfully, the only player who did was the catcher, giving me a little extra time to make the throw.

In my first plate appearance, I walked, reaching base for the first time since my final home run in 2016. The plan was for me to take one more at-bat and call it a night, so when I ended the third inning standing on deck, my nerves ratcheted higher. I was due to lead off the bottom of the fourth, in what would almost certainly be the final act of my career.

That knowledge was stifling, considering how important baseball had been to me for so long. As I approached the on-deck circle one last time, I thought about hitting Wiffle balls in my childhood backyard with my grandfather, lugging around a wooden bat nearly as big as I was. I remembered my dad making that homemade tee out of concrete, a PVC pipe, and a little bit of rubber, and hanging a fishnet between two trees so I could hit balls into it. I thought about crushing two home runs against our high school rival to win a game. I flashed back to my time in Norfolk playing for the Tides as a young adult. I felt such pride in those moments and so many others. I knew dozens of my oldest friends and coaches were in the stands that night at Citi Field, watching my every move. Memories ran in a loop through my head.

I guess life has a way of creating comic relief when people need it most. In the second pitch of that at-bat, I hacked at an outside fastball, popping it up along the first-base line. As the ball dropped, I contorted my body, hoping it would land out of play. Instead, first baseman Peter O'Brien ranged over into foul territory and, with boos raining around him, made the catch a few feet from the stands.

Poor O'Brien. With that catch, he became a lifelong villain in Queens just for doing his job. After the game, a Marlins clubhouse attendant wrote a note on a baseball jokingly scolding O'Brien for catching the ball, then forged my signature beneath it and gave it to him. When O'Brien realized the message was a prank, he sent the ball over to the Mets clubhouse asking me to sign it for real.

"No, really," I wrote before giving it back. "You should have let it drop."

The whole situation seems funnier in retrospect than it was when the moment was fresh. Part of me felt bad for O'Brien as I walked back to the dugout, staring at my bat, a goofy grin on my face. Most of me was just stunned. Was that really it? I wanted so badly to get one more crack, to take one last at-bat, and—who knows?—maybe bloop a single somewhere to make the crowd cheer.

I thought about asking Callaway for the chance but quickly decided just to let things play out, knowing the Mets had other events scripted for the night. I owed them so much for giving me the chance to play one last game and didn't want to mess with their plans. I also feared lobbying for an extra at-bat, striking out, and leaving my final game with a real sour taste in my mouth. When I saw Mickey fiddling with his lineup card, I knew the end had come. I was okay with that.

Briefly, I retook the field for the top of the fifth, before Mickey called me back to the dugout. Time froze again. As Reyes came over for another hug, my eyes watered. The ballpark noise became overwhelming as I headed down the dugout steps, then reached a crescendo when I reemerged to acknowledge the crowd. For once, I didn't mind being the center of attention. The love and respect Mets fans had shown me over the years was indescribable. I wish I could have repaid them with so much more than just a tip of the cap.

IIIIIIIIIIIIII

What followed was a blur. Stopping back in the clubhouse made me emotional again, but I was too busy to focus on it. Still in full uniform, I took an elevator up to the SNY television booth to spend half an inning with longtime broadcasters Gary Cohen, Keith Hernandez, and Ron Darling. I answered most of their questions in a daze, marveling at the sold-out stadium in front of me. Fans massed together on the concourse below the booth, jumping up and down to try to catch a glimpse. The whole thing was surreal. Next up was the radio booth for an interview with legendary play-by-play man Howie Rose, who had treated me so well over the years.

Although I knew I would see all those people again, it felt like I was saying goodbye for the last time. As I wound my way around the stadium, fans lined up for high fives and fist bumps. My family had a suite near the TV booth, so I went in there to say hello to everyone and snap some photos. At that point, the game was only about halfway done, but poor Olivia was starting to melt down. Molly deserves some serious extra credit for that game, which wound up going thirteen innings. I spent the last six or seven of them back on the dugout bench, soaking in the final moments of my career with my teammates.

I also spent them a bit distracted, because the Mets wanted me to deliver a postgame speech to the fans. Once again, I had no idea what to say. None. I thought about it throughout those last three or four innings and couldn't come up with a thing, outside of seventeen different variations of "Thank you." That's really all I wanted to come across, given how much the fans' support had meant to me in the course of my career.

When I first arrived in New York, people warned me that the city loved to build up stars only to chop them down later. I never experienced that. My final game, featuring a sold-out crowd full of enthusiastic people, was the ultimate example of how great Mets fans were to me.

I genuinely think playing in New York made me a better player and a stronger person. I had so much love for everyone, knowing how easy it would have been for the fans to turn on me. During my tenure, I gave them some disappointing individual seasons. The team didn't win nearly as much as I wanted. Fans loved me all the same, unwaveringly, and for that I was so incredibly thankful.

|||||||||||||

In the end, I winged my speech.

"Man," I opened, "I'm glad we won that one."

As I talked, I turned in circles, trying to soak in every inch of the stadium. "This is amazing," I continued. "I can't thank you guys enough for sticking around.

"You know, I was thinking about what to say today and I think I'm all out of tears, so I think we're good to go with that. But this is love. I mean, I can't say anything else. This is love. You guys welcomed me with open arms as a twenty-one-year-old kid. You've seen a lot of strikeouts, a lot of errors, but you had my back from day one. And for that, I can't say thank you enough.

"When I first got called up, all the older players told me that there's passionate fans here. 'They like to boo. They like to get on you.' Well, you guys have had my back. And you guys have welcomed me—a twenty-one-year-old kid from Virginia, welcomed as a New Yorker.

"Coming into today, I didn't know what to expect. I walked through the doors. There were fans here when I arrived this afternoon. And there's a lot of fans still here now, and I love you guys. I love you.

"We've had some pretty good times here. We've had some rough years. But you guys have always had my back. You've always had my back and that means the world to me. I wish I could thank everybody individually, but the best I can do is just say thank you from the bottom of my heart for accepting me. Thank you for cheering for me. And thank you for allowing me to live out my dream in front of you guys each and every single night. Thank you very much."

I'd lied about the tears. As I spoke those final words, my eyes welled up with them again. I took another long look around the stadium, soaking in what I knew would be my final time there as an active player.

"You're going to make me cry again," I said, microphone still in hand. "I love you guys. Have a good night."

And then I walked off the field, hugging a few people in the dugout on my way to the clubhouse. My major league career, officially, was complete.

IIIIIIIIIIIII

I had never been much of a collector, but as I took off my uniform that night, I realized how much of that moment I wanted to save. Into a duffel bag went my dirty pants and pinstriped Mets jersey, along with my batting gloves and helmet. They were all part of a wonderful memory that I wanted to bottle up and keep forever.

I spent a long time in the clubhouse, thanking my teammates, shedding a few more tears, answering every last question from the media. By the time I left, it was around one A.M., but the late hour didn't stop a group of fans from lingering outside the players' parking lot. I signed for them, took pictures with them, laughed and joked with them for at least another hour. Then I headed into Manhattan to bring my career full circle.

I'd never forgotten how, following my first big league game in 2004, Joe McEwing had insisted on taking me to the midtown sports bar Foley's. Despite the late hour, despite my exhaustion, he'd bought me dinner as we celebrated my debut and the career to come. Unfortunately, McEwing was busy coaching the White Sox on the final weekend of the 2018 season, so he couldn't attend my finale. But I wanted to toast the end of my career the same way I'd celebrated the beginning, so I invited all my closest friends and family to meet me at the same bar. By the time I arrived, the kitchen had long since closed. I ordered in pizza for everyone there instead, attacking it like a savage when it finally arrived.

Between slices, I tried to burn into my memory how cool the scene was. In addition to my family and friends, members of the 7 Line—a fan club that often comes to Mets games en masse, filling up entire stadium sections with orange and blue—were at the bar. So was a group of fans that had been there since early evening, watching the game. The bar renamed itself "Wright's" for the weekend, and during those few hours, it really did feel like home. New York had given me so much over fourteen seasons. Never in my wildest dreams had I imagined I would develop such a deep connection with the city.

That night, being around family, friends, and fans gave me comfort. From the time I was young, my dad had instilled in me the idea that I should work hard enough in my career to have no regrets. In part by surrounding myself with people who meant everything to me, I felt like I'd accomplished that. Along the way, I met lots of guys more talented than me. Lots of guys who were better. But I honestly believe I reached my ceiling as an athlete, playing the game the right way and squeezing the most out of my ability. I don't think many players can say that.

Sure, my career could have ended more pleasantly. Retiring at thirty-five was not the way I would have written my script. Battling injuries was not the way I would have chosen to end things. Popping up in my final at-bat was not the happily-ever-after moment I'd envisioned. I couldn't say I was okay with the way it all happened, because I wasn't.

And yet as I scanned the room early that morning, with sunrise rapidly approaching, I felt a sense of closure. My body may have prevented me from authoring the ending that I wanted, but I'd worked hard enough and received enough support to go out, in a small way, on my own terms.

Under the circumstances, I couldn't have asked for anything better.

# EPILOGUE

||||||||||

Each morning, after dropping my daughter Olivia off at school, I head to a gym near my home in Manhattan Beach, California, to tick through the rehab exercises I'll do for the rest of my life. When I have time to add in a light workout, it helps my back feel better. I'll always have good days and bad days, but no longer training as a professional athlete makes things easier. Still, spinal stenosis is not something that's ever going to disappear.

Afternoons, I practice golf a couple days per week, maybe squeezing in three or four holes while my daughters nap. I've become obsessed with correcting flaws in my swing, watching countless You-Tube videos and buying gadgets online. In 2019, I spent a fun weekend at Bethpage Black on Long Island, serving as an ambassador for the PGA Championship. That's all part of my nature. When I find something competitive that I enjoy, I pour myself into it.

On all but the worst mornings, my back is strong enough to handle a golf swing. It's strong enough for me to pick up my daughters, Olivia and Madison, which is mostly what I need it for these days—and hopefully my back will hold up for our newest addition, a boy, due in October 2020. I don't miss the constant questions of how it's going to feel tomorrow, of what sort of pain I'm going to endure. I don't miss the daily physical grind of Major League Baseball, though I do miss the games and especially the camaraderie.

Shortly after my final appearance, I returned to Queens to clean out all the stuff I had accumulated in my locker first at Shea Stadium, then at Citi Field. Old uniforms from various periods of my career. A signed bottle of champagne to celebrate Jason Isringhausen's 300th save. Some cheap wine that Jason Bay jokingly gifted me after my 200th career homer, inscribing it with the message: "Welcome to the club, kid." And so much else.

It could be difficult knowing that locker would soon belong to someone else (Robinson Canó, as it turned out), that I was done accumulating all those mementoes. During my playing career, I always became laser-focused on the upcoming season as soon as the calendar flipped. When I didn't do that in 2019, I felt a void. One day early that first winter, Molly turned to me and said, "You're going to be really annoying come February."

I looked at her and just shook my head. "I know," I replied. "I know."

From time to time, I find myself back at a ballpark, where the smells of fresh-cut grass, spilled beer, or day-old hot dogs tend to draw my mind back to my playing days. That first off-season, the Mets hired a new general manager, Brodie Van Wagenen, who invited me to baseball's annual Winter Meetings as a way to stay involved. It wasn't what I was used to, wearing khakis in a hotel suite alongside a bunch of executives, offering my opinions on potential free agents and trade targets. But wrapping my mind around baseball for three days at least allowed me to scratch my competitive itch. Ultimately, I signed on as an advisor, even drawing on my experiences to help the front office reach a long-term contract agreement with my friend Jacob deGrom.

He, like me, wanted to be a Met for life.

I'm incredibly proud of that aspect of my career, spending it all with one team. I'm incredibly proud that the Mets thought enough of me to name me captain. I'm incredibly proud that I reached a World Series.

Those three things matter more to me than anything in my career, though I'm appreciative of the lesser stuff, too. At the time of my retirement, I was the Mets' all-time leader in hits, runs, and RBI, ranking second only to Darryl Strawberry in home runs. I made seven All-Star Games, won two Gold Gloves and two Silver Sluggers, and finished in the top ten in National League MVP voting four times. I know I played the game the right way. I hope I made my teammates better.

Through my baseball career, I met my wife and grew my family, which is what I'm focused on most these days. For years, people close to me sacrificed conveniences in their lives to make my dream possible. Molly traveled from city to city, often caring for me as I recovered from surgeries. We adjusted the girls' sleep schedules to accommodate mine. The least I could do in retirement was return that favor by making them the center of attention.

People keep asking me if I want to work in television, or coach, or even manage. Usually, I laugh, knowing my family is more than enough. Maybe someday baseball will call again, or I'll discover some new passion to occupy my time. For now, I like being a husband and a dad. I don't think that's ever going to get old.

When Olivia was three years old, I began coaching her T-ball team, which was an absolute thrill. We drove to a local Dick's Sporting Goods and let her pick out her own bat and helmet, both of which she insisted be pink. I gave her one of my old undersized practice gloves, which I had used during infield drills to keep my hands soft. Going through all that baseball gear with Olivia made me flash back to when I was a kid, my dad was the equipment manager, and the two of us would spend hours in a storage shed portioning out balls, catchers' gear, and other items for every Green Run Little League team.

Molly's parents made sure to be in the stands for Olivia's debut, just like my grandparents never missed a game no matter what else was going on in their lives. Looking back on those days through new eyes, as a father, is an indescribable feeling. It takes me back to a time in my life that, thanks to my children, I'm thrilled to experience again.

## ACKNOWLEDGMENTS

||||||||||

Before beginning this project, I had never thought of myself as an author. I almost fell out of my chair when Anthony DiComo approached me about the idea, and I'd like to thank him for the time, effort, energy, and enthusiasm he put into it. Anthony, thanks also for dedicating a good chunk of your career to covering a mostly boring, cliché-giving, sometimes moody third baseman for the New York Mets, and always treating me fairly.

Thank you to the New York Mets organization, from owners Fred and Jeff Wilpon, Saul Katz, and their loved ones on down. Never in my wildest dreams would I have imagined playing baseball for a living. Thank you for allowing me to live out my dreams on a daily basis and especially for allowing me to be a Met for life. Not only do I feel a part of the Mets fraternity, I feel like I'm a part of each of your families as well.

To my former teammates and coaches, my gratitude is immense. From teaching me how to play the game correctly, to helping me dress and act like a big leaguer, to stealing third base with one out to give me a cheap RBI, you guys did it all for me. It was the honor of a lifetime to be your captain, and I felt blessed to make lifelong friends in the process.

I'm not sure I can ever say this enough times, but thank you to the city of New York and to the best fans in baseball. I didn't know what to expect on July 21, 2004, when I flew over Shea Stadium the morning of my major league debut. You made me feel at ease from the start, welcoming a twenty-one-year-old kid with open arms. Every day, I tried to play the game with a blue-collar mentality, like someone in the stands was watching me for the first time. I hope I earned your respect. And to the 7 Line . . . you're simply the best!

Thanks as well to my inner circle. You know who you are. Many of you had been friends and family long before I ever played baseball for a living. You have taught me so many invaluable life lessons. As you probably know by now, I tend to be a fairly guarded, private person by nature, but your encouragement and positivity always kept me focused on achieving my goals.

Anything I've achieved, I've done so because of my parents, Rhon and Elisa, who taught me the value of hard work, dedication, and unconditional love. You guys set the parenting bar extremely high, and I can only hope to follow in your footsteps. The sacrifices you've made and continue to make for me and my brothers can never be repaid.

To my brothers, Stephen, Matthew, and Daniel, thanks for all the fistfights and wrestling matches after hard fouls on the backyard hoop. I didn't know it at the time, but those experiences laid the foundation for my competitive nature. They also taught us to have each other's backs, which we still do to this day.

Finally, thank you to the captain of our family, my beautiful wife, Molly. Your selflessness and the sacrifices you made to accommodate my needs during my career never went unnoticed. I know I don't say this as often as I should, but thank you and I love you. Asking you to marry me on December 20, 2012, was the best decision I've ever made, leading to the three best days of my life: becoming a father to Olivia, Madison, and Brooks. I know my kids will not remember my last game, so hopefully this will remind them that, at one point in their lives, I wasn't just a dorky dad. I love you all more than you will ever know.

—DAVID WRIGHT

On one of my first afternoons as an MLB.com intern in 2007, I stood in the Shea Stadium clubhouse as my mentor, Marty Noble, scanned the banks of lockers to offer me a scouting report on various Mets players. So-and-so was a good guy. So-and-so was a great quote.

"And David," Marty said, motioning to Wright's locker, "is what everyone says he is."

In beginning my acknowledgments for this book, I couldn't think of a more apt description. Throughout this process, David was exactly what I knew he would be from covering him for a dozen seasons: professional, accommodating, open, honest, forthcoming.

He invited me into his home and into his life, for a book that he did not have to write. In doing so, he changed my career. Thank you, David, for allowing me to work on this project with you.

For this manuscript, I interviewed around forty people in addition to David. Not a single one of them had a bad word to say—seriously. As I ate lunch one day with one of David's best friends, Dave Racaniello, I was struck by this quote: "He just does everything the right way, annoyingly so sometimes. He just does everything the right way. It's incredible. There are no skeletons."

Meet David's family, and it's clear why. I'd like to thank the Wrights for helping with this process—his wife, Molly, whose memory puts David's to shame, as well as his parents and brothers, who were all instrumental. And a special thanks to Allan Erbe, who went above and beyond in helping me reconstruct the early years of David's life.

Big thanks are due to my literary agent, Rob Kirkpatrick, who believed in this project long before David's cooperation was a given. Rob asked all the right questions as we shaped the book proposal in multiple different forms. And he knew the right editor: John Parsley at Dutton. It's probably telling that I met John for the first time on the Citi Field concourse. He's a lifelong Mets fan, just like Rob, which made him and his team a perfect fit for the job.

Over a year of work, I found several resources invaluable. Among the most critical was Jay Horwitz, a human Mets encyclopedia who helped in so many ways. Jay spent thirty-nine years as the Mets' head of media relations. He's a friend of David's, which should speak to his character. I'm happy to call Jay a friend of mine as well.

Baseball-Reference.com doesn't receive enough credit for the service it provides sportswriters on a daily basis. I found myself frequenting that site, as well as digging up old stories and video from ESPN, *The New York Times*, the *New York Post*, *Sports Illustrated*, *The Virginian-Pilot*, and MLB.com.

The last of those publications is nearest and dearest to my heart. I've spent my entire career at MLB.com and would like to thank everyone there for their flexibility in allowing me to pursue this project—especially my editors Matthew Leach, Jim Banks, Matt Meyers, and Gregg Klayman. I'd also like to acknowledge pretty much every single person at SNY, which has become a second home to me. The vibes there are incredible.

People often ask how ball writers survive the 162-game grind of a beat. I'm lucky to have great friends with me, including several who played important roles in the pages you just read. Steve Gelbs and Wayne Randazzo, whom Mets fans know well, did so much to help to promote this book. Marc Carig kept me sane with his parking-lot chats. Jared Diamond and others gave me valuable insight on the book-writing process. In my fourteen years covering baseball, too many others have passed through Queens and elsewhere for me to thank individually. But one I will: the late Marty Noble, my predecessor on the Mets beat, as well as a mentor and friend. I wish he were here to see this finished product.

Finally, the most important thank-yous go to my family. Growing up, David had Elisa and Rhon. I had Camille and Tony, the most supportive parents imaginable. (Told you I'd hit my deadline, Mom.) I love you both so much.

To my sister, Christine: you helped me write my first book

about a snowman who came to life (and now, for some reason, won't seem to die). In a lot of ways, you helped me write this one as well. And to Angie and Maggie, the only people reading this who think I'm cooler than David Wright: spending time with you is one of my favorite things in this world.

All my love goes as well to Kate, for her patience and understanding throughout this process. I sacrificed so many hours working in cars, on subways, in apartments, in beach chairs, and elsewhere. Your steadiness throughout did not go unnoticed. (And thanks for not telling my parents about that speeding ticket in Virginia.)

For those not mentioned here, believe me when I say you haven't been forgotten. I'll be waiting for you all with a metaphorical tray of cookies in a metaphorical hotel lobby.

—ANTHONY DiCOMO

# INDEX

||||||||||

## ABOUT THE AUTHORS

|||||||||

**David Wright** is a seven-time All-Star third baseman who played fourteen seasons in the major leagues and was voted the "Face of MLB." He retired as the team's fourth captain and the franchise leader in hits, runs, and RBIs. He is a special advisor in the Mets' front office.

**Anthony DiComo** is the Mets beat writer for MLB.com and the chairman of the Baseball Writers' Association of America's New York chapter. He also is an analyst for the SNY channel and a regular contributor to the MLB Network.